MORE WONDERS
OF THE
INVISIBLE WORLD

MORE WONDERS
OF THE
INVISIBLE WORLD:
OR
THE WONDERS
OF
THE INVISIBLE WORLD

DISPLAYED.
IN FIVE PARTS.

PART I.—An account of the Sufferings of *Margaret Rule*, written by the Rev. *Cotton Mather*.

PART II.—Several Letters to the Author, &c. and his Reply relating to Witchcraft.

PART III.—The Differences between the Inhabitants of *Salem* Village, and Mr. *Parris*, their Minister, in *New-England*.

PART IV.—Letters of a Gentleman uninterested, endeavouring to prove the received opinions about Witchcraft to be Orthodox. With short Essays to their Answers.

PART V.—A short Historical Account of Matters of Fact in that Affair.

TO WHICH IS ADDED
A POSTSCRIPT,
RELATING TO A BOOK ENTITLED "THE LIFE OF SIR WM. PHIPS."

COLLECTED BY
ROBERT CALEF,
Merchant, of Boston, in New-England

PRINTED IN LONDON A.D. 1700.

This unabridged edition has been newly typeset and edited. The text was compiled from various print sources of the original 1700 book. Other than the correction of some small typographical errors, the text retains spelling, capitalization and type styles based primarily on the Salem 1823 edition, except for the first page of the "Epistle" (p. v), which is set as an example of the type and capitalization style of the original London 1700 edition.

Header illustrations and drop-caps are from the Salem 1860 edition.

Notes are by Samuel P. Fowler, Salem 1860 edition, unless otherwise noted.

Cover is adapted from the original London 1700 edition, errors intact.

Classic Reprint edition dedicated to the descendants of Mr. Robert Calef and Mrs. Susannah North Martin.

Copyright 2018 by
Katie Fox
San Francisco, CA
All rights reserved.

ISBN 978-1-947587-02-1
First facsimile print edition, 2018.

Design, typesetting, editing, & back-cover text by Katie Fox
WWW.FOXEDITING.COM

THE EPISTLE TO THE READER,
AND MORE ESPECIALLY TO THE NOBLE BARONS OF THIS AGE, WHEREVER RESIDING.

GENTLEMEN,

YOU that are freed from the Slavery of a corrupt Education; and that in spite of human Precepts, Examples, and Precedents, can hearken to the Dictates of Scripture and Reason:

For your sakes I am content that these Collections of mine, as also my Sentiments, should be exposed to public view; in hopes that having well considered and compared them with Scripture, you will see reason, as I do, to question a belief so prevalent as that here treated of, as also the practice flowing from thence; they standing as nearly connected as cause and effect; it being found wholly impracticable to extirpate the latter without first curing the former.

And if the Buffoon or Satyrical will be exercising their Talents, or if the Biggots wilfully and blindly reject the Testimonies of their own reason, and more sure word, it is no more than what I expected from them.

But you Gentlemen, I doubt not, are willing to Distinguish between Truth and Error; and if this may be any furtherance to you herein, I shall not miss my Aim.

But if you find the contrary, and that my belief herein is any way Heterodox, I shall be thankful for the Information to any Learned or Reverend Person, or others, that shall take that pains to inform me better, by Scripture or sound Reason; which is what I have been long seeking for in this Country in vain.

In a time when not only England *in particular, but almost all* Europe, *had been labouring against the Usurpations of Tyranny and Slavery, the* English, America *has not been behind in a share of the common calamities; more especially,* New-England *has met not only with such calamities as are common to the rest, but with several aggravations enhancing such Afflictions, by the Devastations and Cruelties of the*

THE EPISTLE

Barbarous Indians in their Eastern borders, &c. But this is not all; they have been harast (on many accounts) by a more dreadful Enemy, as will herein appear to the considerate.

Were it, as we are told in *Wonders of the Invisible World*, "that the devils were walking about our streets with lengthened chains, making a dreadful noise in our ears; and brimstone (even without a metaphor) was making a horrid and a hellish stench in our nostrils;" and "that the devil, exhibiting himself ordinarily as a black man, had decoyed a fearful knot of proud, froward, ignorant, envious and malicious creatures, to list themselves in his horrid service, by entering; their names in a book tendered unto them; and that they have had their meetings and sacraments, and associated themselves to destroy the kingdom of our Lord Jesus Christ, in these parts of the world; having each of them their spectres, or devils, commissioned by them, and representing of them to be the engines of their malice, by these wicked spectres seizing poor people about the country, with various and bloody torments, and of those evidently preternatural torments some have died; and that they have bewitched some even so far as to make them self-destroyers, and others in many towns here and there languished under their evil hands—the people, thus afflicted, miserably scratched and bitten; and that the same invisible furies did stick pins in them, and scald them, distort and disjoint them, with a thousand other plagues; and sometimes drag them out of their chambers, and carry them over trees and hills, miles together, many of them being tempted to sign the devil's laws"—"those furies, whereof several have killed more people perhaps than would serve to make a village"—If this be the true state of the afflictions of this country, it is very deplorable, and beyond all other outward calamities miserable. But if, on the other side, the matter be, as others do understand it, that the devil has been too hard for us by his temptations, signs, and lying wonders, with the help of pernicious notions, formerly imbibed and professed; together with the accusations of a parcel of possessed, distracted or lying wenches, accusing their innocent neighbours, pretending they see their spectres, i.e. devils in their likeness, afflicting of them; and that God in righteous judgment (after men had ascribed his power to witches, of commissioning devils to do these things) may have given them over to strong delusions to believe lies, &c. and to let loose the devils of envy, hatred, pride, cruelty and malice against each other, yet still disguised under the mask of zeal for God, and left them to the branding one another with the odious name of witch; and upon the accusation of those above mentioned, brother to accuse and prosecute brother, children their parents, pastors and teachers their immediate flock, unto death; shepherds becoming wolves; wise men infatuated; people hauled to prisons; with a bloody noise pursuing to, and insulting over the (true) sufferers at execution; while some are fleeing from that called justice, justice itself fleeing before such accusations, when once it did but begin to refrain further proceedings; and, to question such practices, some making their escape out of prisons, rather than by an obstinate defence of their innocency to run so apparent hazard of their lives; estates seized, families of children and others left to the mercy of the wilderness (not to mention here the numbers proscribed, dead in prisons or executed, &c.)—All which tragedies, though begun in one town, or rather by one parish, has plague-like spread more than through that country, and by its echo giving a brand of infamy to this whole country throughout the world:—If this were the miserable case of this country in the time thereof, and that the devil be so far prevailed upon us, in our sentiments and actions, as to draw us from so much as looking into the scriptures for our guidance in these pretended intricacies; leading us to a trusting in blind guide, such as the corrupt practices of some other countries, or the bloody experiments of Bodin, and such other authors:—then, though our case be most miserable, yet it must be said of New England, thou hast destroyed thyself and brought this greatest of miseries upon thee.

And now, whether the witches (such as have made a compact by explicit covenant with the devil, having thereby obtained a power to commission him) have been the cause of our miseries; or whether a zeal, governed by blindness and passion, and led by precedent, has not herein precipitated us into far greater wickedness (if not witchcrafts) than any have yet been proved against those that suffered:—to be able to distinguish aright in this matter, to which of these two to refer our miseries, is the design of the present work.

As to the former, I know of no sober man, much less reverend christian, that, being asked, dares affirm, and abide by it, that witches have that power, viz. to commission devils to kill and destroy; and as to the latter, it were well if there were not too much of truth in it, which remains to be demonstrated.

But here it will be said, What need of raking in the coals that lay buried in oblivion? We cannot recal those to life again, that have suffered, supposing it were unjustly; it tends but to the exposing the actors, as if they had proceeded irregularly.

Truly I take this to be just as the devil would have it, so much to fear disobliging men, as not to endeavor to detect his wiles, that so he may the sooner, and with the greater advantages, set the same on foot again (either here or elsewhere), so dragging us through the pond twice by the same cat. And, if reports do not herein deceive us, much the same has been acting this present year in Scotland. And what kingdom or country is it, that has not had their bloody fits and turns at it? And if this is such a catching disease, and so universal, I presume I need make no apology for my endeavours to prevent, as far as in my power, any more such bloody victims or sacrifices; though indeed I had rather any other would have undertaken so offensive, though necessary, a task; yet, all things weighed, I had rather thus expose myself to censure, than that it should be wholly omitted. Were the notions in question innocent and harmless, respecting the glory of God, and well-being of men, I should not have engaged in them; but finding them, in my esteem, so intolerably destructive of both, this, together with my being by warrant called before the justices, in my own just vindication I took it to be a call from God, to my power, to vindicate his truths, against the pagan and popish assertions, which are so prevalent; for though christians in general do own the scriptures to be their only rule of faith and doctrine, Jet these notions will tell us, that the scriptures have not sufficiently, nor at all, described the crime of witchcraft, whereby the culpable might be detected, though it be positive in the command to punish it by death; hence the world has been from time to time perplexed, in the prosecution of the several diabolical mediums of heathenish and popish invention to detect an imaginary crime (not but that there are witches such as the law of God describes) which has produced a deluge of blood; hereby rendering the commands of God not only void but dangerous.

So also they own God's providence and government of the world; and that tempests and storms, afflictions and diseases, are of his sending; yet these notions tell us, that the devil has the power of all these, and call perform them when commissioned by a witch thereto; and that he has a power, at the witch's call, to act and do, without and against the course of nature, and all natural causes, in afflicting and killing of innocents; and this it is that so many have died for.

TO THE READER.

Also it is generally believed, that if any Man has strength, it is from God the Almighty Being: but these notions will tell us, that the devil can make one man as strong as many; which was one of the best proofs, as it was counted, against Mr. Burroughs the minister; though his contemporaries in the schools, during his minority, could have testified, that his strength was then as much superior to theirs as ever (setting aside incredible romances) it was discovered to be since: thus rendering the power of God, and his providence, of none effect.

These are some of the destructive notions of this age; and however the asserters of them seem sometimes to value themselves much upon sheltering their neighbours from spectral accusations, they may deserve as much thanks as that tyrant, that, having industriously obtained an unintelligible charge against his subjects, in matters wherein it was impossible they should be guilty, having thereby their lives in his power, yet suffers them of his mere grace to live, and will be called gracious lord.

It were too Icarian a task for one, unfurnished with necessary learning, and library, to give any just account from whence so great delusions have sprung, and so long continued. Yet, as an essay from those scraps of reading that I have had opportunity of, it will be no great venture to say, that signs and lying wonders have been one principal cause.

It is written of Justin Martyr, who lived in t he second century, that he was before his conversion a great philosopher; first in the way of the stoicks, and after, of the peripateticks, after that of the pythagorean, and after that of the platonist sects; and after all proved of eminent use in the church of Christ: yet a certain author, speaking of one Apollonius Tyaneus, has these words: "That the most orthodox themselves began to deem him vested with power sufficient for a deity; which occasioned that so strange a doubt from Justin Martyr, as cited by the learned Gregory, fol. 37: If God be the creator and lord of the world, how comes it to pass that Apollonius his telisms have so much over-ruled the course of things? for we see that they also have stilled the waves of the sea, and the raging of the winds, and prevailed against the noisome flies, and incursions of wild beasts, &c." If so eminent and early a christian were by these false shews in such doubt, it is the less wonder, in our depraved times, to meet with what is equivalent thereto. Besides this, a certain author informs me, that Julian (afterwards called the apostate) being

THE EPISTLE

instructed in the philosophy and disciplines of the heathen, by Libarius his tutor, by this means he came to love philosophy better than the gospel, and so by degrees turned from christianity to heathenism."

This same Julian did, when apostate, forbid that christians should be instructed in the discipline of the gentiles; which, it seems, Socrates, a writer of the ecclesiastical history, does acknowledge to be by the singular providence of God; christians having then begun to degenerate from the gospel, and to betake themselves to heathenish learning. And in the Mercury for the month of February, 1695, there is this account, "That the christian doctors, conversing much with the writings of the heathen, for the gaining of eloquence, a council was held at Carthage, which forbad the reading of the books of the gentiles."

From all which it may be easily perceived, that in the primitive times of christianity, when not, only many heathen of the vulgar, but also many learned men and philosophers, had embraced the christian faith, they still retained a love to their heathen learning; which, as one observes, being transplanted into a christian soil, soon proved productive of pernicious weeds, which overran the face of the church; hence it was so deformed, as the reformation found it.

Among other pernicious weeds arising from this root, the doctrine of the power of devils, and witchcraft, as it is now and long has been understood, is not the least: the fables of Homer, Virgil, Horace and Ovid, &c. being for the elegancy of their language retained then (and so are to this day) in the schools, have not only introduced, but established, such doctrines, to the poisoning the christian world. A certain author expresses it thus: "That as the christian schools at first brought men from heathenism to the gospel, so the schools carry men from the gospel to heathenism, as to their great perfection." And Mr. I.M. in his *Remarkable Providences*, gives an account, that (as he calls it) an old council did anathematize all those that believed such power of the devils, accounting it a damnable doctrine. But as other evils did afterwards increase in the church (partly by such education) so this insensibly grew up with them, though not to that degree as that any council, I have ever heard or read of, has to this day taken off those anathemas; yet after this the church so far declined, that witchcraft became a principal ecclesiastical engine (as also that of heresy was) to root up all that stood in their way; and besides the ways of trial that we have still in practice, they invented some which were peculiar to themselves; which, whenever they were minded to improve against any orthodox believer, they could easily make effectual. That deluge of blood, which that Scarlet Whore has to answer for, shed under this notion, how amazing is it!

The first in England, that I have read of of any note, since the reformation, that asserts this doctrine, is the famous Mr. Perkins: he, as also Mr. Gaul, Mr. Bernard, &c. seem all of them to have undertaken one task; taking notice of the multiplicity of irregular ways to try them by. Invented by heathen and papists, they made it their business, and main work, herein to oppose such as they saw to be pernicious. And if they did not look more narrowly into it, but followed the first, viz. Mr. Perkins, whose education (as theirs also) had forestalled him into such belief, whom they readily followed, it cannot be wondered at. And that they were men liable to err, and so not to be trusted to as perfect guides, will manifestly appear to him that shall see their several receipts laid down to detect them, by their presumptive and positive ones; and consider how few of either have any foundation in scripture, or reason; and how vastly they differ from each other in both; each having his art by himself, which forty or an hundred more may as well imitate, and give theirs, *ad infinitum*, being without all manner of proof. But though this be their main design, to take off people from those evil and bloody ways of trial, which they speak so much against; yet this does not hinder, to this day, but the same evil ways, or as bad, are still used to detect them by, and that even among protestants; and are so far justified, that a reverend person has said lately here, How else shall we detect witches? And another, being urged to prove by scripture such a sort of witch as has power to send devils to kill men, replied, that he did as firmly believe it, as any article of his faith; and that he (the inquirer) did not go to the scriptures to learn the mysteries of his trade or art. What can be said more to establish their heathenish notions, and to vilify the scriptures, our only rule? and that, after we have seen such dire effects thereof, as has threatened the utter extirpation of this whole country.

And as to most of the actors in these tragedies, though they are so far from defending their actions, that they will readily own that undue steps have been taken, &c. yet it seems they choose that the same should be acted over again, enforced by their example, rather than it should remain as a warning to posterity, as herein they have mist it. So far are they from giving glory to God, and taking the due shame to themselves.

And now, to sum up all in a few words, we have seen a bigoted zeal stirring up a blind and most bloody rage, not against enemies, or irreligious, profligate persons; but (in judgment of charity, and to view) against as virtuous and religious as any they have left behind them in this country, which have suffered as evil doers (with the utmost extent of rigour, not that so high a character is due to all that suffered) and this by the testimony of vile varlets, as not only were known before, but have been further apparent since, by their manifest lives, whoredoms, incest, &c. The accusations of these, from their spectral sight, being the chief evidence against those that suffered; in which accusations they were upheld by both magistrates and ministers, so long as they apprehended themselves in no danger.

And then, though they could defend neither the doctrine nor the practice, yet none of them have, in such a public manner as the case requires, testified against either; though at the same time they could not but be sensible what a stain and lasting infamy they have brought upon the whole country, to the endangering the future welfare not only of this but of other places, induced by their example; if not to an entailing the guilt of all the righteous blood that has been by the same means shed, by heathen or papists, &c. upon themselves, whose deeds they have so far justified, occasioning the great dishonour and blasphemy of the name of God, scandalizing the heathen, hardening of enemies; and, as a natural effect thereof, to the great increase of atheism.

I shall conclude, only with acquainting the reader, that of these collections, the first, containing More Wonders of the Invisible World,[1] I received of a gentleman, who had it of the author, and

---

1. The Proceedings of the Massachusetts Historical Society, in their 1st vol., page 288, inform us that "Calef was furnished with materials for his work by Mr. Brattle of Cambridge and his brother of Boston, and other gentlemen who were opposed to the Salem proceedings." That the judges sought the advice and countenance of the leading ministers we have sufficient proof; also that the principal examining magistrates, John Hathorne and Jonathan Corwin, when faltering in their course at the multiplicity of the complaints from distressed persons, occasioned by supposed witchcraft, were cheered on in their prosecutions by receiving such letters of commendation from the principal inhabitants of Salem Village as the following:—

TO THE READER.

communicated it to use, with his express consent, of which this is a true copy. As to the letters, they are, for substance, the same I sent, though with some small variation, or audition. Touching the two letters from a gentleman, at his request I have forborn naming him. It is great pity that the matters of fact, and indeed the whole, had not been done by some abler hand, better accomplished, and with the advantages of both natural and acquired judgment; but others not appearing, I have enforced myself to do what is done; my other occasions will not admit any further scrutiny therein.

R.C.

August, 11, 1697.

These to the Honered John Hathorne and Jonathan Corwin Esquires— Lieuing at Salem present.

Salem Village this 21st of April 1692——

Much Honered—After most humble and hearty thanks presented to your Honrs. for the great care and paines you have already taken for us, for which you know we are never able to make you Recompence, and we believe you do not expect it of us, therefore a full reward be given you of the Lord God of Israel, whose cause and interest you have espoused, and we trust this shall add to your Crown of Glory in the day of the Lord Jesus— And we beholding continually the tremendous works of Divine Providence, not only every day but every hour; thought it our duty to Inform your Honors of that we conceive you have not heard, which are high and dreadful, of a wheel within a wheel, at which our ears do tingle— Humbly craving continually your prayers and help in this distressed case; So praying Almighty God continually to prepare you, that you may be a terror to evildoers, and a praise to them that do well— We remain yours to serve in what we are able

THOMAS PUTNAM—

The author of the above letter is the worthy parish clerk of Salem Village; and what probably caused his ears to tingle, was the suspicion which began to be entertained against George Burroughs, his former minister, of being a wizard. Nine days after the date of his letter, April 30, 1692, Jonathan Walcott and Thomas Putnam made complaint against Burroughs to the Salem magistrates.

The CONTENTS.

THE EPISTLE TO THE READER v

PART I.

ACCOUNT OF THE SUFFERINGS OF MARGARET RULE. ... 1
ANOTHER BRAND PLUCKT OUT OF THE BURNING, ... 2

PART II.

SEVERAL LETTERS, &c. 17

PART III.

ACCOUNT OF THE DIFFERENCES IN SALEM VILLAGE. . 66

PART IV.

LETTERS OF A GENTLEMAN UNINTERESTED, ENDEAVOURING TO PROVE THE RECEIVED OPINIONS ABOUT WITCHCRAFT TO BE ORTHODOX. 77

PART V.

AN IMPARTIAL ACCOUNT OF THE MOST MEMORABLE MATTERS OF FACT, TOUCHING THE SUPPOSED WITCHCRAFT IN NEW-ENGLAND. 107

POSTSCRIPT, RELATING TO "THE LIFE OF SIR WILLIAM PHIPS." 173

PART I.

ACCOUNT OF THE SUFFERINGS

OF

MARGARET RULE.

SIR,

I NOW lay before you a very entertaining story—a story which relates yet more Wonders of the Invisible World—a story which tells the remarkable afflictions and deliverance of one that had been prodigiously handled by the Evil Angels. I was myself a daily eyewitness to a large part of these occurrences, and there may be produced scores of substantial witnesses to the most of them; yea, I know not of any one passage of the story but what may be sufficiently attested. I do not write it with a design of throwing it presently into the press, but only to preserve the memory of such memorable things, the forgetting whereof would neither be pleasing to God, nor useful to men; as also to give you, with some others of peculiar and obliging friends, a sight of some curiosities. And I hope this apology will serve to excuse me, if I mention, as perhaps I may, when I come to a tenth paragraph in my writing, some things which I would have omitted in a farther publication.

COTTON MATHER.

ANOTHER BRAND
PLUCKT OUT OF THE BURNING,

OR

MORE WONDERS OF THE INVISIBLE WORLD.

SECT. 1. Within these few years, there died in the southern parts, a christian Indian, who, notwithstanding some of his Indian weakness, had something of a better character, of virtue and goodness, than many of our people can allow to most of their countrymen, that profess the christian religion. He had been a zealous preacher of the gospel to his neighbourhood, and a sort of overseer or officer, to whose conduct was owing very much of what good order was maintained among these proselyted savages. This man, returning home from the funeral of his son, was complimented by an Englishman, expressing sorrow for his loss. Now, though the Indians used upon the death of relations to be the most passionate and outrageous creatures in the world, yet this converted Indian handsomely and cheerfully replied, Truly I am sorry, and I am not sorry: I am sorry that I have buried a dear son; but I am not sorry that the will of God is done: I know that without the will of God my son could not have died; and I know that the will of God is always just and good, and so I am satisfied. Immediately upon this, even within a few hours, he fell himself sick, of a disease that quickly killed him; in the time of which disease, he called his folks about him, earnestly persuading them to be sincere in their praying unto God, and to beware of the drunkenness, the idleness, the lying, whereby so many of that nation disgraced their profession of christianity; adding, that he was ashamed, when he thought how little service he had hitherto done for God; and, that if God could prolong his life, he would labour to do better service; but that he was fully sure he was now going to the Lord Jesus Christ, who had bought him with his precious blood; and for his part, he longed to die, that he might be with his glorious Lord; and, in the midst of such passages, he gave up the ghost; but in such repute, that the English people, of good fashion, did not think much of travelling a great way to his interment. Lest my reader do wonder why I have related this piece of a story, I will now hasten to abate that wonder, by telling that whereto this was intended but for an introduction. Know then, that this remarkable Indian being, a little before he died, at work in the wood, making of tar, there appeared unto him a black man, of a terrible aspect, and more than human dimensions, threatening bitterly to kill him, if he would not promise to leave off preaching, as he did, to his countrymen, and promise particularly, that if he preached any more, he would say nothing of Jesus Christ unto them. The Indian was amazed, yet had the courage to answer, I will, in spite of you, go on to preach Christ, more than ever I did; and the God whom I serve will keep me, that you shall never hurt me. Hereupon the apparition, abating somewhat of his fierceness, offered to the Indian a book of a considerable thickness, and a pen and ink, and said, that if he would now set his hand unto that book, he would require nothing further of him; but the man refused the motion with indignation, and fell down upon his knees into a fervent and pious prayer Unto God, for help against the tempter; whereupon the demon vanished.

This is a story which I would never have tendered unto my reader, if I had not received it from an honest and useful Englishman, who is at this time a preacher of the gospel to the Indians; nor would the probable truth of it have encouraged me to have tendered it, if this also had not been a fit introduction unto a yet further narrative.

SECT. 2. It was not much above a year or two after this accident (of which no manner of noise has been made) that there was a prodigious descent of devils upon divers places near the centre of this province; wherein some scores of miserable people were troubled by horrible appearances of a black man, accompanied with spectres, wearing these and those human shapes, who offered them a book to be by them signed, in token of their being listed for the service of the devil; and, upon their denying to do it, they were dragooned with a thousand preternatural torments, which gave no little terror to the beholders of these unhappy people. There was one in the north part of Boston seized by the evil angels many months after the general storm of the late enchantments was over, and when the country had long lain very quiet, both as to molestations and accusations from the invisible World: her name was Margaret Rule, a young woman: she was born of sober and honest parents, yet living; but what her own character was before her visitation I can speak with the less confidence of exactness because I observe that wherever the devils have been let loose, to worry any poor creature among us, a great part of the neighbourhood presently set themselves to inquire, and relate all the little vanities of their childhood, with such unequal exaggerations, as to make them appear greater sinners than any whom the pilot of hell has not yet preyed upon. But it is affirmed, that, for about half a year before her visitation, she was observably improved in the hopeful symptoms of a new creature; she was become seriously concerned for the everlasting salvation of her soul, and careful to avoid the snares of evil company. This young woman had never seen the afflictions of Mercy Short, whereof a narrative has been already given; and yet, about half a year after the glorious and signal deliverance of that poor damsel, this Margaret fell into an affliction, marvellous, resembling hers in almost all the circumstances of it; indeed the afflictions were so much alike, that the relation I have given of the one, would almost serve as the full history of the other; this was to that little more than the second part of the same tune; indeed Margaret's case was in several points less remarkable than Mercy's. and in some other things the entertainment did a little vary.

SECT. 3. It was upon the Lord's day, the 10th of September, in the year 1693, that Margaret Rule, after some hours of previous disturbance in the public assembly, fell into odd fits, which caused her friends to carry her home, where her fits in a few hours grew into a figure that satisfied the spectators of their being preternatural. Some of the neighbours were forward enough to suspect the rise or this mischief in an house hard by, where lived a miserable woman, who had been formerly imprisoned, on the suspicion of witchcraft, and who had frequently cured very painful hurts, by muttering over them certain charms, which I shall not endanger the poisoning of my reader by repeating. This woman had, the evening before Margaret fell into her calamities, very bitterly treated her, and threatened her; but the hazard of hurting a poor woman, that might be innocent, notwithstanding, surmises that might have been more strongly grounded than those, caused the pious people in the vicinity to try, rather, whether incessant supplication to God alone might not procure a quicker and safer ease to the afflicted, than hasty prosecution of any supposed criminal; and accordingly that unexceptionable course was all that was ever followed: yea, which I looked on as a token for good, the afflicted family was as averse, as any of us, to entertain thoughts of any other course.

SECT. 4. The young woman was assaulted by eight cruel spectres, whereof she imagined that she knew three or four; but the rest came still with their faces covered, so that she could never have a distinguished view of the countenance of those whom she thought she knew; she was very careful of my reiterated charges, to forbear blazing their names, lest any good person should come to suffer any blast of reputation, through the cunning malice of the great accuser; nevertheless, having since privately named them to myself, I will venture to say this of them, that they are a sort of wretches, who for these many years have gone under as violent presumptions of witchcraft, as perhaps any creatures yet living upon earth; although I am far from thinking that the visions of this young woman were evidence enough to prove them so. These cursed spectres now brought unto her a book about a cubit long—a book red and thick, but not very broad; and they demanded of her, that she would set her hand to that book, or touch it at least with her hand, as a sign of her becoming a servant of the devil. Upon her peremptory refusal to do what they asked, they did not after renew the proffers of the book unto her, but instead thereof they fell to tormenting of her in a manner too hellish to be sufficiently described—in those torments confining her to her bed for just six weeks together.

SECT. 5. Sometimes, but not always, together with the spectres, there looked in upon the young woman (according to her account) a short and a black man, whom they called their master—a white, exactly of the same dimensions and complexion and voice, with the devil that has exhibited himself unto other infested people, not only in other parts of this country, but also in other countries, even of the European world, as the relation of the enchantments there informs us. They all profest themselves vassals of this devil, and in obedience unto him they addressed themselves unto various ways of torturing her. Accordingly she was cruelly pinched with invisible hands, very often in a day, and the black and blue marks of the pinches became immediately visible unto the standers by. Besides this, when her attendants had left her without so much as one pin about her, that so they might prevent some feared inconveniences, yet she would every now and then be miserably hurt with pins, which were found stuck into her neck, back and arms; however, the wounds made by the pins would in a few minutes ordinarily be cured; she would also be strangely distorted in her joints, and thrown into such exorbitant convulsions as were astonishing unto the spectators in general. They that could behold the doleful condition of the poor family without sensible compassions, might have entrails indeed; but I am sure they could have no true bowels in them.

SECT. 6. It were a most unchristian and uncivil, yea, a most unreasonable thing, to imagine, that the fits of the young woman were but mere impostures; and I believe scarce any but people of a particular dirtiness will harbour such an uncharitable censure. However, because I know not how far the devil may drive the imagination of poor creatures, when he has possession of them, that at another time, when they are themselves, would scorn to dissemble any thing, I shall now confine my narrative unto passages wherein there could be no room left for any dissimulation. Of these, the first that I'll mention shall be this: From the time that Margaret Rule first found herself to be formally besieged by the spectres, until the ninth day following, namely, from the 10th of September to the 18th, she kept an entire fast, and yet she was unto all appearance as fresh, as lively, as hearty, at the nine days end, as before they began; in all this time though she had a very eager hunger upon her stomach, yet, if any refreshment were brought unto her, her teeth would be set, and she would be thrown into many miseries; indeed once or twice or so in all this time, her tormentors permitted her to swallow a mouthful of somewhat that might increase her miseries, whereof a spoonful of rum was the most considerable; but otherwise, as I said, her fast unto the ninth day was very extreme and rigid: however, afterwards there scarce passed a day wherein she had not liberty to take something or other for her sustentation, And I must add this, further, that this business of her fast was carried so, that it was impossible to be dissembled without a combination of multitudes of people, unacquainted with one another, to support the juggle; but be that can imagine such a thing of a neighbourhood, so filled with virtuous.people, is a base man—I cannot call him any other.

SECT. 7. But if the sufferings of this young woman were not imposture, yet might they not be pure distemper? I will not here inquire of our sadducees, what sort of a distemper it is, that shall stick the body full of pins without any hand that could be seen to stick them; or whether all the pin-makers in the world would be willing to be evaporated into certain ill habits of body, producing a distemper; but of the distemper my reader shall be judge, when I have told him something further of those unusual sufferings. I do believe that the evil angels do often take advantage, from natural distempers in the children of men, to annoy them with such further mischiefs, as we call preternatural. The malignant vapours and humours of our diseased bodies may be used by devils, thereinto insinuating as engines of the execution of their malice upon those bodies; and perhaps, for this reason, one sex may suffer more troubles of some kinds from the invisible world than the other; as well as for that reason, for which the old serpent made, where he did, his first address. But I pray, what will you say to this? Margaret Rule would sometimes have her jaws forcibly pulled open, whereupon something invisible would be poured down her throat; we all saw her swallow, and yet we saw her try all she could, by spitting, coughing and shrieking, that she might not swallow; but one time the standers-by plainly saw something of that odd liquor itself on the outside of her neck: she cried out of it, as of scalding brimstone poured into her, and the whole house would immediately scent so hot of brimstone that we were scarce able to endure it—whereof there are scores of witnesses; but the young woman herself would be so monstrously inflamed, that it would have broke a heart of stone to have seen her agonies. This was a thing that several times happened; and several times, when her mouth was thus pulled open, the standers-by clapping their hands close thereupon, the distresses that otherwise followed -would be diverted. Moreover there _was a whitish powder, to us, invisible, sometimes cast upon the eyes of this young woman, whereby her eyes would be extremely incommoded; but one time some of this powder was fallen actually visible upon her cheek, from whence the people in the room wiped it with their handkerchiefs; and sometimes the young woman would also be so bitterly scorched with the unseen sulphur thrown upon her, that very sensible blisters would be raised upon her skin, whereto her friends found it necessary to apply the oils proper for common burnings; but the most of these hurts would be cured in two or three days at farthest. I think I may without vanity pretend to have read not a few of the best systems of physick that have been yet seen in these American regions, but I must confess that I have never yet learned the name of the natural distemper whereto these odd symptoms do belong: however, I might suggest perhaps many a natural medicine which would be of singular use against many of them.

SECT. 8. But there fell out some other matters far beyond the reach of natural distemper. This Margaret Rule once in the middle of the night lamented sadly that the spectres threatened the drowning of a young man in the neighbourhood, whom she named unto the company: well, it was afterwards found that at that very time this young man, having been prest on board a man of war, then in the harbour, was out of some dissatisfaction attempting to swim ashore, and he had been drowned in the attempt, if a boat had not seasonably taken him up; it was by computation a minute or two after the young woman's discourse of the drowning, that the young man took the water. At another time she told us, that the spectres bragged and laughed in her hearing about an exploit they had lately done, by stealing from a gentleman his will soon after he had written it; and within a few hours after she had spoken this, there came to me a gentleman with a private complaint, that having written his will, it was unaccountably gone out of the way; how, or where, he could not imagine; and besides all this, there were wonderful noises every now and then made about the room, which other people could ascribe to no other authors but the spectres; yea, the watchers affirm, that they heard those fiends clapping their hands together with an audibleness wherein they could not be imposed upon; and once her tormentors pulled her up to the ceiling of the chamber, and held her there, before a very numerous company of spectators, who found it as much as they could all do to pull her down again. There was also another very surprising circumstance about her, agreeable to what we have not only read in several histories concerning the imps that have been employed in witchcraft, but also known in some of our own afflicted: we once thought we perceived something stir upon her pillow at a little distance from her; whereupon one present laying his hand there, he to his horror apprehended that he felt, though none could see it, a living creature not altogether unlike a rat, which nimbly escaped from him; and there were divers other persons who were thrown into a great consternation by feeling, as they judged, at other times, the same invisible animal.

SECT. 9. As it has been with a thousand other enchanted people, so it was with Margaret Rule in this particular, that there were several words which her tormentors would not let her hear, especially

MARGARET RULE.

the words Pray or Prayer, and yet she could so hear the letters of those words distinctly mentioned as to know what they meant. The standers by were forced sometimes thus in discourse to spell a word to her;. but because there were some so ridiculous as to count it a sort of spell or a charm for any thus to accommodate themselves to the capacity of the sufferer, little of this kind was done. But that which was more singular in this matter was, that she could not use these words in those penetrating discourses wherewith she would sometimes address the spectres that were about her. She would sometimes for a long while together apply herself to the spectres, whom she supposed the witches, with such exhortations to repentance as would have melted an heart of adamant to have heard them; her strains of expression and argument were truly extraordinary; persons perhaps of the best education and experience, and of attainments much beyond hers, could not have exceeded them; nevertheless, when she came to these words, God, Lord, Christ, Good, Repent, and some other such, her mouth could not utter them; whereupon she would sometimes, in an angry parenthesis, complain of their wickedness in stopping that word, but she would then go on with some other terms that would serve to tell what she meant. And I believe that if the most suspicious person in the world had beheld all the circumstances of this matter, he would have said it could not have been dissembled.

SECT. 10. Not only in the Swedish, hut also in the Salem witchcraft, the enchanted people have talked much of a white spirit, from whence they received marvellous assistances in their miseries. What lately befel Mercy Short, from the communications of such a spirit, hath been the just wonder of us all; but by such a spirit was Margaret Rule now also visited. She says that she could never see his face; but that she had a frequent view of his bright, shining and glorious garments; he stood by her bed-side continually, heartening and comforting her, and counselling her to maintain her faith and hope in God, and never comply with the temptations of her adversaries. She says he told her, that God had permitted her afflictions to befal her for the everlasting and unspeakable good of her own soul, and for the good of many others, and for his own immortal glory; . and that she should therefore be of good cheer, and be assured of a speedy deliverance; and the wonderful resolution of mind wherewith she encountered her afflictions was but agreeable to such expectations. Moreover, a minister having one day with some importunity prayed for the deliverance of this young woman, and pleaded that as she belonged to his flock and charge, he had so far a right unto her as that he was to do the part of a minister of our Lord for the bringing of her home unto God, only now the devil hindered him in doing that which he had a right thus to do; and whereas he had a better title unto her to bring her home to God, than the devil could have unto her to carry her away from the Lord, he therefore humbly applied himself unto God, who alone could right this matter, with a suit that she might be rescued out of satan's hands. Immediately upon this, though she heard nothing of this transaction, she began to call that minister her father, and that was the name whereby she every day before all sorts of people distinguished him. The occasion of it she says was this: the white spirit presently upon this transaction did after this manner speak to her: Margaret, you now are to take notice that such a man is your father; God has given you to him; do you from this time look upon him as your father, obey him, regard him, as your father; follow his counsels, and you shall do well. And though there was one passage more, which I do as little know what to make of as any of the rest, I am now going to relate it: more than three times have I seen it fulfilled in the deliverance of enchanted and possest persons, whom the providence of God has cast into my way, that their deliverance could not be obtained before the third fast kept for them, and the third day still obtained the deliverance; al though I have thought of beseeching of the Lord thrice, when buffeted by Satan: yet I must earnestly entreat all m y readers to beware of any superstitious conceits upon the number three; if our God will hear us upon once praying and fasting before him, it is well; and if he will not vouchsafe his mercy upon our thrice doing so, yet we must not be so discouraged as to throw by our devotion; but if the sovereign grace of our God will in any particular instances count our patience enough tried when we have solemnly waited upon him for any determinate number of times, who shall say to him, What doest thou? And if there shall be any number of instances wherein this grace of our God has exactly holden the same course, it may have a room in our humble observations, I hope, without any superstition. I say then that after Margaret Rule had been more than five weeks in her miseries, this white spirit said unto her, "Well, this day such a man (whom he named) has kept a third day for your deliverance; n o w be of good cheer, you shall speedily be delivered." I inquired whether what had been said of that man was true, and I gained exact and certain information that it was precisely so; but I doubt lest in relating this passage that I have used more openness than a friend should be treated with, and for that cause I have concealed several of the most memorable things that have occurred, not only in this but in some former histories, although indeed I am not so well satisfied about the true nature of this white spirit, as to count that I can do a friend much honour by reporting what notice this white spirit may have thus taken of him.

Sect. 11. On the last day of the week her tormentors (as she thought and said) approaching towards her, would be forced still to recoil and retire as unaccountably, unable to meddle with her; and they would retire to the fire side with their poppets; but going to stick pins into those poppets, they could not (according to their visions) make the pins to enter. She insulted over them with a very proper derision, daring them now to do their worst, whilst she had the satisfaction to see their black master strike them and kick them, like an overseer of so many negroes, to make them to do their work, and re new the marks of his vengeance on them when they failed of doing it. At last, being as it were tired with their ineffectual attempts to mortify her, they furiously said, "Well, you shan't be the last." And after a pause they added, "Go, and the devil go with you, we can do no more;" whereupon they flew out of the room, and me, returning perfectly to herself, most affectionately gave thanks to God for her deliverance. Her tormentors left her extremely weak and faint, and overwhelmed with vapours, which would not only cause her sometimes to swoon away, but also now and then for a little while discompose the reasonableness of her thoughts. Nevertheless her former troubles returned not; but we are now waiting to see the good effects of those troubles upon the souls of all concerned. And now I propose that some of our learned witlings of the coffee-house, for fear lest these proofs of an invisible world should spoil some of their sport, I will endeavour to turn them all into sport; for which buffoonery their only pretence will be, "They can't understand how such things as these could be done;" whereas indeed he that is but philosopher enough to have read but one little treatise, published in the year 1656, by no other man than the chirurgeon of an army, or but one chapter of Helmont, which I will not quote at this time too particularly, may give a far more intelligible account of these appearances than most of these blades can give why and how their tobacco makes them spit, or which way the flame of their candle becomes illuminating. As for that cavil, "The world would be undone if the devils could have such power as they seem to have in several of our stories," it may be answered, that as to many things, the lying devils have only known them to be done, and then pretended unto the doing of those things; but the true and best answer is, that by these things we only see what the devils could have power to do, if the great God should give them that power; whereas now our histories afford a glorious evidence for the being of a God. The world would indeed be undone, and horribly undone, if these devils, who now and then get liberty to play some very mischievous pranks, were not under a daily restraint of some Almighty Superior from doing more of such mischiefs. Wherefore, instead of all apish shouts and jeers at histories which have such undoubted confirmation, as that no man that has breeding enough to regard the common laws of human society, will offer to doubt of them, it becomes us rather to adore the goodness of God, who does not permit such things every day to befal us all, as he sometimes did permit to befal some few of our miserable neighbours.

SECT. 12. And why, after all my unwearied cares and pains to rescue the miserable from the lions and bears of hell, which had seized them, and after all my studies to disappoint the devils in their designs to confound my neighbourhood, must I be driven to the necessity of an apology? Truly the hard representations wherewith some ill men have reviled my conduct, and the countenance which other men have given to these representations, oblige me to give mankind some account of my behaviour. No christian can (I say none but evil workers can) criminate my visiting such of my poor flock as have at any time fallen under the terrible and sensible molestations of evil angels: let their afflictions have been what they will, I could not have answered it unto my glorious Lord, if I had withheld my just counsels and comforts from them; and if I have also with some exactness observed the methods of the invisible world, when they have thus become observable, I have been but a servant of mankind in doing so; yea, no less a person than the venerable Baxter has more than once or twice in the most publick manner invited mankind to thank me for that service. I have not been insensible of a greater danger attending me in this fulfilment of my ministry, than if I had been to take ten thousand steps over a rocky mountain filled with rattle-snakes; but I have considered, he that is wise will observe things; and the surprising explication and confirmation of the biggest part of the bible, which I have seen given in these things, has abundantly paid me for observing them. Now, in my visiting of the miserable, I was always of this opinion, that we were ignorant of that power the devils might have to do their mischiefs in the shapes of some that had never been explicitly engaged in diabolical confederacies, and that therefore, though many witchcrafts had been fairly detected on inquiries provoked and begun by spectral exhibitions, yet we could not easily be too jealous of the snares laid for us in the devices of Satan. The world knows how many pages I have composed and published, and particular gentlemen in the government know how many letters I have written, to prevent the excessive credit of spectral accusations; wherefore I have still charged the afflicted that they should cry out of nobody for afflicting of them; but that, if this might be any advantage, they might privately tell their minds to some one person of discretion enough to make no ill use of their communications; accordingly there has been this effect of it, that the name of no one good person in the world ever came under any blemish by means of an afflicted person that fell under my particular cognizance; yea, no one man, woman or child ever came into any trouble for the sake of any that were afflicted, after I had once begun to look after them. How often have I had this thrown into my dish, "that many years ago I had an opportunity to have brought forth such people as have in the late storm of witchcraft been complained of, but that I smothered all; and after that storm was raised at Salem, I did myself offer to provide meat, drink and lodging for no less than six of the afflicted, that so an experiment might be made, whether prayer with fasting, upon the removal of the distressed, might not put a period to the trouble then rising, without giving the civil authority the trouble of prosecuting those things which nothing but a conscientious regard unto the cries of miserable families could hare overcome the reluctancies of the honourable judges to meddle with." In short, I do humbly but freely affirm it, that there is not a man living in this world who has been more desirous than the poor man I to shelter my neighbours from the inconveniences of spectral outcries; yea, I am very jealous I have done so much that way, as to sin in what I have done; such have been the cowardice and fearfulness whereunto my regard unto the dissatisfaction of other people has precipitated me. I know a man in the world, who has thought he has been able to convict some such witches as ought to die; but his respect unto the publick peace has caused him rather to try whether he could not renew them by repentance; and as I have been studious to defeat the devils of their expectations to set people together by the ears thus, I have also checked and quelled those forbidden curiosities which would have given the devil an invitation to have tarried amongst us, when I have seen wonderful snares laid for curious people, by the secret and future things discovered from the mouths of damsels possest with a spirit of divination. Indeed I can recollect but one thing wherein there could be given so much as a shadow of reason for exceptions, and that is, my allowing of so many to come and see those that were afflicted. Now for that I have this to say, that I have almost a thousand times entreated the friends of the miserable, that they would not permit the intrusion of any company, but such as by prayers or other ways might be helpful to them; nevertheless I have not absolutely forbid all company from coming to your haunted chambers; partly because the calamities of the families were such as required the assistance of many friends; partly because I have been willing that there should be disinterested witnesses of all sorts; to confute the calumnies of such as would say all was but imposture; and partly because I saw God had sanctified the spectacle of the miseries on the afflicted unto the souls of many that were spectators; and it is a very glorious thing that I have now to mention: The devils have with most horrid operations broke in upon our neighbourhood, and God has at such a rate overruled all the fury and malice of those devils, that all the afflicted have not only been delivered, but I hope also savingly brought home unto God, and the reputation of no one good person in the world has been damaged; but instead thereof the souls of many, especially of the rising generation, have been thereby awakened unto some acquaintance with religion; our young people, who belonged unto the praying meetings; of both sexes, apart, would ordinarily spend whole nights by whole weeks together in prayers and psalms upon these occasions, in which devotions the devils could get nothing, but, like fools, a scourge for their own backs; and some scores of other young people, who were strangers to real piety, were now struck with the lively demonstrations of hell evidently set forth before their eyes, when they saw persons cruelly frighted, wounded and starved by devils, and scalded with burning brimstone; and yet so preserved in this tortured state, as that, at the end of one month's wretchedness, they were as able still to undergo another; so that of these also it might now be said, "Behold they pray." In the whole—the devil got just nothing—but God got praises, Christ got subjects, the Holy Spirit got temples, the church got addition, and the souls of men got everlasting benefits.[2] I am not so vain as to say that any wisdom or virtue of mine did contribute unto this good order of things; but I am so just as to say, I did not hinder this good. When therefore there have been those that picked up little incoherent scraps and bits of my discourses in this fruitful discharge of my ministry, and so travestied them in their abusive pamphlets as to persuade the town that I was their common enemy in those very points, wherein, if in anyone thing whatsoever, I have sensibly approved myself as true a servant unto them as possibly I could, though my life and soul had been at stake for it—yea to do like satan himself, by sly, base, unpretending insinuations, as if I wore not the modesty and gravity which became a minister of the gospel—I could not but think myself unkindly dealt withal, and the neglect of others to do me justice in this affair has caused me to conclude this narrative with complaints in another hearing of such monstrous injuries.

---

2. The estimated value of the tragedy of 1692 by Dr. Mather, in a moral and religious point of view, has not as yet been seen or experienced. We are certainly better able to judge of the effect produced by the delusion from our stand-point in 1860, than was Mather from his in 1693. While we are certain that virtue has received no aid from the transaction, it is not so apparent as he supposed "that the devil got just nothing." It has its use, however, as a beacon to warn us from too near an approach to such delusions, or those similar to them of the present day.

☞ The dates of the letters beginning on pages 25, 29 and 32 should have been printed 1693 (instead of 1694) conformably to the practice at that time beginning the year on the 25th of March, and to the dates of other letters in the book. [*From the 1823 edition.*]

PART II.

SEVERAL LETTERS, &c.

Boston, Jan. 11, 1693.

Mr. COTTON MATHER,
Reverend Sir,

INDING it needful on many accounts, I here present you with the copy of that paper which has been so much misrepresented, to the end that what shall be found defective or not fairly represented (if any such shall appear) they may be set right,—which runs thus:

September the 13*th,* 1693. In the evening, when the sun was withdrawn, giving place to darkness to succeed, I with some others were drawn by curiosity to see Margaret Rule, and so much the rather, because it was reported Mr. M—— would be there that night. Being come to her father's house, into the chamber wherein she was in bed, I found her of a healthy countenance, of about seventeen years old, lying very still, and speaking very little; what she did say seemed as if she were light-headed. Then Mr. M—— (father and son) came up, and others with them; in the whole there were about thirty or forty persons; they being set, the father on a stool, and the son upon the bedside by her, the son began to question her:

Margaret Rule, how do you do? then a pause without any answer.

Question, What! do there a great many witches sit upon you? *Answer,* Yes.

Question, Do you not know that there is a hard master? Then she was in a fit. He laid his hand upon her face and nose, but as he said without perceiving breath; then he brushed her on the face with his glove, and rubbed her stomach (her breast not being covered with the bed-clothes) and bid others do so too, and said it eased her—then she revived.

Q. Don't you know there is a hard master? *A.* Yes. .Reply, Don't serve that hard master—you know who.

Q. Do you believe? Then again she was in a fit, and he again rubbed her breast, &c.

About this time, Margaret Perd, an attendant, assisted him in rubbing her. The afflicted spake angrily to her, saying, Don't you meddle with me—and hastily put away her hand. He then wrought his fingers before her eyes, and asked her if she saw the witches? *A.* No.

Q. Do you believe? *A.* Yes.

Q. Do you believe in you know who? *A.* Yes.

Q. Would you have other people do so too—to believe in you know who? *A.* Yes.

Q. Who is it that afflicts you? *A.* I know not, there is a great many of them.

About this time the father questioned, if she knew the spectres. An attendant said, if she did she would not tell. The son proceeded:

Q. You have seen the black man, have you not? *A.* No.

Reply, I hope you never will.

Q. You have had a book offered you, have you not? *A.* No.

Q. The brushing of you gives you ease, don't it? *A.* Yes. She turned herself, and a little groaned.

Q. Now the witches scratch you, and pinch you, and bite you, don't they? *A.* Yes.

Then he put his hand upon her breast and belly, viz. on the clothes over her, and felt a living thing, as he said; which moved the father also to feel, and some others.

Q. Don't you feel the live thing in the bed? *A.* No.

Reply, That is only fancy.

Q. The great company of people increase your torment, don't they? *A.* Yes.

The people about were desired to withdraw. One woman said, I am sure I am no witch, I will not go; so others; so none withdrew.

Q. Shall we go to prayers? Then she lay in a fit as before. But this time, to revive. her, they waved a hat, and brushed her head and pillow therewith.

Q. Shall we go to prayer, &c. spelling the word. *A*. Yes.

The father went to prayer for perhaps half an hour, chiefly against the power of the devil and witchcraft, and that God would bring out the afflicters. During prayer-time, the son stood by, and when they thought she was in a fit, rubbed her and brushed her as before, and beckoned to others to do the like. After prayer he proceeded:

Q. You did not hear when we were at prayer, did you? *A*. Yes.

Q. You don't hear always—you did not hear for some time past, a word or two, did you? *A*. No.

Then turning him about. said, this is just another Mercy Short. Margaret Perd replied, she was not like her in her fits.

Q. What does she eat or drink? *A*. She does not eat at all, but drinks *rum*.[3]

Then he admonished the young people to take warning, &c. saying it was a sad thing to be so tormented by the devil and his instruments. A young man present, in the habit of a seaman, replied, "*This is the Devil all over.*" Then the ministers withdrew. Soon after they were gone the afflicted desired the women to be gone, saying, that the company of the men was not offensive to her; and having hold of the hand of a young man, said to have been her sweetheart

---

3. The affliction of Margaret Rule, like that of the Surrey Demoniac, Richard Dugdale of England, was nothing more than a bad case of delirium tremens. Richard was singularly tossed and buffeted by Satan, when nine ministers undertook to exorcise him, by many months of continued prayer and fasting, and happily succeeded on the 24th of March,1689. The record of the event in forms us,when Satan finally left Richard, he had a terrible fit and vomited, whereon the devil, when he could no longer withstand the ministers, with singular impudence cried, "Now, Dickey, I must leave thee, and must afflict thee no more." It is probable that the success in this famous case of the Surrey Demoniac occurred to the mind of Dr. Mather, when he offered to provide meat, drink, and lodging for no less than six of the possessed of Salem Village, that "the possessed might be scattered sunder," so that an experiment might be made, whether prayer with fasting, upon the removal of the accused, might not put a period to the rising trouble.

formerly, who was withdrawing, she pulled him again into his seat, saying, he should not go to night.

September the 19*th*, 1693. This night I renewed my visit, and found her rather of a fresher countenance than before. About eight persons were present with her. She was in a fit, screaming and making a noise. Three or four persons rubbed and brushed her, with their hands; they said that the brushing put them away, if they brushed or rubbed in the *right place*: therefore they brushed and rubbed in several places, and said that when they did it in the *right place* she could fetch her breath, and by that they knew. She being come to herself was soon in a merry talking fit. A young man came in, and asked her how she did. She answered, very bad, but at present a little better.

He soon told her he must be gone, and bid her good night; at which she seemed troubled, saying that she liked his company, and said she would not have him go till she was well; adding, for I shall die when you are gone. Then she complained they did not put her on a clean cap, but let her lie so like a beast, saying she should lose all her fellows. She said she wondered any people should be so wicked as to think she was not afflicted, but to think she dissembled. A young woman answered, Yes, if they were to see you in this merry fit, they would say you dissembled indeed. She replied, Mr. M—— said this was her laughing time, she must laugh now. She said Mr. M—— had been there this evening, and she enquired how long he had been gone. She said he stayed alone with her in the room half an hour, and said that he told her there were some that came for spies, and to report about town that she was not afflicted; that during the said time she had no fit; that he asked her if she knew how many times he had prayed for her to day; and that she answered, that she could oat tell; and that he replied, he had prayed for her nine times to day. The attendants said that she was sometimes in a fit, that none could open her joints, and that there came an old *iron-jawed* woman and tried, but could not do it; they likewise said, that her head could not be moved from the pillow. I tried to move her head, and found no more difficulty than another person (and so did others) but was not willing to offend by lifting it up, once being reproved for endeavouring it; they saying angrily, you will break her neck. The attendants said Mr. M—— would not go to prayer with her when people were in the room, as they did one night—that night he felt the *live creature*. Margaret Perd and another said they smelt brimstone. I and others said we did not smell any; then they said they did not know what it was. This Margaret said she wished she had been here when Mr. M—— was here. Another attendant said, If you had been here, you might not have been permitted in, for her own mother was not suffered to be present.

Sir, after the sorest affliction and greatest blemish to religion that ever befel this country, and after most men began to fear that some undue steps had been taken, and after his excellency (with their Majesties' approbation as is said) had put a stop to executions, and men began to hope there would never be a return of the like; finding these accounts to contain in them something extraordinary, I writ them down the same nights, in order to attain the certainty of them, and soon found them so confirmed that I have (besides other demonstrations) the whole under the hands of two persons who are ready to attest the truth of it; but not satisfied herewith, I shewed them to some of your particular friends, that so I might have the greater certainty; but was much surprised with the message you sent me, that I should be arrested for slander, and at your calling me one of the worst or liars, making it pulpit news, with the name of pernicious libels, &c. This occasioned my first letter: [as followeth.]

September the 29th, 1693.

Reverend Sir,

I having written from the mouths of several persons, who affirm they were present with Margaret Rule the 13th instant, her answers and behaviour, &c. and having shewed it to several of my friends, as also yours, and understanding you are offended at it, this is to acquaint you that if you and any one particular friend will please to meet me and some other indifferent person with me at Mr. Wilkins's, or at Benj. Harris's, you intimating the time, I shall be ready there to read it to you, as also a further account of proceedings the 19th instant, which may be needful to prevent groundless prejudices, and let deserved blame be cast where it ought. From, sir, yours, in what I may, R.C.

The effects of which, sir, (not to mention that long letter only once read to me) was, you sent me word you would meet me at Mr. Wilkins's; but, before that answer, at yours and your father's complaint, I was brought before their majesties' justice, by warrant, for scandalous libels against yourself, and was bound over to answer at sessions. I do not remember you then objected against the truth of what I had wrote, but asserted it was wronged by omissions; which, if it were so, was past any power of mine to remedy, having given a faithful account of all that came to my knowledge: and, sir, that you might not be without some cognizance of the reasons why I took so much pains in it, as also for my own information, (if it might have been) I wrote to you my second letter to this effect:

November the 24th, 1693.

Reverend Sir,

Having expected some weeks your meeting me at Mr. Wilkins's, according to what you intimated to me, and the time drawing near for our meeting elsewhere, I thought it not amiss to give you a summary of my thoughts in the great concern, which, as you say, has been agitated with so much heat. That there are witches is not the doubt; the scriptures else were vain, which assign their punishment to be by death; but what this witchcraft is, or wherein it does consist, seems to be the whole difficulty: and as it may be easily demonstrated, that all that bear that name cannot be justly so accounted; so that some things and actions, not so esteemed by the most, yet upon due examination will be found to merit no better character.

In your late book you lay down a brief synopsis of what has been written on that subject, by a triumvirate of as eminent men as ever handled it (as you are pleased to call them) viz. Mr. Perkins, Gaule and Bernard, consisting of about thirty tokens to know them by, many of them distinct from, if not thwarting, each other: among all of which I can find but one decisive, viz. that of Mr. Gaule, head iv, and run thus: "Among the most unhappy circumstances to convict a witch, one is a maligning and oppugning the word, work or worship of God, and by any extraordinary sign seeking to seduce any from it. See *Deut.* xiii. I. 2. *Matt.* xxiv. 24. *Acts* xiii. 8, 10. *2 Tim.* iii. 8. Do but mark well the places; and for this very property, of thus opposing and perverting, they are all there concluded arrant and absolute witches." This head, as here laid down and inserted by you, either is a truth or not; if not, why is it here inserted from one of the triumvirate? If it be a truth, as the scriptures quoted will abundantly testify, whence is it that it is so little regarded, though it be the only head well proved by scripture, or that the rest of the triumvirate should so far forget their work as not to mention it? It were to be unjust to the memory of those otherwise wise men, to suppose them to have any sinister design; but perhaps the force of a prevailing opinion, together with an education thereto suited, might overshadow their judgments, as being wont to be but too prevalent in many other cases. But if the above be truth, then the scripture is full and plain, what is witchcraft. And if so, what need of his next head of hanging people without as full and clear evidence as in other cases? Or what need of the rest of the receipts of the triumvirate? What need of praying that the afflicted may be able to discover who it is that afflicts them? or what need of searching for teats for the devil to suck, in his old age; Or the experiment of saying the Lord's prayer, &c. with a multitude more, practised in some places superstitiously inclined? Other actions have been practised for easing the afflicted, less justifiable, if not strongly savouring of witchcraft itself, viz. fondly imagining by the hand, &c. to drive off spectres, or to knock off invisible chains, or by striking in the air to wound either the afflicted or others, &c. I write not this to accuse any, but that all may beware; believing that the devil's bounds are set, which he cannot pass; that devils are so full of malice, that it cannot be added to by mankind; that where he hath power he neither can nor will omit executing it; that it is only the Almighty that sets hounds to his rage, and that only can commissionate him to hurt or destroy any.

These last, sir, are such foundations of truth, in my esteem, that I cannot but own it to be my duty to assert them, when called, though with the hazard of my all; and consequently to detest such as these, that a witch can commissionate devils to afflict mortals; that he can, at his or the witch's pleasure, assume any shape; that hanging or drowning of witches can lessen his power of afflicting, or restore those that were at a distance tormented, with many others depending on these; all tending, in my esteem, highly to the dishonour of God, and the endangering the well-being of a people; and do further add, that as the scriptures are full that there is witchcraft (ut sup.) so 'tis as plain that there are possessions, and that the bodies of the possest have hence been not only afflicted, but strangely agitated, if not their tongues improved to foretel futurities, &c. and why not to accuse the innocent, as bewitching them? having pretence to divination to gain credence. This being reasonable to be expected from him who is the father of lies, to the end he may thereby involve a country in blood, malice and evil-surmising, which he greedily seeks after, and so finally lead them from their fear and dependence upon God, to fear him and a supposed witch, thereby attaining his end upon mankind; and not only so, but natural distempers, as has been frequently observed by the judicious, have so operated as to deceive more than the vulgar, as is testified by many famous physicians and others. And as for that proof of multitudes of confessions, this country may be by this time thought competent judges what credence we ought to give them, having had such numerous instances, as also how obtained.

And now, sir, if herein be any thing in your esteem valuable, let me entreat you not to account it the worse for coming from so mean a hand; which, however you may have received prejudice, &c. am ready to serve you to my power; but. if you judge otherwise hereof, you may take your own methods for my better information. Who am, sir, yours to command, in what I may,   R.C.

In answer to this last, sir, you replied to the gentleman that presented it, that you had nothing to prosecute against me; and said, as to your sentiments in your books, you did not bind any to believe them; and then again renewed your promise of meeting me, as before, though not yet performed. Accordingly, though, I waited at sessions, there was none to object ought against me, upon which I was dismissed. This gave me some reason to believe that you intended all should have been forgotten; but, instead of that, I find the coals are fresh blown up, I being supposed to be represented, in a late manuscript, *More Wonders of the*, &c. as travestying your discourse in your faithful discharge of your duty, &c. and such as see not with the author's eyes, rendered sadducees and witlings, &c. and the arguments that square not with the sentiments therein contained, buffoonery; rarely, no doubt, agreeing with the spirit of Christ, and his dealings with an unbelieving Thomas, yet whose infidelity was without compare less excusable; but the author having resolved long since to have no more than one single grain of patience with them that deny, &c. the wonder is the less. It must needs be that silences come, but wo to him by whom they come. To vindicate myself therefore from such false imputations, of satan-like insinuations, and misrepresenting your actions &c. and to vindicate yourself, sir, as much as is to in my power, from those suggestions, said to be insinuated, as if you wore not the modesty and gravity that becomes a minister of the gospel; which, it seems, some, that never saw the said narratives, report them to contain; I say, sir, for these reasons, I here present you with the first copy that ever was taken, &c. and purpose for a week's time to be ready, if you shall intimate your pleasure to wait upon me, either at the place formerly appointed, or to any other that is indifferent; to the end that, if there shall appear any defects in that narrative, they may be amended.

Thus, sir, I have given you a genuine account of my sentiments and actions in this affair; and do request and pray, that if I err, I may, be shewed it from scripture, or sound reason, and not by quotations out of Virgil; nor Spanish rhetorick. For I find the witlings mentioned are so far from answering your profound questions, that they cannot so much as pretend to shew a distinction between witchcraft in the common notion of it, and possession; nor so much as to demonstrate that ever the jews or primitive christians did believe that a witch could send a devil to afflict her neighbours. But to all these, sir, (ye being the salt of the earth, &c.) I have reason to hope for a satisfactory answer to him, who is one that reverences your person and office; and am, sir, yours to command, in what I may, R.C.

Boston, Jan. the 15*th,* 1694.

Mr. R.C.

Whereas you intimate your desires, that what is not fairly (I take it for granted you mean truly also) represented in a paper you lately sent me, containing a pretended narrative of a visit by my father and self to an afflicted young woman, whom we apprehended to be under a diabolical possession, might be rectified; I have this to say, as I have often already said, that I do scarcely find any one thing in the whole paper, whether respecting my father or self, either fairly or truly represented, Nor can I think that any, that know my parent's circumstances, but must think him deserving a better character by far, than this narrative can be thought to give him. When the main design we managed, in visiting the poor afflicted creature, was to prevent the accusations of the neighbourhood, can it be fairly represented that our design was to draw out such accusations? which is the representation of the paper. We have testimonies of the best witnesses, and in number not a few, that when we asked Rule whether she thought she knew who tormented her, the question was but an introduction to the solemn charges which we then largely gave, that she should rather die than tell the names of any whom she might imagine that she knew. Your informers have reported the question, and report nothing of what follows, as essential to the giving of that question. And can this be termed a piece of fairness? Fair it cannot be, that when ministers faithfully and carefully discharge their duty to the miserable in their flock, little bits, scraps and shreds of their discourses should be tacked together to make them contemptible, when there shall be no notice of all the necessary, seasonable and profitable things that occurred in those discourses; and without which, the occasion of the lesser passages cannot be understood: and yet I am furnished with abundant evidences, ready to be sworn, that will positively prove this part of unfairness, by the above mentioned narrative, to be done both to my father and self. Again, it seems not fair or reasonable that I should be exposed for that which yourself (not to say some others) might have exposed me for if I had not done, viz. for discouraging so much company from flocking about the possest maid; and yet, as I persuade myself, you cannot but think it to be good advice to keep much company from such haunted chambers. Besides, the unfairness doth more appear, in that I find nothing repeated of what I said about the advantage which the devil takes from too much observation and curiosity.

In that several of the questions in the paper are so worded as to carry in them a presupposal of the things inquired after, to say the best of it, is very unfair. But this is not all; the narrative contains a number of mistakes and falsehoods, which, were they wilful and designed, might justly be termed gross lies. The representations are far from true, when 'tis affirmed my father and self being come into the room, I began the discourse: I hope I understand breeding a little better than so. For proof of this, did occasion serve, sundry can depose the contrary.

'Tis no less untrue, that either my father or self put the question, How many witches sit upon you? We always cautiously avoided that expression, it being contrary to our inward belief: All the standers-by will, I believe, swear they did not hear us use it, (your witnesses excepted) and I tremble to think how hardy those woful creatures must be, to call the Almighty, by an oath, to so false a thing. As false a representation 'tis, that I rubbed Rule's stomach, her breast not being covered. The oath of the nearest spectators, giving a true account of that matter, will prove this to be little less than a gross (if not a doubled) lie; and to be somewhat plainer, it carries the face of a lie contrived on purpose (by them at least to whom you are beholden for the narrative) wickedly and basely to expose me: for you cannot but know how much this representation hath contributed to make people believe a smutty thing of me. I am far from thinking but that in your own conscience you believe, that no indecent action of that nature could then be done by me before such observers, had I been so wicked as to have been inclined to what is base. It looks next to impossible that a reparation should be made me for the wrong done to (I hope, as to any scandal) an unblemished, though weak and small, servant of the church of God. Nor is what follows a less untruth, that it was an attendant and not myself who said, If Rule knows who afflicts her, yet she won't tell. I therefore spoke it that I might encourage her to continue in that concealment of all names whatsoever; to this I am able to furnish myself with the attestation of sufficient oaths. 'Tis as far from true, that my apprehension of the imp, about Rule, was on her belly; for the oaths of the spectators, and even of those that thought they felt it, can testify that it was upon the pillow, at a distance from her body. As untrue a representation is that which follows, viz. that it was said unto her, that her not apprehending of that odd, palpable, though not visible, mover, was from her fancy; for I endeavoured to persuade her that it might be but fancy in others, that there was any such thing at all. Witnesses every way sufficient can be produced for this also. It is falsely represented, that my father felt on the young woman after the appearance mentioned, for his hand was never near her; oath can sufficiently vindicate him. 'Tis very untrue, that my father prayed, for perhaps half an hour, against the power of the devil and witchcraft, and that God would bring out the afflicters: witnesses of the best credit can depose, that his prayer was not a quarter of an hour, and that there was no more than about one clause, towards the close of the prayer, which was of this import; and this clause also was guarded with a singular wariness and modesty, viz. If there were any evil instruments in this matter, God would please to discover them: and that there was more than common reason for that petition, I can satisfy any one that will please to inquire of me. And strange it is, that a gentleman that from eighteen to fifty-four hath been an exemplary minister of the gospel; and that, besides a station in the church of God, as considerable as any that his own country can afford, hath for divers years come off with honour, in his application to three crowned heads and the chiefest nobility of three kingdoms; knows not yet how to make one short prayer of a quarter of an hour, but in New-England he must be libelled for it. There are divers other down-right mistakes which you have permitted yourself (I would hope not knowingly and with a malicious design) to be receiver or compiler of, which I shall now forbear to animadvert upon. As for the appendix of the narrative, I do find myself therein injuriously treated; for the utmost of your proof, for what you say of me, amounts to little more than this, viz. Some people told you, that others told them, that such and such things did pass; but you may assure yourself, that I am not unfurnished with witnesses that can convict the same. Whereas you would give me to believe the bottom of these, your methods, to be some dissatisfaction about the commonly received power of devils and witches; I do not only with all freedom ofter you the use of any part of my library, which you may see cause to peruse on that subject, but also, if you and any one else; whom you please, will visit mc at my study, yea, or meet me at any other place, less inconvenient than those by you proposed. I will with all the fairness and calmness in the world dispute the point. I beg of God that he would bestow us many blessings on you, as ever on myself; and out of a sincere wish that you may be made yet more capable of these blessings, I take this occasion to lay before you the faults (not few nor small ones neither) which the paper contained, you lately sent me, in order to be examined by me. In Case you want a true and full narrative or my visit, whereof such all indecent travesty (to say the best) hath been made, I am not unwilling to communicate it; in mean time must take liberty to say, it is scarcely consistent with common civility, much less christian charity, to offer the narrative, now with you, for a true one, till you have a truer; or for a full one, till you have a fuller. Your sincere (though injured) friend and servant, C. MATHER.

The copy of a paper received with the above letter.

I do testify that I have seen Margaret Rule, in her afflictions from the invisible world, lifted up from her bed, wholly by an invisible force, a great way towards the top of the room where she lay; in her being so lifted, she had no assistance from any use of her own arms or hands, or any other part of her body, not so much as her heels touching her bed, or resting on any support whatsoever. And I have seen her thus lifted, when not only a strong person hath thrown his whole weight across her to pull her down, but several other persons have endeavoured, with all their might, to hinder her from being so raised up; which I suppose that several others. will testify as well as myself when called unto it. Witness my hand, SAMUEL AVES.

We can also testify to the substance of what. is above written; and have several times seen Margaret Rule so lifted up from her bed, as that she had no use of her own limbs to help her up; but it was the declared apprehension of us, as well as others, that saw it, impossible for any hands, but some of the invisible world, to lift her.

ROBERT EARLE,

JOHN WILKINS,

DAN. WILLIAMS.

We, whose names are under-written, do testify, that one evening, when we were in the chamber where Margaret Rule then lay, in her late affliction, we observed her to be, by an invisible force, lifted up from the bed whereon she lay, so as to touch the garret floor, while yet neither her feet, nor any other part of her body, rested either on the bed or any other support, but were also, by the same force, lifted up from all that was under her; and all this for a considerable while, we judged it several minutes; and it was as much as several of us could do, with all our strength, to pull her down. All which happened when there was not only we two in the chamber, but we suppose ten or a dozen more, whose names we have forgotten.

THOMAS THORNTON

WILLIAM HUDSON

testifies to the substance of Thornton's testimony, to which he also hath set his hand.

Boston, January 18, 1694.

Mr. COTTON MATHER,

Reverend Sir,

Yours of the 15th instant I received yesterday, and soon found I had promised myself too much by it, viz. either concurrence with, or a denial of, those fundamentals mentioned in mine, of November the 24th, finding this waved by an invitation to your library, &c. I thank God I have the bible, and do judge that sufficient to demonstrate that cited head of Mr. Gaule to be a truth, as also those other heads mentioned as the foundations of religion. And in my apprehension, if it be asked any christian, whether God governs the world, and whether it be he only can commissionate devils, and such other fundamentals, he ought to be as ready as in the question, Who made him? (A little writing certainly might be of more use, to clear up the controverted points, than either looking over many books in a well furnished library, or than a dispute, if I were qualified for it; the inconveniencies of passion being this way best avoided.) And am not without hopes that you will yet oblige me so far, as to consider that letter, and if I err, to let me see it by scripture, &c.

Yours, almost the whole of it, is concerning the narrative I sent to you; and you seem to intimate as if I were giving characters, reflections, libels, &c. concerning yourself and relations; all which were as far from my thoughts, as ever they were in writing after either yourself, or any other minister. In the front you declare your apprehension to be, that the afflicted was under a diabolical possession; and if so, I see not how it should be occasioned by any witchcraft (unless we ascribe that power to a witch, which is only the prerogative of the Almighty, of sending or commissionating the devils to afflict her.) But to your particular objections against the narrative; and to the first. My intelligence not giving me any further, I could not insert that I knew not. And it seems improbable that a question should be put, whether she knew who they were that tormented her, and at the same time to charge her, and that upon her life, not to tell; and if you had done so, I see but little good you could promise yourself or others by it, she being possest, as also having it inculcated so much to her, of witchcraft. And as to the next objection, about company flocking, &c. I profess my ignorance, not knowing what you mean by it. And, sir, that most of the questions did carry with them a presupposing the things inquired after, is evident, if there were such as those relating to the *black man* and a book, and about her hearing the prayer, &c. (related in the said narrative, which I find no objection against.) As to that which is said of mentioning yourself first discoursing, and your hopes that your breeding was better, (I doubt it not, nor do I doubt your father might first apply himself to others) my intelligence is, that you first spake to the afflicted or possessed, for which you had the advantage of a nearer approach. The next two objections are founded upon mistakes: I find not in the narrative any such question, as How many witches sit upon you? nor, that her breast was not covered, in which those material words, *with the bed clothes*, are wholly omitted. I am not willing to retort here your own language upon you; but can tell you, that your own discourse of it publickly, at Sir W.P.'s table, has much more contributed to, &c. As to the reply, If she could she would not tell, whether either or both spake it, it matters not much. Neither does the narrative say, you felt the live thing on her belly; though I omit now to say what further demonstrations there are of it. As to that reply, That is only her fancy, I find the word *her* added. And as to your father's feeling for the live creature after you had felt it, if it were on the bed it was not so very far from her. And for the length of his prayer, possibly your witnesses might keep a more exact account of the time than those others, and I stand not for a few minutes. For the rest of the objections, I suppose them of less moment, if less can be; however, shall be ready to receive them. Those matters of greatest concern I find no objections against. These being all that yet appear, it may be thought that if the narrative be not fully exact, it was near as memory could bear away; but should be glad to see one more perfect (which yet is not to be expected, seeing none wrote at the same time.) You mention the appendix, by which I understand the second visit; and if you be by the possessed belied (as being half an hour with her alone, excluding her own mother, and as telling her you had prayed for her nine times that day, and that now was her laughing time, she must laugh now) I can see no wonder in it: What can be expected less from the father of lies, by whom, you judge, she was possest?

And besides the above letter, you were pleased to send me another paper, containing several testimonies of the possessed being lifted up, and held a space of several minutes to the garret floor, &c. but they omit giving the account, whether after she was down they bound her down, or kept holding her; and relate not how many were to pull her down, which hinders the knowledge what number they must be, to be stronger than an invisible force. Upon the whole, I suppose you expect I should believe it; and if so, the only advantage gained is, that what has been so long controverted between protestants and papists, whether miracles are ceast, will hereby seem to be decided for the latter; it being, for ought I can see, if so, as true a miracle as for iron to swim; and the devil can work such miracles.

But, sir, to leave these little disputable things, I do again pray that you would let me have the happiness of your approbation or confutation of that letter before referred to.

And now, sir, that the God of all grace may enable us zealously to own his truths, and to follow those things that tend to peace, and that yourself may be as an useful instrument in his hand, effectually to ruin the remainder of heathenish and popish superstitions, is the earnest desire and prayer of yours to command in what I may, R.C.

Postscript.—Sir, I here send you the copy of a paper that lately came to my hands; which, though it contains no wonders, yet is remarkable, and runs thus:

An account of what an Indian told Capt. Hill at Saco Fort.

The Indian told him, that the French ministers were better than the English; for before the French came among them there were a great many witches among the Indians; but now there were none; and there were witches among the English ministers, as Burroughs, who was hang'd for it.

Were I disposed to make reflections upon it, I suppose you will judge the field large enough; but I forbear.
As above,　　　　　　　R.C.

Boston, Feb. 19, 1694.

Mr. COTTON MATHER,
　Reverend Sir,

I have received as yet no answer to mine of November the 24th, except an offer to peruse books, &c. relating to the doctrinals therein contained; nor to my last, of January the 18th, in which I again prayed that if I erred I might be shewed it by scripture, viz. in believing that the devil's bounds are set, which he cannot pass—that the devils are so full of malice, that it can't be added to by mankind—that where he hath power, he neither can nor will omit executing it—that it is only the Almighty that sets bounds to his rage, and who only can commission him to hurt or destroy any; and consequently to detest, as erroneous and dangerous, the belief that a witch can commission devils to afflict mortals—that he can at his or the witch's pleasure assume any shape—that the hanging or drowning of witches can lessen his power of afflicting, and restore those that were at a distance tormented by him;—and whether witchcraft ought to be understood, now in this age, to be the same that it was when the divine oracles were given forth, particularly those quoted by mr. Gaule, in that cited head, *Wonders of the Invisible World* (mr. Gaule's fourth head) to discover witches: which do so plainly shew a witch, in scripture sense, to be one that maligns, &c. and that pretends to give a sign in order to seduce, &c. For I have never understood, in my time, any such have suffered as witches, though sufficiently known; but the only witch now inquired after is one that is said to become so by making an explicit covenant with the devil, i.e. the devil appearing to them, and making a compact, mutually promising each to other; testified by their signing his book, a material book, which he is said to keep; and that thereby they are intituled to a power, not only to afflict others, but such as is truly exorbitant, if not highly intrenching upon the prerogative of him who is the Sovereign Being: For who is he that saith, and it cometh to pass, when the Lord commandeth it not?

Such explicit covenant being, as is said, in this age, reckoned essential to complete a witch; yet I finding nothing of such covenant (or power thereby obtained) in scripture, and yet a witch therein so fully described, do pray that if there be any such scriptures I may be directed to them; for as to the many legends in this case, I make no account of them: I read indeed of a covenant with death and with hell, but suppose that to be in the heart (or *mental*) only, and see not what use such an explicit one can be of between spirits, any further than as 'tis a copy of that *mental* which is in the heart. The dire effects and consequences of such notion may be found written in indelible *Roman* characters of blood, in all countries where they have prevailed. And what less can be expected, when men are indicted for that, which it is impossible to prove, so as for any to clear himself of, viz. such explicit covenant with the devil; and then, for want of better evidence, must take up with such as the nature of such secret covenant can bear, as mr. Gaule hath it, i.e. distracted stories, and strange and foreign events, &c. thereby endeavouring to find it, though by its but supposed effects. By the same rule that one is put to purge himself of such compact, by the same may all mankind.

This then being so important a case, it concerns all to know what foundations in scripture are laid for such a structure; for if they are deficient of that warrant, the more eminent the architects are, the more dangerous are they thereby rendered, &c. These are such considerations as I think will vindicate me, in the esteem of all lovers of humanity, in my endeavours to get them cleared; and, to that end, do once more pray, that you would so far oblige me as to give your approbation or confutation of the above doctrinals; but if you think silence a virtue in this case, I shall (I suppose) so far comply with it as not to lose you any more time to look over my papers. And if any others will so far oblige me, I shall not be ungrateful to them.

LETTERS TO

Praying God to guide and prosper you, I am, sir, yours to my power,
R.C.

(He that doth truth cometh to the light.)

Boston, April the 16*th,* 1694.

Mr. COTTON MATHER,

 Reverend Sir,

 Having as yet received no answer to my last, touching the doctrinals therein referred to, though at the delivery of it you were pleased to promise the gentleman that presented it that I should have it, and after that you acquainted the same gentleman you were about it; the length of time since those promises makes me suppose you are preparing something for the press (for I would not question your veracity;) and I think it may not be amiss, when you do any thing of that nature for the public view, that you also explain some passages of some late books of yours and your relations, which are hard to be understood; to instance in a few of many; *Wonders of the Invisible World*, page 17, "Plagues are some of those woes with which the devil causes our trouble." Page 18, "Hence come such plagues as that besom of destruction which within our memory swept away such a throng of people from one English city, in one visitation. Wars are some of those woes with which the devil causes our trouble." Page 16, "Hence 'tis that the devil, like a dragon keeping a guard upon such fruits as would refresh a languishing world, has hindered mankind for many ages from hitting upon those useful inventions. The benighted world must jog on, for thousands of years, without the knowledge of the load stone, printing, and spectacles." Page 10, "It is not likely that every devil does know every language. 'Tis possible the experience, or, if I may call it so, the education, of all devils is not alike." *Cases of Conscience*, page 63, "The devil has inflicted on many the disease called the lycanthropia." *Memorable Providences relating to Witchcraft Disc.* page 24, "I am also apt to think that the devils are seldom able to hurt us in any of our exterior concerns, without a commission from some of our fellow worms. When foul mouth'd men shall wish harm to their neighbours, they give a commission to the devil to perform what they desire; and if God should not mercifully prevent, they would go through with it. Hear this, you that in wild passion will give every thing to the devil; hear it, you that bespeak a rot; a pox, or a plague, on all that shall provoke you; I here indict you as guilty of hellish witchcraft in the sight of God." *More Wonders of the Invisible World*, p. 49, "They each of them have their spectres or devils commissioned by them, and representing them." Page 14, "But such a permission from God for the devil to come down and break in upon mankind, must often times be accompanied with a commission from some of mankind itself." *Enchantments encountered*, "These witches have driven a trade of commissioning their confederate spirits to do all sorts of mischiefs to their neighbours." Page 50, "They have bewitched some, even so far as to make them self-destroyers." Page 144, "As I am abundantly satisfied, that many of the self-murders, committed here, have been the effects of a cruel and bloody witchcraft, letting fly demons upon the miserable Senecas." Page 51, :We have seen some of their children dedicated to the devil, that in their infancy the imps have sucked them." *Cases of Conscience*, page 24, "They bequeath their demons to the children as a legacy, by whom they are often assisted to see and do things beyond the power of nature." Page 21, "There is in Spain a sort of people called Zahurs, that can see into the bowels of the earth." *On Tuesdays and Fridays, and to add that in page* 49; the words are, "For the law of God allows of no revelation from any other spirit but himself, *Isa.* viii. 19. It is a sin against God to make use of the devil's help, to know that which cannot be otherways known; and I testify against it as a great transgression, which may justly provoke that Holy One of Israel to let loose devils on the whole land. Although the devil's accusation may be so far regarded, as to cause an inquiry into the truth of things, (*Job* i. 11, 12, and ii. 5, 6) yet not so as to be an evidence or ground of conviction; for the devil's testimony ought not to be taken in whole nor in part." It is a known truth, that some unwary expressions of the primitive fathers were afterwards improved for "the introducing and establishing of error, as their calling the Virgin Mary the mother of God, &c. Hence occasion and advantage were taken to propagate the idolizing of her. The like might be said of the eucharist. These assertions, above rehearsed, being apparently liable to a like malconstruction, are no less dangerous, are therefore, as I said, highly needful to be explained, and that in a most public manner. For were they to be understood literally, and as they are spoken, it must seem as if the authors were introducing among christians very dangerous doctrines, such as, were they asserted by the best of men, yet ought to be rejected by all, &c. viz. That 'tis the devil that brings the most of evils upon mankind, by way of infliction, that do befal them; and that the witch can commission him to the performance of these; with many other as dangerous doctrines, and such as seem in their tendency to look favourably upon the antient pagan doctrines of this country, who believed that God did hurt to none, but good to all, but that the devil must be pleased by worshiping, &c. from whom came all their miseries, as they believed. For what were all this, but to rob God of his glory in the highest manner, and give it to a devil and a witch? Is it not he that hath said, Shall there be evil in a city, and the Lord hath not done it? But if any are fond of their own notions, because some eminent men before now have asserted them, they may do well to compare them with that excellent saying (*Wonders of the Invisible World*, p. 7) "About this devil there are many things, whereof we may reasonably and profitably be inquisitive; such things I mean as are in our bibles revealed to us; according to which if we do not speak on so dark a subject, but according to our own uncertain and perhaps humoursome conjectures, there is no light in us." Or that other, p.75, "At every other weapon the devil will be too hard for us." For 'tis most certain that other notions, weapons and practices have been taken up with, and that the event has been answerable: the devil has been too hard for such as have so done. I shall forbear to instance from the dogmatical part, and shall mention some practices that as much need explaining; *Mem. Provid. Rel. to Witchc.* pages 29, 30,31; where account is given that it was prayed for that the afflicted might be able to declare, whom she apprehended herself afflicted by, together with the immediate answer of such prayer. To this you once replied, when it was mentioned to you, that you did not then understand the wiles of satan.

To which I have nothing to object, but it might be a good acknowledgment. But considering that the book is gone forth into all the world, I cannot but think the salve ought to be proportioned to the sore, and the notice of the devil's wiles as universal as the means recommending them. Another practice is, (pages 20, 21,) "There was one singular passion that frequently attended her; an invisible chain would be clapt about her, and she in much pain and fear cry out when they began to put it on: once I did with my own hand knock it off as it began to be fastened about her." If this were done by the power or virtue of any ordinance of divine instruction, it is well; but would have been much better if the institution had been demonstrated; or was there any physical virtue in that particular hand? But supposing that neither of these will be asserted by the author, I think it very requisite, that the world may be acquainted with the operation, and to what art or craft to refer their power of knocking off invisible chains. And thus, sir, I have faithfully discharged what in this I took to be my duty, and am so far from doing it to gain applause, or from a spirit of contradiction, that I expect to procure me many enemies thereby; but (as in case of a fire) where the glory of God and the good and welfare of mankind are so nearly concerned, I thought it my duty to be no longer an idle spectator; and can and do say, to the glory of God, in this whole affair, I have endeavoured to keep a conscience void of offence, both towards God and towards man; and therein at the least have the advantage of such as are very jealous they have done so much herein, as to sin in what they have done, viz. in sheltering the accused; such have been the cowardice and fearfulness, into which a regard to the dissatisfaction of other people have precipitated them; which by the way must needs acquaint all, that for the future other measures are resolved upon (by such) which, how bloody they may prove when opportunity shall offer, is with him who orders all things according to the counsel of his own will. And now, that the song of angels may be the emulation of men, is the earnest desire and prayer of; sir, yours to command in what I may, R.C.

Glory to God in the highest, and on earth peace, and good will towards men.

Boston, March the 1*st,* 1694.

Mr. B——,

Worthy Sir,

After more than a year's waiting for the performance of a reiterated promise from one under singular obligations, and a multitude of advantages to have done it sooner, the utmost compliance I have met with is (by your hands) the sight of four sheets of rescinded papers. But I must first be obliged to return them in a fortnight, and not copied, which I have now complied with: and having read them, am not at all surprised at the author's caution, not to admit of such crude matter and impertinent absurdities, as are to be found in it. He seems concerned that I take no notice of his several books, wherein, as he saith, he has unanswerably proved things. To this I might reply, that I have sent him letters of quotations out of those books, to know how much of them he will abide by; for I thought it hard to affix their natural consequences, till he had opportunity to explain them. And saith, that he hath sent me mr. Baxter's *World of Spirits*, an ungainsayable book, &c. (though I know no ungainsayable book but the bible;) which book, I think, no man that has read it will give such a title to but the author. He speaks of my reproaching his public sermons; of which I am not conscious to myself unless it be about his interpretation of a thunder storm (that broke into his house) which savoured so much of enthusiasm.

As to those papers, I have (as I read them) quoted in the margin where, in a hasty reading, I thought it needful; of which it were unreasonable for him to complain, seeing I might not take a copy, thereby to have been enabled more at leisure to digest what were needful to be said on so many heads; and as I have not flattered him, so, for telling what was so needful, with the hazard of making so many enemies by it, I have approved myself one of his best friends. And besides his own sense of the weakness of his answer, testified by the prohibition above, he has wholly declined answering to most of those things that I had his promise for; and what he pretends to speak to, after mentioning, without the needful answer or proof, drops it.

His first main work, after his definition of a witch, which he never proves (without saying any thing to mr. Gaule's scriptural description, though so often urged to it, and though himself has in his book recommended and quoted it) is to magnify the devil's power, and that as I think beyond and against the scripture; this takes him up about 11 pages; and yet in page 22d he again returns to it, and, as *I* understand it, takes part with the pharisees against our Saviour in the argument; for they charge him that he cast out devils through Beelzebub: our Saviour's answer is, (*Matt.* xii. 25) *Every kingdom divided against itself is brought to desolation; and every city or house divided against itself shall not stand; and if satan cast out satan, he is divided against himself; how shall then his kingdom stand?*

And yet, notwithstanding this answer, together with what follows, for further illustration our author is it seems resolved to assert, that our Saviour did not in this answer deny that many did so, viz. cast out devils by Beelzebub; and, page 23, grants that the devils have a miraculous power, but yet it must not be called miraculous, and yet can be distinguished, as he intimates, only by the conscience or light within, to the no small scandal of the christian religion: though our Saviour and his apostles account this the chief or principal proof of his godhead, (*John* xx. 30, 31. *John* x. 37, 38. *John* v. 30. *Mark* xvi. 17, 18. *Acts* ii. 22. and iv. 30. with many others) and that miracles belong only to God, who also governs the world, (*Ps.* cxxxvi. 4. *Jer.* xiv. 22. *Isa.* xxxviii. 8. *Ps.* lxii. 11, *Lam.* iii. 37. *Amos* iii, 6.) But, to forbear quoting that which the scripture is most full in, do only say, that he that dares assert the devil to have such a miraculous power, had need have other scriptures than ever I have seen.

In page 12, our author proceeds, and states a question to this effect: If the devil has such powers, and cannot exert them without permission from God, what can the witch contribute thereunto? Instead of an answer to this weighty objection, our author first concedes, that the devils do ordinarily exert their powers, without the witches contributing to it; but yet, that, to the end to increase their guilt, he may cheat a witch, by making her believe herself the author of them. His next is, If witchcraft be, as I suppose it is, the skill of applying the plastic spirit of the world, &c. then the consent of the witch doth naturally contribute to that mischief that the devil does. And his last answer runs to this effect: Is it not the ordination of God, that where the devil can get the consent of a witch for the hurting of others, the hurt shall as certainly be as if they had set mastiff dogs upon them, or had given them poison into their bowels? and God's providence must be as great in delivering from one as from the other. And this it seems is not only his belief, but the most orthodox and the most learned answer that our author could pitch upon: If witchcraft be, as I suppose it is, &c. and is it not the ordination of God, that, &c. What is all this but precarious, and begging the question, and a plain dropping the argument he cannot manage? However, to amuse the ignorant, and to confound the learned, he hooks in a cramp word, if not a nonentity, viz. plastic spirit of the world; for who is it either knows that there is a plastic spirit, or what it is, or how this can any way serve his purpose?

He then proceeds to scripture instances of witches, &c. and where I thought it needful, I have, as I said, shewed my dissent from his judgment. He accounts it unreasonable to be held to the proof of his definition of a witch; which he makes to consist in a covenant with the devil; and chooses rather a tedious process about a pistol to defend him from it, which indeed is one particular way whereby murder has been committed, and so the doer becomes culpable. But his definition of a witch, which, as I said, still remains to be proved, is to this effect: that a witch is one that covenants with and commissions devils to do mischiefs; that she is one in covenant, or that by virtue of such covenant she can commission him to kill. The not bringing scripture to prove these two is a sufficient demonstration there is none; and so our author leaves off just where he began, viz. in a bare assertion, together with his own bigoted experiences, hinting also at multitudes of histories to confirm him in the belief of his definition. Here being all that I take notice of to be considerable.

And now, sir, if you think fit, improve your friendship with the author, for the glory of God, the sovereign being, the good and welfare of mankind, and for his real and true interest. As you see it convenient, put him in mind, that the glory of God is the end why mankind was made, and why he hath so many advantages to it: that the flames we have seen, threatening the utter extirpation of the country, must owe their original to these dangerous errors (if not heresies) which, if they remain unextinguished, may and most likely will be acted over again: that it is more honour to own an error in time, than tenaciously after full conviction to retain it. But if our author will again vindicate such matters, please to acquaint him, that I shall not any more receive his papers, if I may not copy and use them; and that when he does, instead of such abstruse matters, I still pray his determination in those things I have his promise for. And thus begging pardon for thus long detaining you, I am, sir, yours to command, R.C.

Boston, March 18, 1694.

To the Ministers, whether English, French or Dutch.

I, having had not only occasion, but renewed provocation, to take a view of the mysterious doctrines which have of late been so much contested among us, could not meet with any that had spoken more, or more plainly, the sense of those doctrines (relating to witchcraft) than the rev. mr. C.M.; but how clearly and consistent, either with himself or the truth, I need not now say, but cannot but suppose his strenuous and zealous asserting his opinions has been one cause of the dismal convulsions we have here lately fallen into. Supposing that his books of *Memorable Providences relating to Witchcraft*, as also his *Wonders of the Invisible World*, did contain in them things not warrantable, and very dangerous, I sent to him a letter of quotations out of those books, &c. that so, if it might have been, I might understand what tolerable sense he would put upon his own words; which I took to be a better way of proceeding, than to have affixed what I thought to be their natural consequences; and, lest I might be judged a sceptic, I gave him a full and free account of my belief relating to those doctrines, together with the grounds thereof; and prayed him, that if I erred I might be shewed it by scripture; and this I had his reiterated promise for. But after more than a year's waiting for the performance thereof, all that is done in compliance therewith is, that in February last he sent me four sheets of his writing, as his belief; but before I might receive it I must engage to deliver it back in a fortnight, and not copied. A summary account of which I shall give you, when I have first acquainted you what the doctrines were which I sent to him for his concurrence with, or confutation of, and to which I had his promise, as above.

These by way of question, viz. Whether that fourth head, cited and recommended by himself (in *Wonders of the Invisible World*) of mr. Gaule, ought to be believed as a truth; which runs thus: "Among the most unhappy circumstances to convict a witch, one is a maligning and oppugning the word, work and worship of God, and seeking by an extraordinary sign to seduce any from it. *Deut*. xiii. 1, 2. *Matt*. xxiv. 24. *Acts* xiii. 3, 10. 2 *Tim*. iii, 8. Do but mark well the places; and for this very property of thus opposing and perverting, they are all there concluded arrant and absolute witches."

And if in witchcraft the devil by means of a witch does the mischief, how is it possible to distinguish it from possession? both being said to be performed by the devil; and yet, without all infallible distinction, there can be no certainty in judgment. And whether it can be proved that the jewish church, in any age before, or in our Saviour's time, even in the time of their greatest apostasy, did believe that a witch had power to commission devils to do mischief?

So much to the questions. These were sent as my belief: That the devil's bounds are set, that he cannot pass; that the devils are so full of malice, that it cannot he added to by mankind; that where he hath power, he neither can nor will omit executing it; that it is only the Almighty that sets bounds to his rage, and that only can commission him to hurt or destroy. And now I shall give you the summary account of his four sheets above mentioned, as near as memory could recollect, in ten particulars.

1. That the devils have in their natures a power to work wonders and miracles; particularly that the pharisees were not

mistaken in asserting that the devils might be cast out by Beelzebub; and that our Saviour's answer does not oppose that assertion; and that he hath the power of death; that he can make the most solid things invisible, and can invisibly bring poison, and force it down people's throats.

2. That to assert this natural, wonderful power of the devil, makes most for the glory of God, in preserving man from its effects.

3. Yet this power is restrained by the Almighty, as pleaseth him.

4. That a witch is one that makes a covenant with the devil.

5. That by virtue of such a covenant, she arrives at a power to commission him.

6. That God has ordained that when the devil is called upon by the witch, though he were before restrained by the Almighty, the desired mischiefs ordinarily shall as certainly be performed, as if the witch had lodged poison in the bowels of her neighbour, or had set mastiff dogs on them.

8. That that God which restrained an Abimelech and a Laban from hurting, does also restrain the witch from calling upon or improving the devil, when he will not have his power so exerted.

9. That to have a familiar spirit, is to be able to cause a devil to take bodily shapes, whereby either to give responses, or to receive orders for doing mischief.

10. That this is the judgment of most of the divines in the country, whether English, Dutch, or French.

This, as I said, I took to be the most material in the four sheets sent to me as his belief, and is also all the performance he has yet made of his several promises; which ten articles being done only by memory, lest through mistake or want of the original I might have committed any errors, I sent them to him, that, if there were any, they might be rectified: but instead of such an answer as might be expected from a minister and a learned gentleman, one mr. W. shewed me a letter writ by mr. C.M. to himself, which I might read, but neither borrow nor copy, and so, if I were minded, could give but a short account of it.

And passing over his hard language, which, as I am conscious to myself I never deserved, (relating to my writing in the margin of the four sheets, and to these ten articles) so I hope I understand my duty better than to imitate him in retorting the like. Among his many words in his said letters, I meet with two small objections; one is against the word miracle in the first article; the word, I say, not the matter; for the works he attributes to the devil are the same, in their being above or against the course of nature and all natural causes; yet he will not admit of these to be called miracles; and hence he reckons it the greatest difficulty he meets with in this whole affair, to distinguish the works of the devil from miracles. And hence also he concedes to the devil the power to make the most solid things invisible and invisibly to drink poison, and force it clown people's throats, &c. which I look upon to be as true miracles as that 2 *Kings*, vi. 18; and this is the sense I understand the word in; and in this sense he himself, in the four sheets, admits it; for he has an objection to this effect, viz. If the devils have such power, &c. then miracles are not ceased; and where are we then? His answer is, where! Even just where we were before, say I: so that it seems the only offence here is at my using his words. His second objection (for weight) is against the whole ninth article, and wonders how it is possible for one man so much to misunderstand another; yet, as I remember, he, speaking of the witch of Endor, in the said four sheets, says, she had a familiar spirit, and that a spirit belonging to the invisible world, upon her calling, appeared to Saul, &c. and if so, it is certain he gave responses. He also tells of Balaam, that it was known that he could set devils on people to destroy them; and therefore how this objection should bear any force I see not. The rest of the objections are of so small weight, that once reading may be sufficient to clear them up; and if this be not so, he can, when he pleases, by making it publick, together with the margins I writ, convince all people of the truth of what he asserts. But here it is to be noted, that the 2d, 3d, 4th and 5th articles he concedes to, as having nothing to object against them, but that they are his belief; and that the 6th and 7th he puts for answer to an objection which he thus frames, viz. If the devil have such powers, but cannot exert them but by permission from God, what can the witch contribute thereto?

And thus I have faithfully performed what I undertook; and do solemnly declare, I have not intentionally in the least wronged the gentleman concerned, nor designed the least blemish to his reputation; but if it stands in competition with the glory of God, the only almighty being, his truths and his people's welfare, I suppose these too valuable to be trampled on for his sake, though in other things I am ready to my power (though with denying some part of my own interest) to serve him. Had this gentleman declined or detracted his four sheets, I see not but he might have done it, and which I think there was cause enough for him to have done; but to own the four sheets, and at the same time to disown the doctrine contained in them, and this knowing that I have no copy, renders the whole of the worse aspect.

And now I shall give you a further account of my belief, when I have first premised, that it is a prevailing belief in this country, and elsewhere, that the scriptures are not full in the description of, and in the way and means how to detect, a witch, though positive in their punishment to be by death; and that hence they have thought themselves under a necessity of taking up with the sentiments of such men or places that are thought worthy to give rules to detect them by; and have accordingly practised viz. in searching for teats for the devil to suck; trying whether the suspected can say the Lord's prayer; and whether the afflicted falls at the sight, and rises at the touch, of the supposed witch; as also by the afflicted or possessed giving account who is the witch.

Touching these, my belief is, that 'tis highly derogatory to the wisdom of the wise Lawgiver, to assert, that he has given a law by Moses, the penalty whereof is death, and yet no direction to his people, whereby to know and detect the culpable, till our triumvirate, messrs. Perkins, Gaule and Bernard, had given us their receipts; and, that that fourth head of mr. Gaule, being so well proved by scripture, is a truth, and contains a full and clear testimony who are witches culpable of death, and that plainly and from scripture, yet not excluding any other branch, when as well proved by that infallible rule; and, that the going to the afflicted or possessed, to have them divine who are witches by their spectral sight, is a great wickedness, even the sin of Saul (for which he also died) but with this difference, the one did it for augury, or to know future events; the other, in order to take away life; and, that the searching for teats, the experiment of their saying the Lord's prayer, the falling at the sight and rising at the touch of the supposed criminal, being all of them foreign from scripture, as well as reason, are abominations to be abhorred and repented of; and, that our Salem witchcraft, either respecting the judges and juries, their tenderness of life, or the multitude and pertinency of witnesses, both afflicted and confessors, or the integrity of the historians, is as authentic, and made as certain, as any event of that kind in the world: And yet who is it that now sees not through it, and that these were the sentiments that have procured the sorest affliction, and most lasting infamy, that ever befel this country, and most like so to do again, if the same notions be still entertained? and, finally, that these are those last times, of which the Spirit speaks expressly, *Tim.* iv. 1?

And now, ye that are fathers in the churches, guides to the people, and the salt of the earth, I beseech you consider these things; and if you find the glory of God diminished by ascribing such power to witches and devils; his truths opposed by these notions; and his people aspersed in their doctrines and reputations, and endangered in their lives—I dare not dictate you—you know your duty as watchmen—and the Lord be with you.

But if you find my belief contrary to sound doctrine, I entreat you to shew it me by the scripture; and in the mean time blame me not if I cannot believe that there are several Almighties; for to do all sorts of wonders, beyond and above the course of nature, is certainly the work of Omnipotency. So also, he that shall commission or empower to these, must also be almighty; and I think it not a sufficient salvo, to say they may be restrained by the Most High; and hope you will not put any hard construction on these my endeavours to get information (all other ways failing) in things so needful to be known. Praying the Almighty's guidance and protection, I am

Yours to the utmost of my power,   R.C.

Boston, Sept. the 20*th*, 1695.

Mr. SAMUEL WILLARD,

Reverend Sir,

My former, of March the 18th, directed to the Ministers (and which was lodged with yourself) containing several articles which I sent as my belief praying them if I erred to shew it me by scripture, I have as yet had no answer to, either by word or writing, which makes me gather that they are approved of as orthodox, or at least that they have such foundations as that none are willing to manifest any opposition to them; and therefore, with submission, &c. I think that that late seasonable and well-designed dialogue, intituled, *Some Miscellaneous Observations,* &c. of which yourself is the supposed author, and which was so serviceable in the time of it, is yet liable to a malconstruction, even to the danger of reviving what it most opposed, and of bringing those practices again on foot, which in the day of them were so terrible to this whole country. The words, which I suppose so liable to misconstruction, are, p. 14,

B. *Who informed them?* S. *The spectre.* B. *Very good, and that's the devil turned informer. How are good men like to fare, against whom he hath particular malice? It is but a presumption, and wise men will weigh presumptions against presumptions. There is to be no examination without grounds of suspicion. Some persons credit nothing to be accounted too good to be undermined so far as to be suspected on so slight a ground; and it is an injury done them to bring them upon examination, which renders them openly suspected. I will not deny but for persons already suspected, and of ill fame, it may occasion their being examined.* In which, these words, *'tis but a presumption, &c.* and *some persons credit, &c.* and *I will not deny but for persons already suspected, &c.* I take to be waving the discussion of those points, the speaking to which might at that time have hindered the usefulness and success of that book, rather than any declaring the sentiments of the author. But notwithstanding, many persons will be ready to understand this as if the author did wholly leave it with the justice, to judge who are ill persons, such as the devil's accusations may fasten upon; and that the devil's accusation of a person is a presumption against them of their guilt; and that, upon such presumptions, they may be had to examination, if the justice counts them persons of ill fame; for the author I suppose knows that the bare examination will leave such a stain upon them (and it would be well if their posterity escaped it!) as the length of a holy and unblamable life will be found too short to extirpate. And if the justice may go thus far with the devil's evidence, then the addition of a story or two of some cart overset; or persons taken sick after a quarrel, might as well be thought sufficient for their commitment, in order to their trial, as 'tis called, (though this too often has been more like a stage play, or a *tragicomic* scene) and so that otherways useful book may prove the greatest snare to revive the same practices again.

These things being so liable, as I said, to such malconstruction, it were needful that men might be undeceived, and the matter more fully demonstrated, viz. That the devil's accusation is not so much as any presumption against the life or reputation of any person; (for how are good men like to fare, if his malicious accusations may be taken as a presumption of their guilt?) and, that his accusations, as they are no presumption against persons of unspotted fame, so neither are to be heard, or any ways regarded, against persons though otherways of ill life, much less for their having long since had their names abused by his outcries, or by the malice of ill neighbours; and, that justice knows no difference of persons; that, if this evidence be sufficient to bring one person, 'tis so to bring any other, to examination, and consequently to the utmost extent of odium which such examination will certainly expose them to; for who can know any other, but that as the one may be maliciously accused by devils and a devilish report gone before it, so that another, who has not been so much as accused before, being more cunning or more seeming religious, might yet be more guilty; the whole depending upon invisible evidence, of which invisible stuff, though we have had more than sufficient, yet I find (among other reverend persons) your name to a certain printed paper, which runs thus:

Certain Proposals, made by the President and Fellows of Harvard College to the reverend Ministers of the Gospel, in the several churches of New-England.

First. To observe and record the more illustrious discoveries of the Divine Providence in the government of the world, is a design so holy, so useful, so justly approved, that the too general neglect of it in the churches of God is as justly to be lamented.

2. For the redress of that neglect, although all christians have a duty incumbent on them, yet it is in a peculiar manner to be recommended unto the Ministers of the gospel to improve the special advantages which are in their hands, to obtain and preserve the knowledge of such notable occurrences as are fought out by all that have pleasure in the great works of the Lord.

3. The things to be esteemed memorable, are specially all unusual accidents in the heaven, or earth, or water; all wonderful deliverances of the distressed; mercies to the godly; judgments on the wicked; and more glorious fulfilments of either the promises or threatenings in the scriptures of truth; with apparitions, possessions, enchantments, and all extraordinary things, wherein the existence and agency of the Invisible World is more sensibly demonstrated.

4. It is therefore proposed, that the Ministers throughout this land would manifest their pions regards unto the works of the Lord, and the operation of his hands, by reviving their cares to take written accounts of such *Remarkables*; but still well attested with credible and sufficient witnesses.

5. It is desired that the accounts, thus taken, of these remarkables, may be sent to the President or Fellows of the

college, by whom they shall be carefully reserved for such a use to be made of them, as may by some fit assembly of Ministers be judged most conducing to the glory of God, and the service of his people.

6. Though we doubt not that love to the name of God will be a sufficient motive to all good men to contribute what assistance they can unto this undertaking; yet, for further encouragement, some singular marks of respect shall be studied for such good men, as will actually assist it, by taking pains to communicate any important passages proper to be inserted in this collection.

INCREASE MATHER, Pres.

James Allen,	*John Leverette,*
Char. Morton,	*Will. Brattle,*
Sam. Willard,	*Neb. Walter,*
Cotton Mather,	Fellows.

Cambridge, March 5, 1694.

NOTE.— It is known that Dr. Increase Mather designed to publish a book concerning things rare and wonderful, occurring around him. It would seem from this circular addressed to the clergy, that he was desirous of collecting materials for the work.

Here being an encouragement to all good men to send in such remarkables as are therein expressed, I have sent in the following; not that I think them a more sensible demonstration of the being of a future state (with rewards and punishments) or of angels good and bad, &c. than the scriptures of truth hold forth, &c.; or than any of those other demonstrations God hath given us; for this were treacherously and perfidiously to quit the post to the enemy. The sadducee, deist and atheist would hereby be put in a condition so triumphantly to deny the existence and agency thereof, as that a few stories told (which at best must be owned to be fallible and liable to misrepresentations) could not be thought infallibly sufficient to demonstrate the truth against them. I have heard that in logick a false argument is reckoned much worse than none; yet, supposing that a collection of instances may be many ways useful, not only to the present but succeeding ages, I have sent you the following remarkables, which have lately occurred, the certainty of which, if any scruple it, will be found no hard matter to get satisfaction therein. But here, not to insist on those less occurrences, as the sudden death of one of our late justices; and a like mortality that fell upon the two sons of another of them; with the fall of a man that was making provision to raise the new northern bell, which, when it was up, the first person, whose death it was to signify, was said to be a child of him, who, by printing and speaking, had had as great a hand in procuring the late actions as any, if not the greatest; and the splitting the gun at Salem, where that furious marshal, and his father, &c, were rent to pieces, &c. As to all these, if must be owned, that no man knows love or hatred by all that is before him, much less can they be more sensible demonstrations of the existence and agency of the invisible world, than the scriptures of truth afford, &c. though the rich man in the parable might think otherwise, &c. who was seeking to send some more sensible demonstrations thereof to his brethren, &c. In that tremendous judgment of God upon this country, by the late amazing prosecution of the people here, under the notion of witches; whereby twenty suffered as evil doers, (besides those that died in prison) about ten more condemned, and a hundred imprisoned, and about two hundred more accused, and the country generally in fears when it would come to their turn to be accused; and the prosecution and manner of trial such, that most would have chosen to have fallen into the hands of the barbarous enemy, rather than (under that notion) into the hands of their brethren in church fellowship; and, in short, was such an affliction as far exceeded all that ever this country hath laboured under—

Yet in this mount God is seen. When it was thus bad with this distressed people, a full and a sudden stop is put, not only without, but against, the inclination of many; for out of the eater came forth meat: those very accusers, which had been improved as witnesses against so many, by the providence of the Most High, Yet in this mount God is seen. When it was thus bad with this distressed people, a full and a sudden stop is put, not only without, but against, the inclination of many; for out of the eater came forth meat: those very accusers, which had been improved as witnesses against so many, by the providence of the Most High, and perhaps blinded with malice, are left to accuse those in most high esteem, both magistrates and ministers, as guilty of witchcraft; which shewed our rulers, that necessity lay upon them to confound that which had so long confounded the country, as being themselves unwilling to run the same risk: this, that was in the event of it, to this country, as life from the dead, is most easy with Him, in whose hands are the hearts of all men, and was a very signal deliverance to this whole country. N o less observable was it, that though at the time when the devil's testimony, by the afflicted, was first laid aside, there were great numbers of (real or pretended) afflicted; yet when this was once not judged of validity enough to be any longer brought into the court against the accused as evidence, the affliction generally ceased, and only some remainders of it in such places, where more encouragement was given to the actors, God seeming thereby plainly to decipher that sin of going to the devil, &c. as the rise and foundation of those punishments.

And thus, reverend, I have, as I understand it, performed my duty herein, for the glory of God, and the well-being of men. And for my freedom used in this and former writings, relating to the actors in this tragedy, I shall not apologize, but give you the words of one to whom some can afford the title of venerable (when he is arguing for that which they have undertaken to assert, though at other times more diminutive epithets must serve); it is the reverend mr. R. Baxter, in his book, *the Cure of Church Divisions*, pages 257, 258.

"But[I pray you mark it] the way of God is to shame the sinner, how good soever in other respects, that the sin may have the greater shame, and religion may not be ashamed,as if it allowed men to sin: nor God, the author of religion, be dishonoured; nor others be without the warning: but the way of the devil is, to hide or justify the sin, as if it were for fear of disparaging the goodness of the persons that committed it; that so he may hereby dishonour religion and godliness itself, and make men believe it is but a cover for any wickedness, and as consistent with it as a looser life is, and that he may keep the sinner from repenting, and blot out the memory of that warning which should have preserved after ages from the like falls. Scripture shameth the professors (though a *David*, a *Solomon*, *Peter*, *Noah*, or *Lot*) that the religion profest may not be ashamed, but vindicated. Satan would preserve the honour of professors, that the religion professed may bear the shame; and so it may fall on God himself."

And now that all have had a hand in any horrid and bloody practices may be brought to give glory to God, and take the due shame to themselves; and that our watchmen may no longer seek to palliate, (much less give thanks for such, &c. thereby making them their own) and that the people may no longer perish for want of knowledge in the midst of such means of light, nor God be any longer dishonoured by false sentiments in these matters, is the earnest desire and prayer of, sir, yours to my power,

R.C.

Mr. COTTON MATHER,

Reverend Sir,

Having long since sent you some doctrinals as to my belief, together with my request to you, that if I erred you would be pleased to show it me by scripture, viz. That the devil's bounds are set, which he cannot pass; that the devils are so full of malice that it cannot be added to by mankind; that where he hath power he neither can nor will omit executing it; that 'tis only the Almighty that sets bounds to his rage, and that only can commission him to hurt and destroy, &c. But instead of such an answer as was promised and justly expected, you were pleased to send me a book, which you since called an ungainsayable one; which book till lately I have not had opportunity so fully to consider. And to the end you may see I have now done it, I have sent to you some of the remarkables contained in the said book, intituled, "*The Certainty of the World of Spirits,*" *written by Mr.* R.B. *London, printed* 1691. It is therein conceded (preface) that to see devils and spirits ordinarily would not be enough to convince atheists. Page 88, Atheists are not to be convinced by stories; their own senses are not enough to convince them any more than sense will convince a papist from transubstantiation. (*D. Laderd.*) P.4, No spirit can do any thing but by God's will and permission. Preface, 'Tis the free will of man that gives the devils their hurting power; and without our own consent they cannot hurt us. It is asserted, p. 222, 223, That it is a perverse opposition of popery which causes many protestants not to regard the benefits we receive by angels. And ministers are faulty, that do not pray and give thanks to God for their ministry; and that neglect to teach believers, what love and what thanks they owe to angels. P. 225, Most good people look so much to God and to ministers, that they take little notice of angels, which are God's great ministers. P. 234, The author dares not, as some have done, judge the catholic church to become antichristian idolaters, as soon as they gave too much worship to saints and angels. P. 7, The blessed souls shall be like the angels, therefore may appear here. P. 3, 4, 'Tis hard to know whether it be a devil or a human soul that appears, or whether the soul of a good or a bad person; p, 61, or the soul of some dead friend that suffers, and yet retains love, &c. P. 222, No doubt the souls of the wicked carry with them their former inclinations of covetousness, revenge, &c. P. 7, When revengeful things are done, as on murderers, defrauders, &c. it seems to be from the revengeful wrath of some bad soul; if it be about money or lands, then from a worldly-minded one; some significations of God's mercy to wicked souls after this life. P. 4, 'Tis a doubt whether, Besides the angels (good and bad) and the souls of men, there is not a third sort, called fairies and goblins. It is unsearchable to us how far God leaves spirits to free will in small things, suspending his predetermining motion. P. 246, The devils have a marvellous power, if but a silly wretched witch consent. P. 10, 202, The stories of witches and spirits are many ways useful, particularly to convince atheists, and confirm believers, and to prove the operation of spirits. P. 232, To help men to understand that devils make no small number of laws, and rulers in the world, and are authors of most of the wars, and of many sermons, and of books that adorn the libraries of learned men. P. 6, 102, The devil's lying with the witch is not to be denied, and is more to exercise the lust of the witch than of the devil, who can also bring in another witch without opening the door, and so perform it by one witch with another. P. 105, Witches can raise storms, sell winds, &c. as is commonly affirmed. P. 107, In America it is a common thing to see spirits, day and night. P. 95, 96, 97, 110, Stories of a child that could not be cured of witchcraft, because the emberweeks were past; vomited a knife a span long, cart nails, &c. and neither eat nor drank, fifteen days and nights together; a long piece of wood, four knives, and two sharp pieces of iron, every one above a span long, taken out of the stomach, &c. hair, stones, bones, vomited, &c. a thousand pounds of blood lost by one person in a year's time. P. 250, A story that makes the author think it possible that such great things, as he mentions, should be gotten down and up people's throats. P. 164, Partial credibility spoils many a good story. P. 125, The devil's substance enters into the possessed. P. 174, Distracted are possessed. P. 149, A sick woman, while she lay in bed, went to see her children. P. 151, A dog appeared like a fly or a flea. P. 165, Some knowing agents direct thunderstorms, though the author knows not who; and that they so often fall on churches, he knows not why. P. 2, 80, Mr. I.M. and mr. C.M. recommended, together with Bodin, &c. P. 237, A crispian, if through ignorance he believes not what he saith, may be a christian.

In this, sir, I suppose that if I have not wronged the sense of the author in the places quoted (which I trust you shall not find I have done) I cannot be thought accountable for the errors or contradictions to himself or to the truth, if any such be found, particularly what he grants in the preface, of the free will of man giving the devil his hurting power; this being not only more than those called witch-advocates would desire to be conceded to them, but is a palpable and manifest overturning the author's design in all his witch stories; (for who would consent to have the devil afflict himself?) as also his concession, that no spirit can do any thing but by God's will and permission; I cannot persuade myself but you must be sensible of their apparent contradictoriness to the rest. Others there are of a very ill aspect; as, p. 234, the catholicks are much encouraged in their adoration of angels and saints, if that were so innocent as not to render them antichristian idolaters; and that, p. 4, if admitted, will seem to lay an ungainsayable foundation for the pagan, indian and diabolist's faith, by telling us it is beyond our search to know how far God leaves the devils to free will, to do what they please, in this world, with a suspension of God's predetermination; which if it were a truth, what were more rational than to oblige him that has such power over us? The atheists also would take encouragement if it were granted that we cannot know how far God suspends his predetermining motion: they would thence affirm, we as little know that there is a predetermining motion, and consequently whether there be a God, and p. 165 would abundantly strengthen them, when such a learned, experienced and highly-esteemed christian shall own that he knows not who it is that governs the thunder-storms: for it might as well discover ignorance, who it is that disposes of earthquakes, gun-shot, and afflictions that befal any, with the rest of mundane events, I design not to remark all that in the book is remarkable, such as the departed souls wandering again hither to put men upon revenge, &c, savouring so much of Pythagoras's transmigration of souls, and the separation of the soul from the body without death, as in the case of her that went to see her children, while yet she did not stir out of her bed, which seems to be a new speculation; unless it determines in favour of transubstantiation, that a body may be at the same time in several places, Upon the whole; it is ungainsayable, that that book, though so highly extolled, may be justly expected to occasion the staggering of the weak, and the hardening of unbelievers in their infidelity. And it seems amazing, that you should not only give it such a recommendation, but that you should send it to me, in order (as I take it) to pervert me from the belief of these fundamental doctrinals (above recited) though I account them more firm than heaven and earth. But that which is yet more strange to me, is, that mr. B's friends did not advise him better, than in his declined age to emit such crude matter to the publick. As to the sometime reverend author, let his works praise the remembrance of him; but for such as are either erroneous and foisted upon him, or the effect of an aged imbecility, let them be detected, that they may proceed no further.

I am not ignorant that the manner of education of youth, in, I think, almost all christian schools, hath a natural tendency to propagate those doctrines of devils heretofore solely profest among ethnicks, and particularly in matters of witchcraft, &c. For, notwithstanding the council of Carthage, taking notice that the christian doctors did converse much with the writings of the heathens for the gaining of eloquence, forbad the reading of the books of the gentiles; yet it seems this was only a bill without a penalty, which their successors did not look upon to be binding. He that should in this age take a view of the schools, might be induced to believe that the ages since have thought, that without such heathen learning a man cannot be so accomplished, as to have any pretence to academick literature; and that the vulgar might not be without the benefit of such learning, some of their disciples have taught them to speak english, which bas given me the opportunity to send you these following verses.

Virg. Bucolicks-Ecl. 13.
Sure love is not the cause their bones appear:
Some eyes bewitch my tender lambs, I fear.

Ecl. 8.
For me these herbs in Pontus, Mæris chose;
There ev'ry powerful drug in plenty grows,
Transform'd to a wolf I often Mæris saw,
Then into shady woods himself withdraw:
Oft he from deepest sepulchres would charm
Departed souls; and from another's farm,
Into his own ground, corn yet standing take.
Now from the town my charms bring Daphnis back.
Vanquish'd with charms, from heaven the moon descends,
Circe with charms transform'd Ulysses' friends;

Charms in the field will burst a poisonous snake.
Now from the town, &c.

Ovid's Metam. Lib. 7.

Her arms thrice turns about, thrice wets her crown
With gather'd dew, thrice yawns, and kneeling down,
Oh night! thou friend to secrets! you, clear fires,
That with the moon succeed when day retires;
Great Hecate thou knowst, and aid imparts,
To our design, your charms and magick arts:
And thou, oh earth, that to magicians yields
Thy powerful simples; air, winds, mountains, fields,
Sort murmuring springs, still lakes, and rivers clear,
Ye gods of woods, ye gods of night, appear;
By you, at will, I make swift streams retire
To their first fountain, while their banks admire;
Seas rough make smooth; clear skies with clouds deform;
Storms turn to calms, and make a calm a storm.
With spells and charms, I break the viper's jaw,
Cleave solid rocks, oaks from their fissures draw;
Whole woods remove, the airy mountains shake;
Earth force to groan, and ghosts from graves awake.

Lib. 14.

——————her journey takes
To Rhegium, opposite to Zante's shore,
And treads the troubled waves, that loudly roar;
Running with unwet feet on that profound,
As if sh' had trod upon the solid ground.
This with portentous poison she pollutes,
Besprinkled with the juice of wicked roots;
In words dark and perplexed, nine times thrice,
Enchantments utters with her wicked voice, &c.

These fables of the heathens (though in themselves of no more validity than the idle tales of an indian, or the discourses of a known romancer) are become the school-learning, not to say the faith, of christians, and are the scriptures brought (instead of that most sure word) if not to prove doctrine, yet as illustrations thereof. *Cases of Conscience concerning Witchc.* page 25: *Remarkable Providences*, page 250. This perhaps might he the cause that in England, a people otherwise sober and religious, have for some ages in a manner wholly refused admitting those not so educated to the work of the ministry. Such education and practice have so far prevailed, that it has been a means of corrupting the christian world, almost to that degree as to be ungainsayable;. for though there is reason to hope that these diabolical principles have not so prevailed (with multitudes of christians) as that they ascribe to a witch and a devil the attributes peculiar to the Almighty; yet how few are willing to be found opposing such a torrent, as knowing that in so doing they shall be sure to meet with opposition to the utmost, from the many, both of magistrates, ministers and people; and the name of sadducee, atheist, and perhaps witch too, cast upon them most liberally, by men of the highest profession in godliness; and if not so learned as some of themselves, then accounted only fit to be trampled on, and their arguments (though both rational and scriptural) as fit only for contempt. But though this be the deplorable dilemma,, yet some have dared from time to time (for the glory of God, and the good and safety of men's lives, &c.) to run all these risks. And that God who has said, *My glory I will not give to another*, is able to protect those that are found doing their duty herein against all opposers; and, however otherways contemptible, can make them useful in his own hand, who has sometimes chosen the weakest instruments, that his power may be the more illustrious.

And now, reverend sir, if you are conscious to yourself, that you have, in your principles or practices, been abetting to such grand errors, I cannot see how it can consist with sincerity, to be so convinced in matters so nearly relating to the glory of God, and lives of innocents, and at the same time so much to fear disparagement among men, as to trifle with conscience, and dissemble an approving of former sentiments. You know that word, *He that honoureth me I will honour, and he that despiseth me shall be lightly esteemed*. But if you think that in these matters you have done your duty, and taught the people theirs; and that the doctrines cited from the above mentioned book are ungainsayable; I shall conclude in almost his words, He that teaches such doctrine, if through ignorance he believes not what he saith, may be a christian; but if he believes them, he is in the broad path to heathenism, devilism, popery, or atheism. It is a solemn caution, (*Gal.* i. 8) *But though we, or an angel from heaven, preach any other gospel unto you than that which we have preached unto you, let him be accursed.* I hope you will not misconstrue my intentions herein, who am, reverend sir, yours to command in what I may, R.C.

MR. MATHER, &c.

To the Ministers in and near Boston.

Jan. 12, 1696.

Christianity had been but a short time in the world, when there was raised against it, not only open profest enemies, but secret and inbred underminers, who sought thereby to effect that which open force had been so often baffled in. And notwithstanding that primitive purity and sincerity, which in some good measure was still retained, yet the cunning deceivers and apostate hereticks found opportunity to beguile the unwary, and this in fundamentals.

Among others which then sprung up, with but too much advantage, in the third century, the maniche did spread his pestiferous sentiments, and taught the existence of two beings, or causes of all things, viz. a good and a bad: but these were soon silenced by the more orthodox doctors, and anathematized by general councils. And at this day the american indians, another sort of maniche, entertaining (thus far) the same belief, hold it their prudence and interest to please that evil being, as well by perpetrating other murders, as by their bloody sacrifices, that so he may not harm them. The iron teeth of time have now almost devoured the name of the former; and as to the latter, it is to be hoped that as christianity prevails, among them, they will abhor such abominable belief.

And as those primitive times. were not privileged against the spreading of dangerous heresy, so neither can any now pretend to any such immunity, though professing the enjoyment of a primitive purity.

Might a judgment be made from the books of the modern learned divines, or from the practice of courts, or from the faith of many who call themselves christians, it might be modestly, though sadly, concluded, that the doctrine of the manic he, at least great part of it, is so far from being forgotten, that it is almost every where profest. We in these ends of the earth need not seek far for instances in each respect to demonstrate this. The hooks here printed and recommended, not only by the respective authors, but by many of their brethren, do set forth that the devil inflicts plagues,[4] wars,† diseases,‡ tempests,¤ and can render the most solid things invisible,§ and call do things above and against the course of nature, and all natural causes.

---

4. *Wonders of the Invisible World p. 17, 18.——†p. 18. ——‡Cases of Conscience, p. 63.——¤ Remarkable Providences: p. 124.
——§Wonders of the Invisible World, p. 141.

Are these the expressions of orthodox believers? or are they not rather expressions becoming a maniche, or a heathen, as agreeing far better with these than with the sacred oracles, our only rule? the whole current whereof is so diametrically opposite thereto, that it were almost endless to mention all the divine cautions against such abominable belief; he that runs may read, *Ps.* lxii. 11, and cxxxvi. 4. *Lam.* iii. 37. *Amos* iii. 6 . *Let.* iv. 22. *Ps.* lxxviii. 26, and clxviii. 6, 8. *Job* xxxviii. 22 to 34.

These places, with a multitude more, do abundantly testify, that the asserters of such power to be in the evil being, do speak in a dialect different from the scriptures, (laying a firm foundation for the Indians' adorations, which agrees well with what A. Ross sets forth, in his *Mistag. Poetic*, p. 116, that their ancients did worship the furies and their god *Averinci*, that they might forbear to hurt them.)

And have not the courts in some parts of the world, by their practices, testified their concurrence with such belief; prosecuting to death many people upon that notion, of their improving such power of the evil one, to the raising of storms; afflicting and killing of ethers, though at great distance from them; doing things in their own persons above human strength; destroying cattle, flying in the air, turning themselves into cats, dogs, &c.? which by the way must needs imply something of goodness to be in that evil being, who, though he has such power, would not exert it, were it not for this people, or else that they can some way add to this mighty power.

And are the people a whit behind in their belief? is there any thing above mentioned, their strong faith looks upon to be too hard for this evil being to effect?

Here it will be answered, God permits it. Which answer is so far all owning the doctrine, that the devil has in his nature a power to do all these things, and can exert this power, except when he is restrained, that it is in effect to say that God has made nature to fight against itself; that he has made a creature, who has it in the power of his nature to overthrow nature, and to act above and against it. Which he that can believe may as well believe the greatest contradiction. That being which can do this in the smallest thing, can do it in the greatest. If *Moses*, with a bare permission, might stretch forth his rod, yet he was not able to bring plagues upon the Egyptians, or to divide the waters, without a commission from the Most High; so neither can that evil being perform any of this without a commission from the same power. The scripture recites more miracles wrought by men than by angels good and bad. Though this doctrine be so dishonourable to the only Almighty Being, as to ascribe such attributes to the evil One, as are the incommunicable prerogative of him, who is the alone Sovereign Being, yet here is not all; but, as be that steers by a false compass, the further he sails the more he is out of his way; so, though there is in some things a variation from, there is in others a further progression in, or building upon, the said doctrine of the maniche.

Men in this age are not content barely to believe such an exorbitant power to be in the nature of this evil being; but have imagined that he prevails with many to sign a book, or make a contract with him, whereby they are enabled to perform all the things above mentioned. Another account is given hereof; viz. That by virtue of such a covenant they attain power to commission him. And though the two parties are not agreed which to put it upon, whether the devil empowers the witch, or the witch commissions him; yet both parties are agreed in this, that one way or other the mischief is effected, and so the criminal becomes culpable of death. In the search after such a sort of criminals, how many countries have fallen into such convulsions, that neither the devastations made by a conquering enemy, nor the plague itself, have been so formidable.

That not only good persons have thus been blemished in their reputations, but much innocent blood hath been shed, is testified even by those very books: *Cases of Conscience*, p. 33. *Remarkable Provid.* p. 179. *Memor. Provid.* p. 28.

And (to add) what less can be expected, when men, having taken up such a belief of covenanting, afflicting and killing witches, and, comparing it with the scripture, finding no footsteps therein of such a sort of witch, have thereupon desperately concluded, that though the scripture is full in it, that a witch should not live, yet that it has not at all described the crime, nor means whereby the culpable might be detected?

And hence they are fallen so far as to reckon it necessary to make use of those diabolical and bloody ways, always heretofore practised, for their discovery; as finding that the rules, given to detect other crimes, are wholly useless for the discovery of such.

This is that which has produced that deluge of blood mentioned, and must certainly do so again, the same belief remaining.

And who can wonder, if christians that are so easily prevailed with to lay aside their swords as useless, and so have lost their strength, are (with Samson) led blindfold into an idol temple, to make sport for enemies and infidels, and to do abominable actions, not only not christian, but against even the light of nature and reason? And now, reverend fathers, you who are appointed as guides to the people, and whose lips should preserve knowledge; who are set as shepherds, and as Watchmen; this matter appertains to you. I wrote to you formerly under this head, and acquainted you with my sentiments, requesting" that if I erred, you would be pleased to show it me by scripture; but from your silence I gather that you approve thereof. For I may reasonably presume, that you would have seen it your duty to have informed me better, if you had been sensible of any error. But if in this matter you have acquitted yourselves becoming the titles you are dignified with, you have cause of rejoicing in the midst of calamities that afflict a sinning world.

Particularly, if you have taught the people to fear God, and trust in him, and not to fear a witch or a devil—That the devil has no power to afflict any with diseases, or loss of cattle, &c. without a commission from the Most High—That he is so filled with malice, that whatever commission he may have against any, he will not fail to execute it—That no mortal ever was, or can be, able to commission him, or to lengthen his chain in the least, and that he who only can commission him is God; and that the scriptures of truth not only assign the punishment of a witch, but give sufficient rules to detect them by; and that, according to mr. Gaule's fourth head, a witch is one that hates and opposes the word, work and worship of God, and seeks by a sign to seduce therefrom—That they who are guilty according to that head, are guilty of witchcraft, and by the law given to Moses were to be put to death:—If you have taught the people the necessity of charity, and the evil of entertaining so much as a jealousy against their neighbours for such crimes, upon the devil's suggestions to a person pretending to a spectral or diabolical sight; who litter their oracles from malice, frenzy, or a satanical delusion—That to be inquisitive of such, whose spectres they see, or who it is that afflicts, in order to put the accused's life in question, is a wickedness beyond what Saul was guilty of in going to the witch—That to consult with the dead, by the help of such as pretend to this spectral sight, and so to get information against the life of any person, is the worst sort of necromancy—That the pretending to drive away spectres, i.e. devils, with the hand, or by striking these to wound a person at a distance, cannot be without witchcraft, as pretending to a sign in order to deceive in matters of so high a nature—That 'tis ridiculous to think, by making laws against feeding, employing or rewarding of evil spirits, thereby to get rid of them—That their nature requires no Sucking to support it—That it is a horrid injury and barbarity to search those parts, which even nature itself commands the concealing of, to find some excrescence to be called a teat for these to suck; which yet is said sometimes to appear as a fleabite:—Finally, if you have taught the people what to believe and practise, as to the probation of the accused, by their saying or not saying the Lord's prayer, and as to praying that the afflicted. may be able to accuse, and have not shunned in these matters to declare the whole mind of God; you have then well acquitted yourselves (in time of general defection) as faithful watchmen. But if, instead of this, you have, some by word and writing propagated, and others recommended, such doctrines, and abetted the false notions, which are so prevalent in this apostate age, it is high time to consider it. If when authority found themselves almost nonplust in such prosecutions, and sent to you for your advice what they ought to do,[5] and you have then thanked them for what they had already done (and thereby encouraged them to proceed in those very bypaths already fallen into) it so much the more nearly concerns you. *Ezek.* xxiii. 2 to 8.

To conclude: This whole people are invited and commanded to humble their souls before God, as for other causes, for the errors that may have been fallen into in these prosecutions on either hand, and to pray that God would teach us what we know not, and help us wherein we have done amiss, that we may do so no more.[6]

This more immediately concerns yourselves; for 'tis not supposed to be intended, that God would shew us these things by inspiration; but that such who are called to it should shew the mind of God in these things on both hands, i.e. whether there has been any error in excess or deficiency, or neither in the one nor the other. And if you do not thus far serve the publick, you need not complain of great sufferings and unrighteous discouragements, if people do not

---

5. Cases of Conscience, vlt.

6. Vide the proclamation for a fast, to be the 14th inst. as set forth by authority.

applaud your conduct, as you might otherways have expected.[7] But if you altogether hold your peace at such a time as this is, your silence, at least seemingly, will speak this language; that you are not concerned, though men ascribe the power and providence of the Almighty to the worst of his creatures—that if other ages or countries improve the doctrine and examples given them, either to the taking away of the life or reputations of innocents, you are well satisfied. Which, that there may be no shadow of a reason to believe but that your conduct herein may remove all such jealousies, and that God would be with you in declaring his whole mind to the people, is the earnest desire and prayer of, reverend sirs, yours to my utmost, R.C.

Mr. Benjamin Wadsworth,
Reverend Sir,

After that dreadful and Severe persecution of such a multitude of people, under the notion of witches, which, in the day thereof, was the sorest trial and affliction that ever befel this country; and after many of the principal actors had declared their fears and jealousies, that they had greatly erred in those prosecutions; and after a solemn day of fasting had been kept, with prayers that God would shew us what we knew not, viz. what errors might therein have been fallen into, &c.; and after most people were convinced of the evil of some, if not of most, of those actions; at such a time as this, it might have been justly expected that the ministers would make it their work to explain the scriptures to the people; and from thence to have shown them the evil and danger of those false notions, which not only gave some occasion, but in a blind zeal hurried them into those unwarrantable practices, so to prevent a falling into the like for the future.

But instead of this, for a minister of the gospel (pastor of the old meeting) to abet such notions, and to stir up the magistrates to such prosecutions, and this without any cautions given, is what is truly amazing, and of most dangerous consequence.

It is a truth, witchcraft is, in the text then insisted on, reckoned up as a manifest work of the flesh, viz. *Gal*, v. 19. But it is as true, that in recounting those other works (which are indeed manifest

---

7. The declaration, as drawn by the Deputies with the assistance of the Ministers; but received a nonconcurrence.

fleshly works) the magistrate was not stirred up against those others; as if the rest were either not to be taken notice of by him, or as if all zeal against murder, adulteries, &c. was swallowed up and overshadowed by this against witchcraft.

The description that was then given, was, that they were such as made a covenant with the devil, and sold themselves to the evil angels. It seems faulty, when such minister is inquired of, and requested to give the reasons, or grounds in scripture, of such description, for such minister to assert that it is the inquirer's work to disprove it. And his saying further, in answer, that there are many things true, that are not asserted in scripture, seems to speak this language, viz. that the law of God is imperfect, in not describing this crime of witchcraft, though it be therein made capital.

These perfect oracles inform us, concerning Ahab, that he sold himself to work wickedness; which may signify to us, that great height of wickedness be had arrived at; which yet might be, without his being properly, or justly, accounted a witch; any more than those that are said to have made a covenant with death, and with hell, &c. Can it be thought that all those, or such as are there spoken of, are witches, and ought to suffer as witches?

As the servants and people of God have made a solemn, explicit covenant with him, (*Josh.* xxiv. 25. *Nehem.* ix 33, &c.) so no doubt a covenant has been made by heathen indian nations, to serve and adore the devil; yet even for this, it were very hard to affix the character of a witch upon each of those heathen that so do, and accordingly to execute them as such. It is also possible, that some that have been called christians have sealed a writing, signed with their own blood. or otherways, thereby covenanting to bc the devil's servants, &.c. but from far other grounds, or inducements, than what sways with the indians; these heathen hoping to please him, that so he may not harm them. But these having been educated and confirmed in the belief that by virtue of such covenant they shall have a knowledge and power more than human assisting them; this may have prevailed with some to so horrible a wickedness; for none can seek evil for evil's sake; but as the serpent, in his first tempting man, made use of the knowledge of good and evil, so to teach men that such effects do usually follow such covenant is properly the work of the serpent; for, without this, what inducement, or temptation, could they have to make such a covenant?

These, having thus chosen a false god, may well be accounted the worst sort of idolaters. Yet it does not hence follow, that, in a scripture sense, they are thereby become witches, till they have, or rather till they pretend to have, assistances answerable: and do thereby endeavour to deceive others; which endeavours to deceive, by a sign, may be without any previous covenant.

But supposing none of all those several sorts of covenants was intended, it remains that the covenant that was understood to be intended, in that discourse at the old meeting, is agreeable to the late dangerous notion that has so much prevailed, viz. That the devil appears to the persons; that they and the devil make mutual engagements each to other, confirmed by signing to the devil's book; and are from hence enabled. not only to know futurities, and things done at a distance, but are also thereby empowered to do harm to their neighbours, to raise storms, and do things above and against the course of nature. This being the notion that has occasioned the shedding so much blood in the world, it may be thought to need explaining.

For as reason knows nothing of all afflicting, covenanting witch, so it seems as foreign from scripture in general, as it is from the text then insisted on; which speaks of such wickednesses as are manifestly the works of the flesh: but such communication with spirits, the flesh doth manifestly dread even as death itself: Therefore the usual salutation of the holy angels to the best of men was, fear not; and experience shews, that the most wicked are most affrighted at the apprehensions of the appearances of devils; therefore such an explicit covenanting cannot be a manifest work of the flesh.

Yet this is manifest, that the belief of the witches power to do the things above mentioned, is an ancient belief of the heathen; and that from them it was received by the papists, as a part of their faith, who have since improved upon it and brought in the notion of a covenant. But it seems yet a further improvement, lately made by protestants, that such witches can commission devils to do those mischiefs, thereby setting the witch in the place of God; for though few of the papists are known to be thus absurd, yet when such doctrines have been preached and printed in New-England, they have met with none to oppose, but many to encourage them. Other considerable additions, or new improvements, have been made here; as the art to knock off invisible chains with the hand, to drive away spectres (i.e. devils) by brushing, and spelling words to the afflicted,

&c. What has followed upon these notions, and upon such improvements, is needless here to repeat; it were unaccountable to recount that effusion of blood that has been hereby occasioned; such remaining scars, and such yet. bleeding wounds, as are to be found; which "none can wholly pretend ignorance of.

And if blood shall be required of that watchman that seeth the sword coming, and gives not the needful warning, how much more of such as join with the enemy. to bring in the sword to destroy them, over whom he was placed a watchman!

And if the law of God be perfect, and exceeding broad, as being given forth by the Omniscient Lawgiver, it is exceeding high presumption and arrogance, and highly destructive to the lives of innocents, for any to pretend to give another, and a pretended better, description of a crime made thereby capital, with new rules to try such offenders by.

Reverend sir, the matter, being of such high concern, requires (and it is again prayed) that you would be pleased to consider, and give the grounds from scripture, or reason, of such definition; or else that you would explode it, as inconsistent with both. From, reverend sir, yours to my utmost, R.C.

PART III.

ACCOUNT OF THE DIFFERENCES

IN

SALEM VILLAGE.

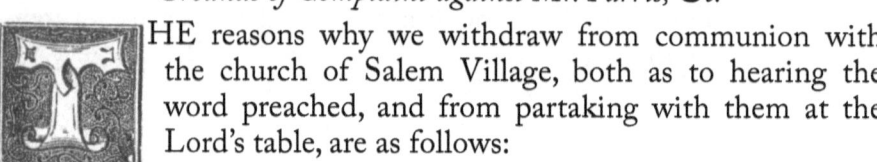

Grounds of Complaint against Mr. Parris, &c.

THE reasons why we withdraw from communion with the church of Salem Village, both as to hearing the word preached, and from partaking with them at the Lord's table, are as follows:

Why we attend not on publick prayer, and preaching the word, there are,

1. The distracting and disturbing tumults, and noises, made by the persons under diabolical power and. delusions; preventing sometimes our hearing, understanding, and profiting by, the word preached. we, having after many trials and experiences found no redress in this matter, accounted ourselves under a necessity to go where we might hear the word in quiet.

2. The apprehension of danger of ourselves being accused as the devil's instruments to afflict the persons complaining, we seeing those, that we have reason to esteem better than ourselves, thus accused, blemished, and of their lives bereaved: for seeing this, thought it our prudence to withdraw.

3. We found so frequent and positive preaching up some principles and practices by mr. Parris, referring to the dark and dismal mystery of iniquity working among us, was not profitable, but offensive.

4. Neither could we in conscience join with mr. Parris, in many of the requests which he made in prayer, referring to the trouble then among us and upon us: therefore thought it our most safe and peaceable way to withdraw.

The reasons why we hold not communion with them at the Lord's table, are, because we find ourselves justly aggrieved and offended with the officer who does administer, for the reasons following:

1. From his declared and published principles, referring to our molestations from the invisible world: differing from the opinion of the generality of the orthodox ministers of the country.

2. His easy and strong faith and belief of the fore-mentioned accusations, made by those called the afflicted.

3. His laying aside that grace (which above all we are to put on) viz. charity towards his neighbours, and especially those of his church. when there is no apparent reason but for the contrary.

4. His approving and practising unwarrantable and ungrounded methods, for discovering what he was desirous to know referring to the bewitched or possessed persons, as in bringing some to others, and by them pretending to inform himself and others, who were the devil's instruments to afflict the sick and maimed.

5. His unsafe, unaccountable oath, given by him against sundry of the accused.

6. His not rendering to the world so fair (if so true) account of what he wrote on examination of the afflicted. .

7. Sundry unsafe, if sound, points of doctrine, delivered in his preaching, which we find not warrantable (if christian).

8. His persisting in these principles, and justifying his practice; not rendering any satisfaction to us, when regularly desired, but rather offending and dissatisfying ourselves.

We, whose names are under written, heard this paper read to our pastor, Mr. Samuel Parris, the 21st of April, 1693.

Nathaniel Jigarson,	*Peter Cloyce,* senior;
Edward Putman,	*Samuel Nurse,*
Aaron Way,	*John Tarboll,*
William Way,	*Thomas Wilkins.*

Mr. Parris's Acknowledgment.

For as much as it is the undoubted duty of all christians to pursue peace, *Psal.* xxxiv. 14, even to a reaching of it, If it be possible; (*Amos* xii. 18, 19) and whereas, through the righteous, sovereign and awful Providence of God, the grand enemy to all christian peace has been of late tremendously let loose in divers places hereabout, and more especially among our sinful selves, not only to interrupt that partial peace which we sometimes enjoyed, but also, through his wiles and temptations, and our weakness and corruptions, to make wider breaches, and raise more bitter animosities between too many of us; in which dark and difficult dispensations, we have been all or most of us of one mind for a time, and afterwards of differing apprehensions; and at last we are but in the dark, upon serious thoughts of all; and after many prayers, I have been moved to present to you (my beloved flock) the following particulars, in way of contribution towards a regaining of christian concord, if so be we be not altogether unappeaseable, irreconcileable, and so destitute of that good spirit, which is first pure, then peaceable, gentle, and easy to be entreated, *James* iii. 17. viz.

1. In that the Lord ordered the late horrid calamity (which afterward plague-like spread in many other places) to breakout first in my family, I cannot but look upon as a very sore rebuke, and humbling providence, both to myself and mine, and desire so we may improve it.

2. In that also in my family were some of both parties, viz. accusers and accused, I look also upon as an aggravation of that rebuke, as an addition of wormwood to the gall.

3. In the means which were used in my family, though totally unknown to me or mine (except servants) till afterwards, to raise spirits and apparitions in no better than a diabolical way, I do also look upon as a further rebuke of Divine Providence. And by all, I do humbly own this day, before the Lord and his people that God has been righteously spitting in my face, *Numb.* xii. 14. And I desire to lie low under all this reproach, and to lay my hand on my mouth.

4. As to the management of these mysteries, as far as concerns myself, I am very desirous upon further light to own any errors I have therein fallen into, and can come to a discerning of; in the mean while I do acknowledge, upon after-considerations, that were the same troubles again, (which the Lord of his rich mercy forever

prevent) I should not agree with my former apprehensions in all points. As for instance,

1. I question not but God sometimes suffers the devil, as of late, to afflict in shape of not only innocent, but pious persons; or so to delude the senses of the afflicted, that they strongly conceit their hurt is from such persons, when indeed it is not.

2. The improving of one afflicted, to inquire by who afflicts the other, I fear may be, and has been, unlawfully used to satan's great advantage.

3. As to my writing, it was put upon me by authority, and therein I have been very careful to avoid the wronging of any.

4. As to my oath, I never meant it, nor do I know how it can be otherwise construed, than as vulgarly, and every one understood, yea, and upon inquiry it may be found so worded also.

5. As to any passage in preaching, or praying, in the sore hour of distress and darkness, I always intended but due justice on each hand, and that not according to men, but God, who knows all things most perfectly; however, through weakness or sore exercise, I might sometimes yea, and possibly sundry times, unadvisedly express myself.

6. As to several that have confessed against themselves, they being wholly strangers to me, but yet of good account with better men than myself, to whom also they are well known, I do not pass so much as a secret condemnation upon them; but rather, seeing God hath so amazingly lengthened out satan's chain, in this most formidable outrage, I much more incline to side with the opinion of those that have grounds to hope better of them.

7. As to all that have unduly suffered in these matters, either in their persons or relations, through the clouds of human weakness, and satan's wiles and sophistry, I do truly sympathize with them; taking it for granted, that such as know themselves clear of this great transgression, or that have sufficient grounds so to look upon their dear friends, have hereby been under those sore trials and temptations, that not an ordinary measure of true grace would be sufficient to prevent a bewraying of remaining corruption.

8. I am very much in the mind, and abundantly persuaded, that God, for holy ends, though for what in particular is best known to himself, has suffered the evil angels to delude us on both hands; but how far on the one side, or the other, is much above me to say; and if

we cannot reconcile till we come to a full discerning of these things, I fear we shall never come to nn agreement, or at soonest not in this world.

9. Therefore, in fine, the matter being so dark and perplexed, as that there is no present appearance that all God's servants should be altogether of one mind in all circumstances, touching the same, I do most heartily, fervently and humbly beseech pardon of the merciful God, through the blood of Christ, for all my mistakes and trespasses in so weighty a matter; and also all your forgiveness of every offence, in this or other affairs, wherein you see or conceive that I have erred and offended; professing, in the presence of the Almighty God, that what I have done has been, as for substance, as I apprehended was duty, however through weakness, ignorance, &c. I may have been mistaken. I also through grace promising each of you the like of me, so again I beg, entreat and beseech you, that satan, the devil, the roaring lion, the old dragon, the enemy of all righteousness, may no longer be served by us, by our envy and strifes, where every evil work prevails whilst these bear sway, (*James* iii. 14, 15, 16) but that all from this day forward may be covered with the mantle of love, and we may on all hands forgive each other heartily, sincerely and thoroughly, as we do hope and pray that God for Christ's sake would forgive each of ourselves, (*Matt.* xviii. 21, to the end.) *Coloss.* iii. 12, 1,3, *Put on therefore (as the elect of God, holy and beloved) bowels of mercies, kindness, humbleness of mind, meekness, long-suffering: forbearing one another, and forgiving one another: if any men have a quarrel against any; even as Christ forgave you, so also do ye.* Eph. iv. 31, 32, *Let all bitterness, and anger, and clamour, and evil-speaking, be put away from you, with all malice. And be ye kind one to another, tender-hearted, forgiving one another even as God for Christ's sake hath forgiven you.* Amen. Amen.

SAMUEL PARRIS.

Given to the dissenting brethren, for their consideration, at their request. *November* 26, 1694.

The Elders and Messengers of the churches met at Salem Village, April 3, 1695, to consider and determine what is to be done, for the composure of the present unhappy differences in that place; after solemn invocation of God in Christ for his direction, do unanimously declare, as followeth, viz.

SALEM VILLAGE.

1. We judge that although in the late and dark time of the confusions, wherein satan had obtained a more than ordinary liberty, to sift this plantation, there were sundry unwarrantable and uncomfortable steps taken by mr. Samuel Parris, the pastor of the church in Salem Village, then under the hurrying distractions of amazing afflictions; yet the said Mr. Parris, by the good hand of God brought unto a better sense of things, hath so fully exprest it, that a christian charity may and should receive satisfaction therewith,

2. Inasmuch as divers christian brethren, in the church of Salem Village, have been offended at mr. Parris, for his conduct in the time of their difficulties, which have distressed them; we now advise them charitably to accept the satisfaction which he hath tendered in his christian acknowledgment of the errors therein committed; yea, to endeavour, as far as it is possible, the fullest reconciliation of their minds unto communion with him, in the whole exercise of his ministry, and with the rest of the church. *Matt.* vi. 12, 14. *Luke* xviii. 3. *James* v. 16.

3. Considering the extreme trials and troubles which the disaffected brethren in the church of Salem Village have undergone, in the day of sore temptation which hath been upon them; we cannot but advise the church to treat them with bowels of much compassion, instead of more critical or rigorous proceedings against them for the infirmities discovered by them, in such an heartbreaking day; and if, after a patient waiting for it, the said brethren cannot so far overcome the uneasiness of their spirits, in the remembrance of the disasters that have happened, as to sit under his ministry, we advise the church with all tenderness to grant them admission to any other society of the faithful, whereunto they may be desirous to be dismissed. *Gal.* vi. 1,2. *Psal.* ciii. 13, 14. *Job* xix. 21.

4. Mr. Parris having, as we understand, with much fidelity and integrity acquitted himself, in the main course of his ministry, since he hath been pastor of the church of Salem Village; about his first call whereunto, we look upon all contests now to be both unreasonable and unseasonable; and our Lord having made him a blessing to the souls of not a few, both old and young, in this place, we advise that he be accordingly respected, honoured and supported, with all the regards that are due to a painful minister of the gospel. *1 Thess.* v. 12, 13. *1 Tim.* v. 17.

5. Having observed that there is in Salem Village a spirit full of contention and animosity, too sadly verifying the blemish which

hath heretofore lain upon them; and that some complaints against mr. Parris have been either causeless or groundless, or unduly aggravated; we do, in the name and fear of the Lord, solemnly warn them to consider whether, if they continue to devour one another, it will not be bitterness in the latter end; and beware lest the Lord be provoked thereby utterly to deprive them of those which they should count their precious and pleasant things, and abandon them to all the desolations of a people that sin away the mercies of the gospel. *James* iii. 16. *Gal.* v. 15. 2 *Sam.* ii. 26. *Isa.* y. 45. *Matt.* xxi. 43.

6. If the distempers in Salem Village should be (which God forbid) so incurable, that mr. Parris, after all, find that he cannot with any comfort and service continue in his present station, his removal from thence will not expose him to any hard character with us; nor, we hope, with the rest of the people of God, among whom we live. *Matt.* x. 14. *Acts* xxii. 13. All which advice we follow with our prayers, that the God of peace would bruise Satan under our feet. Now the Lord of peace himself give you peace always by all means.

Jos. Bridgham,	*Jer. Dummer,*	*James Allen,* ,
Samuel Chickley,	*Neh. Jewitt,*	*Samuel Tory,*
William Tory,	*Ephr. Hunt,*	*S. Willard,*
Jos. Boynton,	*N. Williams,*	*E. Payson,*
R. Middlecutt,	*Incr. Mather,*	*C. Mather,*
John Walley,	*S. Phillips.*	

To the Reverend Elders of the three churches of Christ at Boston, with others the Elders and Brethren of other churches, late of a Council at Salem Village.

We whose names are hereunto subscribed, are bold once more to trouble you with our humble proposals:—That whereas there have been long and uncomfortable differences among us, chiefly relating to mr. Parris; and we having, as we apprehend, attended all probable means for a composure of our troubles: and whereas we had hopes of an happy issue, by your endeavours among us, but now are utterly frustrated in our expectations, and that instead of uniting, our rent is made worse, and our breach made wider:

We humbly query, whether yourselves, being straightened of time, might not omit such satisfactory liberty of debating the whole of our controversy; whereby yourselves had not so large an opportunity of understanding the case, nor the offended so much reason to be satisfied in your advice: We therefore humbly propose, and give full liberty of proving and defending of what may be charged on either hand, leaving it to yourselves to appoint both time and place,

1. That if yourselves please to take the trouble, with patience once more to hear the whole case,.

2. or that you will more plainly advise mr. Parris (the case being so circumstanced that he cannot, with comfort or profit to himself or others, abide in the work of the ministry among us) to cease his labours, and seek to dispose himself elsewhere, as God in his providence may direct; and that yourselves would please to help us in advising to such a choice, wherein we may be more unanimous; which we hope would tend much to a composure of our differences.

3. Or that we may without any offence take the liberty of calling some other proved minister of the gospel, to preach the word of God to us and ours; and that we may not be denied our proportionable privilege, in our public disbursements in the place.

So leaving the whole case with the Lord and yourselves, we subscribe our names.

Signed by 16 young men, from 16 upwards; and 52 householders, and 18 church members. This was delivered to the ministers, May 3, 1695.

The copy of a paper that was handed about, touching those differences.

As to the contest between mr. Parris and his hearers, &c. it may be composed by a satisfactory answer to *Levit.* xx. 6, "And the soul that turneth after such as have familiar spirits, and after wizards, to go a whoring after them, I will set my face against that soul, and will cut him off from among his people." *1 Chron.* x. 13., 14, "So Saul died for his transgression, which he committed against the Lord, even against the word of the Lord, which he kept not; and also for asking counsel of one that had a familiar spirit, to inquire of it; and inquired not of the Lord; therefore he slew him." &c.

Some part of the determination of the Elders and Messengers of the churches, met at Salem Village, April 3, 1695, relating to the differences there.

If the distemper in Salem Village should be (which God forbid) so incurable that mr. Parris, after all, find that he cannot with any comfort and service continue in his present station, his removal from thence will not expose him to any hard character with us, nor, we hope, with the rest of the people of God. among whom we live. *Matt.* x. 14, *And whosoever shall not receive you, nor hear your words; when you depart out of that house, or city, shake off the dust of your feet, &c. Acts* xxii. 18. All which advice we follow with our prayers, that the God of peace would bruise satan under our feet. Now the Lord of peace give you peace always, by all means, &c.

Quest. Whether Mr. Parris's going to Abigail Williams and others, whom he supposed to have a spectral sight, to be informed who were witches and who afflicted those pretended sufferers by witchcraft, in order to their being questioned upon their lives upon it, were not a turning after such as had familiar spirits; and a greater wickedness than Saul was guilty of, in that he did not intend thereby bodily hurt to any others?

And whether, in a crime of such a high nature, the making a slender and general confession, without any proposals of reparations, or due time for probation, ought so far to be accounted sufficient, from such a pastor to his people?

And whether such as were accused, or the surviving friends and relations of those that were any ways sufferers by accusations so by him proved, are in duty and conscience bound to continue their respect, honour and support to him, in the ministry, after such known departures from the rule of God's word, and after such dire effects as followed thereupon, under the penalty of the dust shaken from his feet, testifying against them, even so as to render them in a worse case than those of Sodom and Gomorrah?

To the Honourable Wait Winthrop, Elisha Cook and Samuel Sewall, Esquires, arbitrators, indifferently chosen, between Mr. Samuel Parris and the inhabitants of Salem Village.

The remonstrances of several aggrieved persons in the said village, with further reasons why they conceive they ought not to hear mr. Parris, nor to own him as a minister of the gospel, nor to contribute any support to him as such, for several years past; humbly offered as fit for consideration.

We humbly conceive that having, in April, 1693, given our reasons why we could not join with mr. Parris in prayer, preaching, or sacraments; if these reasons are found sufficient for our withdrawing,

SALEM VILLAGE.

(and we cannot yet find but they are) then we conceive ourselves virtually discharged, not only in conscience, but also in law; which requires maintenance to be given to such as are orthodox, and blameless; the said mr. Parris having been teaching such dangerous errors, and preached such scandalous immoralities, as ought to discharge any (though ever so gifted otherways) from the work of the ministry.

Particularly in his oath against the lives of several, wherein he swears that the prisoners with their looks knock down those pretended sufferers. We humbly conceive, that he that swears to more than he is certain of, is equally guilty of perjury with him that swears to what is false. And though they did fall at such a time, yet it could not be known that they did it, much less could they be certain of it; yet .did swear positively against the lives of such, as he could not have any knowledge but they might be innocent. .

His believing the devil's accusations, and readily departing from all charity to persons, though of blameless and godly lives, upon such suggestions; his promoting such accusations; as also his partiality therein, in stifling the accusations of some, and at the same time vigilantly promoting others, as we conceive, are just causes for our refusal, &c.

That mr. Parris's going to Mary Walcut, or Abigail Williams, and directing others to them, to know who afflicted the people in their illnesses—we understand this to be a dealing with them that have a familiar spirit, and an implicit denying the providence of God, who alone, as we believe, can send afflictions, or cause devils to amid any; this we also conceive sufficient to justify such refusal. That mr. Parris, by these practices and principles, has been the beginner and procurer of the sorest afflictions, not to this Village only, but to this whole country, that did ever befal them.

We, the subscribers, in behalf of ourselves, and of several others of the same mind with us, (touching these things) having some of us had our relations by these practices taken off by an untimely death; others have been imprisoned, and suffered in our persons, reputations and estates; submit the whole to your honours decision, to determine whether we are or ought to be any ways obliged to honour, respect and support such an instrument of our miseries; praying God to guide your honours to act herein as may be for his glory, and the future settlement of our village in amity and unity.

John Tarboll, Samuel Nurse, Jos. Putman, Dan. Andrew,
      Attorneys for the people of the village.

Boston, July 21, 1697.

According to the order of the aforesaid arbitrators, the said mr. Parris had some of his arrears paid him, as also a sum of money for his repairs of the ministerial house of the said village, and is dismissed therefrom.

NOTE.— Writers have generally supposed that Mr. Parris, after his dismission from Salem Village, removed to Concord, Massachusetts. But it is now certain that he received a call to preach in Stowe, by the inhabitants of that town, Nov. 29, 1697, and on the 4th of January, 1698, the Selectmen were ordered "to make a rate of ten pounds for Mr. Parris, our present minister" He is said to have preached in Concord, Mass., in 1705. It is certain that he commenced preaching in Dunstable in October, 1708, and continued to preach in that town three years. He died in Sudbury, Feb. 27, 1720, aged 67 years.

PART IV.

LETTERS

OF A GENTLEMAN UNINTERESTED,

ENDEAVOURING TO PROVE THE RECEIVED OPINIONS
ABOUT WITCHCRAFT TO BE ORTHODOX.

Sir,

I TOLD you I had some thoughts concerning witchcraft, and an intention of conferring with the gentleman who has published several treatises about witchcraft, and persons afflicted by them, lately here in New-England; but since you have put those three books into my hands, I find myself engaged in a very hard province, to give you my opinion of them. I plainly foresee, that should this scribbling of mine come to public view, it would displease all parties, but that is the least. Moreover it is so far out of my road to set my thoughts to consider a matter on every side, which in itself is so abstruse, and every step I advance therein, if I miss truth (which is a narrow and undivided line) I must tumble down headlong into the gulph of dangerous error. Yet, notwithstanding, I have forced myself to send these few lines, if so be I may clear to you a truth you now seem to be offended at, because of the ill consequences which (you think) lately have and again may be drawn from it, by the ill conduct of some men. I am not ignorant that the pious frauds of the ancient, and the inbred fire (I do not call it pride) of many of our modern, divines, have precipitated them to propagate and maintain truth as well as falsehoods, in such an unfair manner, as has given advantage to the enemy to suspect the whole doctrine, these men have profest, to be nothing but a mere trick. But it is certain, that as no lover of truth will justify an illegitimate corollary, though drawn from a true proposition; so neither will he reject a truth, because some or many men take unfair means to prove it, or draw false consequences from it. The many heresies among christians must not give a mortal wound to the essence of the christian religion; neither must any one christian doctrine be exterminated, because evil men make use of it as a cloak to cover their own self-ends; particularly, because some men, perhaps among all sorts of christians, have, under pretence of witchcraft, coloured their own malice, pride and popularity, we must not therefore conclude (1.) that there are no witches; (2.) or that witches cannot be convicted by such clear and undeniable proof, as the law of God requires in the case of death; (3.) or that a witch so convicted ought not to be put to death.

1. That there are witches, is manifest from the precept of Moses, *Thou shalt not suffer a witch to live*. Exod. xxii. 13. For it is certain God would not have given a vain and unintelligible law, as this must be, of putting witches to death, if there are no witches. But you object, that this doth not answer our case, for we have formed another idea of witches than what can be gathered from the scriptures; you quote four places, viz. *Deut.* xiii. *Matt.* xxiv. *Acts* xiii. 2 *Tim.* iii. from all which you infer, that witchcraft is a maligning and oppugning the word, works and worship of God, and by an extraordinary sign seeking to seduce any from it; and this you readily grant. But then you say, What is this to witches now a days, who are said to have made an explicit covenant with the devil, and to be empowered by him to the doing of things strange in themselves, and besides their natural course? This you say does not follow; and herein indeed consists the whole controversy; therefore it is necessary, that first of all we clear this point, laying aside those prejudices we may have from the fatal application of this doctrine to some who were (in your judgment) really, at least in law, and before men, innocent. In a word, we are seeking after truth, and truth shall and will be truth, in spite of men and devils. I do not repeat this caution to forestall you to believe, the doctrine of witchcraft, as it is above defined, without inquiring into the reason and truth of it; only I desire you to inquire into it, as a thing doubtful. For no man can be certain of a negative, unless either the affirmative imply a contradiction, or he can prove it by certain testimony; to neither of which you pretend; only you alledge it cannot be proved by scripture, i.e. you cannot prove it, nor have seen it proved by any other you have read on that subject. I am

not so vain as to think I can do better than the learned authors you have consulted with (though I know not what they have done, for I had no other book but the bible, to make use of on this occasion;) but because I am satisfied myself, and am willing to communicate my reasons, which I divide into three heads. 1. The appearance of angels. 2. The nature of possession; and, 3d, The scripture notion of witchcraft.

1. Good angels did appear to Abraham, and did eat, *Gen.* xv. It seems he washed their feet; it is certain he saw and heard them; therefore there is no impossibility in angels being conversant with men. God is true, and whatever is contained in sacred writ is true; if we poor shallow mortals do not comprehend the manner how, that argues only our weakness and ignorance in this dark prison of flesh, wherein we are enclosed during our abode in this vale of misery, but doth not in the least infringe the verity of scripture; it is sufficient that we undoubtedly know they have appeared unto men in bodily shape, and done their errand they were sent on from God. Now if good angels have appeared, why may not bad? Surely the devils, because fallen and evil, have not therefore lost the nature of angels; neither is there any contradiction in their appearing in a bodily shape, now after, any more than before, their fall. But you will say you must allow of the appearances of good angels, because of the scripture testimony; but not of bad, seeing there is no place of scripture that clearly proves it. *Matt.* iv, The words in the gospel do as plainly signify the devil's outward appearance to our Saviour, when he was tempted, as can be expres'd; *And when the tempter came to him he said—but he answered.* The same form St. Luke useth to signify the appearance of Moses and Elias, in the transfiguration: *And behold there talked with him two men*; for what follows, ver. 31, *who appeared*, is used to signify (not their appearance, but) the manner of their appearance in great glory. But you will urge, that it is very easy to be understood, that Moses and Elias did appear, because they had human bodies; but that it is unintelligible to you, how the devil, being a spirit, can appear, a spirit being a substance void of all dimensions; therefore the words in the history must not be taken in a literal sense. Do not mistake: though some philosophers are of opinion (which whether true or false is all one to our present argument) that a spirit's substance is extended, and hath, besides length, breadth and depth, a fourth dimension, viz. essential spissitude; yet the same do not say, that pure substance is perceptible

by our bodily senses; on the contrary, they tell us, that spirits are clothed with vehicles, i.e. they are united to certain portions of matter, which they inform, move and actuate. Now this we must not reject as impossible, because we cannot comprehend the formal reason, how a spirit acts upon matter: for who call give the reason, that, upon the volition of the human soul, the hand should be lifted up, or any ways moved? for to say the contraction of the muscles is the mechanic cause of voluntary motion, is not to solve the question, which recurs, Why, upon volition, should that contraction ensue which causes that motion? All that I know the wisest man ever said upon this head is, that it is the will of the Creator, who has ordered such a species of thinking creatures, by a catholic law, to be united to such portions of matter, so and so disposed; or, if you will, in the vulgar phrase, to organized bodies; and that there should be between them and the several bodies they are united to a mutual reaction and passion. Now you see how little we know of the reason of that which is most near to us, and most certain, viz. the soul's informing the body, yet you would think it a bad argument, if one should, as some have done, conclude, from this our ignorance, that there was nothing in us but matter; it is no otherways than to deny a spirit's acting a vehicle. The plainest and most certain things when denied are hardest to be proved; therefore the axiom saith well, *contra principia, &c.* There are some certain truths, which are rather to be explained to young beginners than proved, upon which all science is built; as every whole is more than its part; and of this sort I take these two following: 1. That there are two substances, *corpus* and *mens*, body and spirit, altogether different, for the ideas we have of them are quite distinct. 2. That a spirit can actuate, animate or inform a certain portion of matter. and be united to it; from whence it is very evident, that the devil, united to a portion of matter (which hereafter I'll call a vehicle) may fall under the cognizance of our senses, and be conversant with us in a bodily shape. Where then is the reason or need to run to a metaphorical and forced interpretation, when the words are so plain, and the literal sense implieth no contradiction, nor any greater difficulty than (as has been said) what ariseth from the union of the soul and body, which is most certain? Now after all to say, God will not permit the devil so to appear, is to beg the question, without saying any thing to the preceding argument; and it is against the sense of almost all mankind; for in all ages, and all places, there have been many witnesses of the appearances of dæmons, all of whom, that taught any thing contrary to the right worship of the true God, were certainly evil ones: and it were most presumptuous, barely to assert that all these witnesses were always deceived, and it is impossible they could all agree to deceive.

2. We come to consider the nature of possession. The man possest (*Luke* viii. 27) had a power more than natural, for he brake the bands, which he could not have done with his own strength. Now from whom had he this power? The scripture saith, he had devils a long time, and oftentimes it had caught him, &c. he was kept bound with chains and in fetters, and he brake the bands, and was driven of the devil into the wilderness. This power then was immediately from the devil, and whatsoever a possessed person does, or suffers, beyond his natural power, he is enabled by the dæmon so to do; or, to speak more properly, it is the dæmon who acteth the same, as is plain from St. Mark's relation of this passage, v. 2 *v. A man with an unclean spirit.* 3 *v. And no man could bind him, no, not with chains.* 6 *v. But when he saw Jesus afar off, he came and worshipped him;* and the same he, 7 *v.* said, *I adjure thee by God that thou torment me not;* and 9 *v. My name is Legion, for we are many.* 10 *v. And he besought him much: that he would not send them away out of the country.* It is manifest from hence, that it was not the poor man who was possest, but the devils who possessed him, by whom the chains had been plucked asunder, and the fetters broken in pieces. Now here is divine testimony, that the devils have actuated a human body to the doing of things beyond the natural strength of that body, as it was simply united to its human soul: how much more then can the devil actuate any other portion of simple matter, earth, air, fire or water, and make it a fit organ for himself to act in!

But enough of this already: let us rather inquire how the devil enters into the body of the possest, to move it at his pleasure. This I think he cannot do as a mere spirit, or by any never so strict union with the human soul; for in that case he is only a tempter or seducer, and nothing above human strength can be done: but here there being something performed (the bonds broken) by a force which could not proceed from human strength, it necessarily follows that the devils entered into the possest, otherways qualified them as a mere spirit; he did not enter without some portion of matter, to which he was united, by the intermedium whereof he acted upon and actuated the human body. Again, if it is said that the devil entered as a mere spirit, and immediately acted upon and moved that body, it follows, the devil hath a vehicle, a certain portion of matter (that body) to actuate and dispose of at will; which is absurd: 1, Because it asserts what it seems to deny, viz. the devil's having a vehicle to act immediately upon; and to be united to a portion of matter (as has been said before) is the same thing. 2, It fights against the catholic law of the union of soul and body, by which the Omnipotent hath ordained the voluntary motion of a human body to depend upon the will of its human soul, and those that are not voluntary to proceed either from its own mechanism or material force; hence we may certainly conclude, that it is by the intervening of the devil's vehicle, that he enters into the body of the possest. But what if you and I cannot agree about this notion of possession, must we therefore reject the truth itself, and run to a far-fetched and intolerable sense of the words? No, our opinions do not alter the nature of things; it is certain there were persons possest, and it is as certain that the devil entered into them, either with or without a vehicle; it is all one which part of the contradiction you take, the consequence is the same, viz. That the devil doth act immediately upon matter. There is another acceptation of the word possession in scripture, (*Acts* xvi. 17) where one is said to be possest with a spirit of divination, the word commonly used to the priestess of Apollo, who gave responses; and it seems this damsel was such an one, for she brought her masters much money, or gain, by soothsaying, till they were full of the god. Now if the history of them be true, that they were demented, and knew not themselves what they uttered, (as they word it) their case is not different, but the same with the foregoing; but if they understood what they spoke, then had they familiar spirits, whereof there is frequent mention made in the old testament, and one good king is commended for having cut off them that had such; therefore I think the meaning of the word was very obvious in his time; neither was it ever controverted being joined with any other name than spirit, familiar, one of our own family: that is, oft, every day, conversant with us, and almost ever ready upon call to attend us. But the consideration of them, who have familiar spirits, falleth under the head of witchcraft, which we are to consider in the third place.

3. Witchcraft, to inquire into the scripture notion of it, and compare whether it be the same with that above defined. The cabalistick learning would be of great use in this search, and afford us much light; there is little doubt but that there are many great truths not commonly known. And our Saviour expressly cautions his

disciples that they do not throw their pearls before swine: therefore it is no wonder that some doctrines, while unquestionably true, are not so fully described, because the authors who treat of them are afraid, lest evil men should be the more depraved by being informed: but I am in no such fear; nor can I give you any other thoughts but what are obvious to any man, from the plain sense of the scripture. Our definition we'll divide into two propositions, and handle them severally. 1 Proposition, The witch is empowered by the devil to do things strange in themselves, and beside their natural course. 2 Prop. The manner how the witch is empowered to do those strange things, is by explicit compact, or covenant, with the devil. For clearing of the first, we will consider the four places above cited, wherein a witch is called a false prophet, a false Christ, a sorcerer, a resister of the truth, and is said to shew signs to seduce the people to seek after other gods: whence let us note three things. 1. That those terms, witch, false Christ, false prophet and sorcerer, are all synonimous, i.e. signify the same thing. 2. That a witch doth do things strange in themselves, and beyond their natural course: for it were most ridiculous to alledge that our blessed Saviour, when he said, *there shall arise false Christs, and shall shew great signs and wonders, in so much that (if it were possible) they should deceive the very elect*, meant that cunning cheats should arise, and shew legerdemain tricks; the words will in no wise bear it, and I believe you are far from thus interpreting them; so it is manifest they signify not a feigned, but a real, doing of things, beyond their natural course; therefore the sorceries of Elymas and Simon were not simple delusions, but real effects, that could not have been produced by physical causes in the ordinary course of nature. 3. That the end of the witches' shewing these signs, is to seduce the people to seek after other gods; from which premises I infer, that the witches have the power of doing those wonders, or strange things, immediately from the devil: they are without the reach of nature, and therefore above human power, and no mere man can effect them; the witch then who does them must have the power of doing them from another; but who is the other? God will not give his testimony to a lie; and to say God did at any time empower a witch to work wonders, to gain belief to the doctrine of devils, were with one breath to destroy root and branch of all revealed religion; no, it cannot be, it is only God's permission, who proveth his people, whether they love him with all their heart, and with all their soul. Therefore the witch has a power of doing wonders, or strange things, immediately from the devil. 2

Proposition, we will subdivide into these two. 1. That there is an express covenant between the witch and the devil. 2. That it is not reasonable to suppose this covenant to be transacted mentally. 1. The devil cannot communicate this power, by never so strict a union with the soul of the witch; for in that case be is only a tempter, and nothing above human power can be done, as has been already proved; therefore the devil, who improves the witch to do things above human power, must either appear in an external shape, and instruct him how, and upon what terms, he will enable him to do those wonders; or else he must enter into the body of the witch, and possess it. The demoniacs in the gospel are such whom the devils invade by main force, their soul having no further command of their bodies, which are subjected to the will of the devils; whose end is to wound and torment those miserable creatures, to throw them into the fire, and into the water: but the witch, who likewise is possessed, is not treated in such an outrageous manner; his dæmon is tame and familiar unto him, and suffers him for a time to live quietly, without any further molestation, than prompting him to do his utmost endeavour to withdraw men from God; he is not bereaved of his senses as the poor lunatic, but is conscious of all he does, and willeth all his crimes: he receiveth power from the devil to do wonders, and doth them to serve the devil's turn. Therefore there must be a covenant, an express covenant, between the devil and him, viz. that he shall obey the devil and serve him, and that the devil shall both enable him so to do, and also reward him for so doing; for if there is no contract between them, how comes the witch to know he has a supernatural power? or how can he so peremptorily pretend to do that which is so much above his natural power, not knowing he has a supernatural one enabling him to do the same? There can be no doubt but there was a very intimate commerce between satan and him who is called by St. Paul thou child of the devil, not as other unholy men, but in an especial manner, as being the enemy of all righteousness, who would not cease to pervert the right ways of the Lord. It is not to be supposed that he entered into this so near a relation with satan, with which he is stigmatized, that others may beware of him, without his own knowledge and consent. And is not this a covenant, an express covenant, on his part, to serve the devil incessantly; and on the devil's, to empower him to act his sorceries wherewith he bewitched the people? Now I think I have from scripture fully satisfied you of the truth of what I offered in a discourse at ———. But, since, you have told me an explicit covenant with the devil signifies the devil's appearing in a bodily shape to the witch, and their signifying an express covenant, which you say cannot be proved from scripture. It were most unreasonable to imagine that the ceremonies of this hellish mystery are particularly set down in the word of God; therefore we must gather by analogy and reason the matter how this express covenant is transacted; and to that end I will set down these following considerations.

1. Under the law God did ordain his people in all their matters to have recourse immediately to himself, and depend upon him for counsel, which they were ready to obey, with full assurance of aid and protection from him against their enemies. This the devil imitateth by setting up of oracles among the heathen, to which all the kings, nations and mighty conquerors upon earth, did come, and paid their humblest adoration to the god (as the devil blasphemously called himself) of the temple, in which they were imploring his direction and assistance in their doubtful and prosperous affairs. Again, God instituted sacrifices to put men in mind of their duty to the Creator, to whom they owe all things, even themselves; but the devil is not contented with the bare imitation hereof; the acknowledgment and worship he receiveth from the deluded world is not enough, though they offer up unto him innumerable hecatombs, unless they cause their children to pass through the fire unto him, to whom no sacrifice is so well pleasing as that of human blood. And there is no reason to think, that now, under the economy of the gospel, the devil hath left off to vie with God, and thereby to ensnare men. No, it is rather to be feared that his kingdom doth now more prevail; for by how much the light is greater, so much greater is their condemnation who do not receive it: it is reasonable to suppose that (seeing the Son of God, when he came to transact with men the wonderful covenant of their redemption, took upon him their nature, and was perfect man) the devil likewise doth counterfeit the same, in appearing in an human shape to them who receive him, and confederate themselves with him, and become his vassals.

2. Consider, it is not probable that those false apostles mentioned, *2 Cor.* xi. 13, erred only in ceremonies or circumstances, or that their errors, though great, did proceed rather from their ignorance than from the perverseness of their minds. *1 Cor.* iii. 15. For, for such we may have charity and hope, that God will be merciful unto them, if they sincerely do the best they know, though they dissent in some, nay many things, from the practices and belief of the christian

church; but those St. Paul threatens with a heavy curse, that their end shall be according to their works; therefore it seems they immediately struck at the very root and being of the christian religion, and were the same with them spoken of, *2 Tim.* iii. 6, but with this difference, that they did not resist, but, beholding the miracles and signs which were done by the true apostle of our Lord, wondered, and believed also, and were baptized; yet, being sorcerers, they were unwilling to lose that great esteem they had obtained; as it is related of Simon, who had bewitched the people of Samaria, giving out that he himself was some great one, to whom they all gave heed, from the least to the greatest, saying, this man is the great power of God; therefore he could not brook that Peter or John should have a greater power than himself; but offered them money, that on whomsoever he laid hands, he (that person) should receive the Holy Ghost; which shews him, who thus designed to make merchandise of the Spirit, though baptized, to have been no true believer, but still a sorcerer, in the gall of bitterness, and in the bond of iniquity. Such were those deceitful workers, who, not being able barefaced to resist, did put on christianity as a mask, that they might undermine the truth, and introduce the doctrines of devils. Samaria and Paphos were not the only two places where the devil had such agents; there was no part of the earth where his kingdom was not established, and where he had not his emissaries before the preaching of the gospel; and since the text telleth us he hath his ministers, who imitate their master, by being transformed into the apostles of Christ, as he himself is transformed into an angel of light: whose design, in being thus transformed, cannot be to impose upon the Almighty; for whatever shape he appears in, he cannot hide his ugliness from the eyes of him who is omniscient; therefore he appeareth thus in the shape of an angel of light, either to tempt and seduce the blessed spirits to rebel against God, or to ensnare wicked men, who by their heinous crimes (being lovers of themselves, covetous, boasters, proud, blasphemers) were before disposed to be fit instruments to serve him, and to enter into league with him. Surely I, who am ignorant of the laws by which the intellectual world is governed, dare not affirm that it is impossible for satan so to appear, as to hide his deformities from the good angels, and under that vail to tempt them: but certain I am that it is more consonant to reason, to think that the apostle's intention here was to teach that the devil appeared as a glorified angel unto men, to gain ministers, whom he might imbue with the poison of his black art, and (when he had gotten full possession of them) instruct them by his own example to transform themselves into the apostles of Christ, that under that vizard they might with the greater advantage promote his ends, and join with him in doing the utmost despite to the spirit of grace.

3d Consideration: It is against the nature of this covenant, that it should be consummated by a mental colloquy between the devil and the witch. I know not how many articles it consists of; but it is certain, from what has been already proved, that the renouncing of Christ to be the Son of God, and owning the devil to be, and worshiping him as God, are the two chiefs, to which our Saviour, who was accused of casting out devils by Beelzebub, i.e. of being confederated with Beelzebub, was tempted to consent: *If thou be the son of God, command that these stones be made bread*: and again, *throw thyself down from hence; for it is written, he will give his angels charge over thee*; and again, *all these things will I give thee, if thou wilt fall down and worship me*. Whence it is evident that here the devil laboured to insinuate into our Lord, either to do things rash and unwarrantable, or to suspect his sonship, revolt from God his father, and worship satan, that he might obtain the glory of the world. Now it has been already said, that when Jesus was tempted, the devil appeared unto him in a bodily shape; therefore it is agreeable to reason, that he doth appear in the same manner to all them, whom he also tempteth to worship him: moreover, the form of renouncing a covenant ought to bear resemblance to the form of entering into the same covenant; therefore men who are received into the mystical body of Christ by God's minister, who in God's stead expressly covenanteth with and then administereth the sacrament of baptism unto them, must in the like manner go out of, or renounce, the said covenant; and of them there are two sorts, one who, through the perverseness of their own hearts, the lucre of the world, the fear of men more than of God, abjure their Saviour, turn apostates, turks, or pagans. The other sort is of them who contract with the devil to be his subjects, in the initiation of whom it is not to be supposed that the devil will omit any material circumstance which tends both to bring them into and confirm them in his service. To effect which, his outward appearance, when he receives his catechumens, is of greater force than any mental contract; for many wicked men who have denied God and Christ, not only in their practice, but also blasphemously in profession, yet have repented, and at last obtained some hope of mercy. I dare not say it is impossible for a witch to repent, and find mercy; the secrets of the Almighty are too high for me; but it is certain that these wretches are strangely hardened, by what passes between them and the devil, in a bodily shape, particularly their worshiping him, which necessarily implies his outward appearance unto them; for no man can love evil as evil, because the law of self-preservation, deeply rooted in all men, determineth their will to pursue that which seems good, and fly from that which seems evil to them; out the inbred notion that every man has of the devil, is, that he is an enemy and destroyer of mankind, therefore every man hath a natural aversion from him, and consequently cannot formally worship him as such, because the object of worship must be esteemed to be propitious and placable by the worshipers; otherwise, if fear alone be the adequate cause of adoration, it follows that the devils and damned in hell do worship God, which is contrary to scripture, which saith they blasphemed, because of their pains; whence it follows, that they who worship the devil must have changed the innate idea that they had of him, viz. that he is an implacable worrier of men, and take him to be benign at least to his own; but this change cannot be wrought by any suggestion of satan into the minds of men, whom indeed he mentally tempteth to lust, pride and malice; but it is his greatest artifice to cause his insinuations to arise in the hearts of men, as their own natural thoughts; and if conscience discovers their author, and opposes them, then he varnishes them over with the specious colours of pleasure, honour and glory; and so represents them as really good, to be willed and desired by the soul, which judgeth of all things without agreeing to the ideas she hath of them; but because most objects have two, and some many, faces, and she not always attends, therefore she often errs in her choice; nevertheless it is impossible for her to love an object, whose simple idea is evil; but the idea we have of the devil is such, for we cannot represent him in our minds any otherwise than the great destroyer of men, therefore no mental temptation can make us believe this our grand enemy to be ever exorable by, or in any measure favourable to us; whence it evidently follows, that the devil, to work this change of opinion his worshipers have of him, must appear unto them in a bodily shape, and impose upon them, whom, because of their great corruption and sinfulness, God hath wholly left, and given up to strong delusions, that they should believe a lie, and the father of lies; who, now appearing in a human shape, telleth them that he is not such a monster as he has been represented to them by his enemy, who calls himself God, which title of right belongs to him; and that he (if they contract to be his servants) will both amply reward them, by giving them power to do many things very suitable to their abominable depraved nature, that the christians, whatever opinion they may pretend to have of their God, cannot so much as pretend to, and also that he will protect and defend them against him, whom heretofore they have mistaken for the Almighty, and his pretended Son Christ, whom they must abjure before they can be received by or expect any benefit from him. Upon no other consideration is it possible for any man to worship the devil; for the atheists, who deny the being of a God, do likewise deny the existence of any spirit good or bad; therefore their drinking the devil's health, even upon their knees (though a most horrid crime) cannot be construed allY part of worship. paid to him, whom they assert to be a chimera, a mere figment of statesmen to keep the vulgar in awe. Now I have evinced to you that there are witches; that the witch receiveth power from the devil to do strange things; that there is an express covenant between the devil and the witch; that this covenant cannot be transacted mentally, but that the devil must appear in a bodily shape to the witch; therefore I conclude, that a witch in the scripture is such, who has made an explicit covenant with the devil, and is empowered by him to do things strange in themselves, and beside their natural course.

II. I persuade myself you do not expect from me any essay concerning the methods how witches mayor ought to be convicted; I wish those gentlemen, whose eminent station both enables them to perform it, and likewise makes it their duty so to do, may take this province upon them, and handle it so fully as to satisfy you herein. I once intended to have provided some materials for this work, by defining four principal things relating to witchcraft, viz. 1. witch-fits. 2. The imps that are said to attend on the witch. 3. The transportation of the witch through the air. 4. Lastly, the invisibility of the witch. But upon second thought, that it was foreign from my purpose, who am not concerned to compose a just treatise of witchcraft, which would require more vacant time than my present circumstances will allow; only I proposed to give you my opinion privately; therefore I will venture to make use of an argument, which sheweth neither art nor learning in the author; and it is this, That seeing there are witches, and that the law of God doth command them to be put to death, therefore there must be means to convict them, by clear and certain proof, otherwise the law were in vain; for no man can be justly condemned, who is not fairly convicted by full and certain evidence.

III. In the last place we are to inquire, whether a witch ought to be put to death or no? You answer in the negative; because you say that that law, Thou shalt not suffer a witch to live, is *judicial*, and extendeth only to the people of the Jews; but our Saviour, or his apostles, have not delivered any where any such command, therefore they ought to be suffered to live. This indeed seems somewhat plausible at first view, but ,upon thorough examination hath no weight in it at all, for these reasons, 1. All penal laws receive their sanction from him or them who have the sovereign power in any state; as, Thou shalt not commit adultery, is a moral law, and obligatory over the consciences of men in all places and ages; but that the adulterers shall be put to death, is a judicial law, and in force only in that state, where it is enacted by the sovereign. 2. The government of the Jews was a theocracy, and God himself condescended to be their King, not only as he is King of kings; for in that sense he is, always was, and ever will be, supreme Lord and Governor of all his creatures; but in an especial manner to give them laws for the government of their state, and to protect them against their enemies; in one word, to be immediately their Sovereign. 3. Our Saviour's kingdom was not of this world; he was no judge to divide so much as an inheritance between two brethren; nay, he himself submitted patiently to the unjust sentence of the governor of the country in which he lived; therefore both the rewards and punishments annexed to his laws are spiritual, and then shall have their full accomplishment, when the Son of Man at the last day shall pronounce, *come unto me ye blessed, and depart ye cursed into everlasting fire.* 4. That sovereigns, who have received the gospel of our Lord, have not therefore lost their power of enacting laws for the ruling and preserving their people, and punishing malefactors even with death; so that the criminal is as justly condemned to die by our municipal, as he was heretofore by the judicial law among the Jews. How much more then ought our law to advert against the highest of all criminals, those execrable men and women, who, though yet alive, have listed themselves under satan's banner, and explicitly sworn allegiance to him, to fight against God and Christ! Indeed all unholy men afford great matter to the devils of blaspheming; but these wretches have confederated themselves with the devils, to blaspheme and destroy all they can. And do you think that these common enemies of God and mankind ought to be suffered to live in a christian commonwealth? especially considering that we have . a precedent of putting them to death from God himself, when he acted as King over his own peculiar people. But methinks I hear you saying, All this doth not satisfy me, for I am sure nothing can be added to the devil's malice; and if he could, he certainly would, appear, and frighten all men out of their wits. I answer, 1. We must not reject a truth, because we cannot resolve all the questions that may be proposed about it; otherwise all our science must he turned into scepticism, for we have not a comprehensive knowledge of any one thing.—2. When you say, that if the devil could, he would appear and frighten all men—the lawful consequence is, not that he cannot appear at all, for we have undoubtedly proved the contrary, but that we are ignorant of the bounds that the Almighty hath set to him, whose malice indeed, if he were not restrained, is so great as to destroy all men; but the goodness of our God is greater, who hath given us means to escape his fury, if we will give earnest heed to the gospel of our Saviour, which only is able to comfort us against the sad and miserable condition of our present state; for not only the devils, but likewise all do conspire against us to work our ruin. The deluge came and swept away all the race (save eight persons) of mankind: the fire will in time devour what the water has left; and all this cometh to pass because of sin: but we, who have received the Lord Jesus, look for new heavens, and a new earth, wherein dwelleth righteousness. Therefore he, if we purify ourselves as he is pure, will save us (for when he appears we shall be made like unto him, to whom be glory forever, Amen) from the great destruction that must come,upon all the world, and inhabitants thereof. Farewell.

March 8, 1693.

BOSTON, *March* 20, 1693.

Worthy Sir,

The great pains you have taken for my information and satisfaction in those controverted points relating to witchcraft, whether it attain the end or not, cannot require less than suitable acknowledgments and gratitude; especially considering you had no particular obligation of office to it, and when others, whose proper province it was, had declined it. It is a great truth, that the many heresies among the christians (not the lying miracles, or witchcrafts, used by some to induce to the worship of images, &c.) must not give a mortal wound to christianity or truth; but the great question in these controverted points still is, What is truth? And in this search, being agreed in the judge or rule, there is great hopes of the issue. That there are witches, is plain from that rule of truth, the scriptures, which commands their punishment by death. But what that witchcraft is, or wherein it does consist, is the whole difficulty. That head cited from mr. Gaule, and so well proved thereby (not denied by any) makes the work yet shorter; so that it is agreed to consist in a maligning, &c. and seeking by a sign to seduce, &c. not excluding any other sorts or branches, when as well prayed by that infallible rule. That good angels have appeared, is certain; though that instance of those to Abraham may admit of a various construction; some divines supposing them to be the Trinity;. others, that they were men-messengers, as *Judges* ii. 1; and others, that they were angels. But though this, as I said, might admit of a debate, yet I see no question of the angel Gabriel's appearance, particularly to the blessed virgin; for though the angels are spirits, and so not perceptible by our bodily eyes without the appointment of the Most High, yet he, who made all things by his word in the creation, can with a word speak things into being. And whether the angels did assume matter (or a vehicle) and by that appear to the bodily eye; or whether by the same word there were an idea framed in the mind, which needed no vehicle to represent them to the intellects, is with the All-wise, and not for me to dispute. If we poor shallow mortals do not comprehend the manner how, that argues only our weakness. Two other times did this glorious angel appear. *Dan.* viii. 16. *Dan.* ix. 21. The first of these times was in vision, as by the text and context will appear. The second was the same as the first; which, being considered as it will, ascertains that angels have appeared, so that it is at the will of the sender how they shall appear, whether to the bodily eye, or intellect only. *Matt.* i. 20. The appearance of the angel to Joseph was in a dream, and yet a real appearance; so was there a real appearance to the apostle, but whether in the body or out of the body he could not tell; and that they are sent, and come not of their own motion. Luke i.26, *And in the sixth month the angel Gabriel was sent from God.* Dan. ix. 23, *At the beginning of thy supplication the commandment came forth, and I am come.* v. 21, *Being caused to fly swiftly, &c.* But from these places may be set down, as undoubted truths or conclusions,

1. That the glorious angels have their mission and commission from the Most High.

2. That without this they cannot appear to mankind. And from these two will necessarily flow a third:

3. That if the glorious angels have not that power to go till commissioned, or to appear to mortals, then not the fallen angels; who are held in chains of darkness to the judgment of the great day. Therefore to argue, that because the good angels have appeared, the evil may or can, is to me as if, because the dead have been raised to life by holy prophets, therefore men, wicked men, can raise the dead. As the sufferings, so the temptations, of our Saviour were (in degree) beyond those common to man. He being the second Adam, or public head, the strongest assaults were now improved; and we read that he was tempted, that he might be able to succour them that are tempted; as also that he was led of the Spirit into the wilderness, that he might be tempted, &c. But how the tempter appeared to him who was God Omniscient; whether to the bodily eye, or to the intellect, is as far beyond my cognizance, as for a blind man to judge of colours. But from the whole set down this fourth conclusion:

4. That when the Almighty Free Agent has a work to bring about for his own glory, or man's good, he can employ not only blessed angels, but the evil ones, in it, as *2 Cor.* xii. 7, *And lest I should be exalted above measure, there was given to me a thorn in the flesh, the messenger of satan to buffet me.* 1 *Sam.* xvi. 14, 15 & 23, *An evil spirit from the Lord troubled him, &c.* It is a great truth, that we understand little, very little, and that in common things; how much less then in spirituals, such as are above human cognizance! But though upon the strictest scrutiny in some natural things we can only discover our ignorance, yet we must not hence deny what we do know, or suffer a rape to be committed upon our reason and senses in the dark. And to say that the devil by his ordinary power can act a vehicle, i.e. some matter distinct from himself, who is wholly a spirit, and yet this matter not to be felt nor heard, and at the same .... time to be seen; or may be felt, and not heard, nor seen, &c. seems to me to be a chimera, invented at first to puzzle the belief of reasonable creatures, and since calculated to a roman latitude, to uphold the doctrine of transubstantiation; who teach, that under the accidents of bread is contained the body of our Saviour, his human body, as long, and as broad, &c. for here the power of the Almighty must not be confined to be less than the devil's, and it is be that has said, *hoc est meum*

corpus. As to the consent of almost all ages, I meddle not now with it, but come to the fifth conclusion:

5. That when the Divine Being will employ the agency of evil spirits for any service, it is with him to determine how they shall exhibit themselves, whether to the bodily eye, or intellect only; and whether it shall be more or less formidable. To deny these three last, were to make the devil an independent power, and consequently a God. As to the nature of possessions by evil spirits, for the better understanding of it, it may be needful to compare it with its contraries; and to instance in Samson, of whom it was foretold, that he should begin to deliver Israel. And how was he enabled to this work? *Judges* xiii. 25, *The spirit of the Lord began to move him at times in the camp, &c.* Chap. xv. 13, 14. *v. And they bound him with two new cords, and brought him up from the rock; and when they came to Lehi, the Philistines shouted against him; and the spirit of the Lord came mightily upon him, and the cords that were upon his arms became as flax, that was burnt with fire, and his bands loosed from his hands, &c.* I might instance further; but this may suffice to show that he had more than a natural strength, as also whence his strength was, viz. he was empowered by the spirit from God. And now will any say, that it was not Samson, but the spirit, that did these things; or, that these being things done, bonds broken, &c. by a force that could not proceed from human strength, that therefore the spirit entered into him otherwise qualified than as a mere spirit; or, that the spirit entered not without some portion of matter, and by the intermediation thereof acted Samson's body? If any say this and more too, this doth not alter the truth, which remains, viz. that, the spirit of God did enable Samson to the doing of things beyond his natural strength. And now what remains but, upon parity of reason, to apply this to the case of possession? which may be summed up in this sixth conclusion:

6. That God, for wise ends, only known to himself, may and has empowered devils to possess and strangely to actuate human bodies, even to the doing of things beyond the natural strength of that body. And for any to tell of a vehicle, or matter used in it, I must observe that general rule, *Coloss.* ii. 3, "Beware lest any spoil you through philosophy, and vain deceit, after the tradition of men, after the rudiments of the world, and not after Christ." To come next to that or witchcraft, and here taking that cited head of mr. Gaule, to be uncontroverted, set it as a seventh conclusion:

7. That witchcraft consists in a maligning and opposing the word, work and worship of God, and seeking by any extraordinary sign to seduce any from it. *Deut*. xiii. 12. *Matt*. xxiv. 24. *Acts* xiii. 8, 10. 2 *Tim*. iii. 8. Do but mark well the places; and for this very property of thus opposing and perverting, they are all there concluded arrant and absolute witches; and it will be easily granted, that the same that is called witch, is called a false Christ, a false prophet, and a sorcerer, and that the terms are synonymous; and that what the witches aim at is, to seduce the people to seek any other gods. But here the question will be, whether the witch really do things strange in themselves, and beyond their natural course, and all this by a power immediately from the devil. In this inquiry, as we have nothing to do with unwritten verities, so but little with cabalistic learning, which might perhaps but lead us more astray; as in the instance of their charging our Saviour with casting out devils by Beelzebub; his answer is, if satan be divided against himself, his kingdom hath an end. But seeing all are agreed, set this eighth conclusion:

8. That God will not give his testimony to a lie. To say that God did at any time empower a witch to work wonders,[8] to gain belief to the doctrine of devils, were with one breath to destroy the root and branch of all revealed religion. And hence it is clear the witch has no such wonder-working power from God. And must we then conclude she has such a miraculous power from the devil? If so, then it follows, that either God gives the devil leave to empower the witch to make use of this seal, in order to deceive, or else that the devil has this power independent of himself. To assert the first of these were in effect to say, that though God will not give his testimony to a lie, yet that he may empower the devil to set to it God's own seal, in order to deceive. And what were this but to overthrow all revealed religion? The last, if asserted, must be to own the devil to be an unconquered enemy, and consequently a sovereign deity, and deserving much thanks, that he exerts his power no more. Therefore in this dilemma it is wisdom for shallow mortals to have recourse to

---

8. Jos. Glanvil, in his *Saducismus Triumpbalus*, published in London in 1681, and which was considered good authority in the trials in 1692, says "a witch is one who can do or seem to do strange things beyond the known power of art and ordinary nature by virtue of a confederacy with evil spirits." It was the strict application of the above rule or test, in the case of George Burroughs, that cost him his life.

their only guide, and impartially to inquire, whether the witches really have such a miraculous or wonder-working power. And it is remarkable that the apostle, *Gal.* v. 20, reckons up witchcraft among the works of the flesh; which were it indeed a wonder-working power, received immediately from the devil, and wholly beyond the power of nature, it were very improper to place it with drunkenness, murthers, adulteries, &c. all manifest fleshly works. 'Tis also remarkable that witchcraft is generally in scripture joined with spiritual whoredom, i.e. idolatry. This thence will plainly appear to be the same; only pretending to a sign, in order to deceive, seems to be yet a further decree; and in this sense Menasseh and Jezebel, *2 Chron.* xxxiii. 6; *2 Kings* ix. 22, used witchcraft and whoredoms. *Nahum* iii. 4, the idolatrous city is called mistress of witchcrafts. But to instance in one place instead or many. *2 Thess.* ii. 3 to 12, particularly 9 and 10 *v*. *Even him, whose coming is after the working if satan, with all power and signs, and lying wonders, and with all deceivableness. And for this cause God shall send them strong delusions that they should believe a lie, that they all might be damned, who believed not the truth, &c.* This that then was spoken in the prophecy of that man of sin, that was to appear, how abundantly does history testify the fulfilment of it, particularly to seduce to the worship of images! Have not the images been made to move, to smile, &c.? Too tedious were it to mention the hundredth part of what undoubted history doth abundantly testify. And hence do set down this Ninth conclusion:

9. That the man of sin, or seducer, &c. makes use of lying wonders to the end to deceive, and that God in righteous judgment *may send strong delusions that they should believe a lie, that they might be damned, who believe not the truth, &c.*

'Tis certain that the devil is a proud being, and would be thought to have a power equal to the Almighty; and it cannot but be very grateful to him to see mortals charging one another with doing such works by the devil's power, as in truth is the proper prerogative of the Almighty, Omnipotent Being. The next head should have been about an explicit covenant between the witch and the devil, &c. But in this, the whole of it, I cannot persuade myself but you must be sensible of an apparent leaning to education (or tradition) the scriptures being wholly silent on it; and supposing this to fall in as a dependent on what went before, I shall say the less to it; for if the devil has no such power to communicate upon such compact, then the whole is a fiction; though I cannot but acknowledge you have said so much to uphold that doctrine, that I know not how any could have done more. However, as I said, I find not myself engaged (unless scripture proof were offered) to meddle with it: for as you have in such cases your reason for your guide, so I must be allowed to use that little that I have, and do only say, that as God is a spirit, so he must be worshiped in spirit and in truth; so also that the devil is a spirit, and that his rule is in the hearts of the children of disobedience, and that an explicit covenant of one nature or another can have little force, any further than as the heart is engaged in it. And so I pass to the last, viz. whether a witch ought to be put to death; and without accumulation of the offence do judge, that where the law of any country is to punish by death such as seduce and tempt to the worship of strange gods (or idols, or statues) by as good authority may they, no doubt, punish these as capital offenders,. who are distinguished by that one remove, viz. to their seducing is added a sign, i.e. they pretend to a sign in order to seduce. and thus, worthy sir, I have freely given you my thoughts upon yours, which you so much obliged me with the sight of; and upon the whole, though I cannot in the general but commend your caution in not asserting many things contended for by others, yet must say, that in my esteem there is retained so much as will secure all the rest: (to instance) if a spirit has a vehicle, i.e. some portion of matter which it acts, &c. hence as necessarily may be inferred that doctrine of *incubus* and *succubus*, and why not that also of procreation by spirits both good and bad? Thus was Alexander the Great, the British Merlin, and Martin Luther, and many others, said to be begotten. Again, if the witch had such a wonder-working power, why not to afflict? Will not the devil thus far gratify her? And have none this miraculous power, but the covenanting witch? Then the offence lies in the covenant; then it is not only hard, but impossible, to find a witch by such evidence as the law of God requires; for it will not be supposed that they call witness to this covenant; therefore it will here be necessary to admit of such as the nature of such covenant will bear (as Mr. Gaule hath it in his fifth head, i.e.) the testimony of the afflicted, with their spectral sight, to tell who afflicts themselves or others; the experiment of saying the Lord's prayer, falling at the sight, and rising at the touch, searching for teats, (i.e. excrescences of nature) strange and foreign stories of the death of some cattle, or oversetting some cart. And what can juries have better to guide them to find out this covenant by?

It is matter of lamentation, and let it be for a lamentation, to consider how these things have opened the floodgates of malice, revenge, uncharitableness and bloodshed, and what multitudes have been swept away by this torrent.

In *Germany*, countries depopulated; in *Scotland*, no less than 4000 are said to have suffered by fire and halter at one heat.

Thus we may say with the prophet, *Isa.* lix. 10, *We grope for the wall like the blind, and we grope as if we had no eyes: we stumble at noonday as in the night, we are in desolate places as dead men:* and this by seeking to be wise above what is written, in framing to ourselves such crimes and such ordeals (or ways of trial) as are wholly foreign from the direction of our only guide, which should be a light to our feet, and a lanthorn to our paths; but instead of this, if we have not followed the direction, we have followed the example, of pagan and papal Rome, thereby rendering us contemptible and base before all people, according as we have not kept his ways, but have been partial in his law.

And now, that we may, in all our sentiments and ways, have regard to his testimonies, and give to the Almighty the glory due to his name, is the earnest desire and prayer of, sir, yours to command,

R.C.

Sir,

Since your design of giving copies of our papers, if not to the public, at least out of your hands, I find myself obliged to make a reply to your answer, lest silence should be construed an assent to the positions whereby, I think, truth would be scandalized.

I remember that some have taught that it is not certain there is any such thing really in being as matter; because the ideas which we have of our own and all other bodies may be caused to arise in us by God, without the real existence of the objects they represent. But this opinion is not only absurd and false, but likewise atheistical, destroying the veracity of the Almighty, whom it asserts to have determined us by a fatal necessity to believe things to be, which are not; and I wonder that you should allude unto it, because that angels have appeared in a dream, in a vision; for we dream also of trees, birds, &c. Are there therefore no such things in nature, because we sometimes dream to see and hear them, when we are asleep? St. Paul in his vision was so far from believing the objects that were represented to him to come by the intermedium of his senses, that he declares, he does not know whether he was in the body or out of the body; therefore the instance is in no wise proper. For Abraham and the Blessed Virgin did see and hear; and if there were not such things really, as were represented to them by their senses, they were deluded, by being made to believe they saw and heard what was flat. There is none who denieth God causeth thoughts to arise in men's minds; but thence to infer he maketh objects which are not, by forming their ideas ill our minds, to appear to us through the ministry of our senses as though they were, is a piece not only of vain, but very dangerous, philosophy.

It is true, the good angels will not appear without the appointment of God; they will not do anyone action, but according to the laws he has prescribed to them. But you say they cannot, (which does not follow from your premises) supposing their not appearing to proceed from the defect of their power, and not the rectitude of their will; which fallacy has deceived you into a third conclusion: for the fallen angels are not so held under chains of darkness, but that they can, and do, go to and fro on the earth, seeking whom they may devour. Before their fall they could have appeared if sent, and would not then do any thing without a divine command; but now they have rebelled against God, and do all they can to despite him; therefore their not appearing now (if it were true they never did, they never shall, appear) must proceed from a restraint they are under, which is accidental, not essential to their nature; so that the true conclusion is, the fallen angels, while they are under forcible restraint from God to the contrary, cannot appear. But what this (being cleared from the ambiguity you express it in) maketh to the purpose, I know not, unless God had promised for a determinate time to detain them under this restraint.

I do not understand what you intend by the dead being raised by holy men; the most natural inference is, that, in imitation of them, wicked men, by their enchantments calling on a dæmon to appear in the shape of the dead, will pretend that they also can raise the dead.

The Romanists are much obliged to you for making transubstantiation (so much contended for by them) to be of as old a date as the appearance of devils, and that the one implieth no more contradiction than the other: if so, we do well to think seriously whether we are not guilty of great sin in separating from them; nor certainly whatever private men's notions in this age may be, yet it is matter of great moment, that all antiquity (the sadducees, the elder brethren of our Hobbists, excepted) hath believed the appearance of evil spirits and their delusions.

I should be too officious if I offered to explain how matter, real matter, may fall under the cognisance of one of our senses, and not the rest. It is for you to shew the impossibility thereof, if you will build any thing upon your assertion; to prove which, your first argument is (it seems to me) a chimera; which is not enough, when there are many to whom it seems to be a truth. Your second is very dangerous, and highly derogatory of the honour of God, between whom and the devil you make comparison more than once, as the power of the Almighty must not be considered to be less than the devil's. And again, to deny these three last were to make the devil an independent power. and consequently a God. These expressions (which cannot but be very pleasing to the devil, who vainly boasts himself to be a being without dependence) are altogether groundless, and very unmeet to proceed from a christian. Consider what you are doing; to establish a doctrine (the contrary whereof the greatest part of mankind does believe) you run upon such precipices, as, if you are mistaken, (and that is not impossible) must totally destroy all religion, natural and revealed; for suppose it were generally believed, according to you, that the devil cannot appear, because if he could he must be a God, independent, an unconquered enemy, and he doth appear to us as we hear be hath to multitudes, both of the past and present ages; in such a case what remains for us to do, but to, fall down and worship him?

Upon the head of possession, you have recourse to that instance of Samson, who was empowered by God to the doing of things beyond the natural strength of common men; and thence you say, we may at least learn the nature of possession by evil spirits. This comparison is indeed very odious, and I had rather think you have fallen into it unawares; for what greater blasphemy, than that God and the devil do act the bodies, which the one and the other do possess, in the same manner? If the hypothesis I laid down had not pleased you, yet you ought not (for fear of being deceived by vain philosophy) to have run to so horrible all extreme, as to assimilate God's manlier of working to the devil's, which necessarily implies, that either their powers are equal, or at least that they do not differ in kind, but in degree only; than which nothing can be more impious or absurd: for the most possible perfect creature is infinitely distant from the Creator, and there can be no comparison between them.

On the head of witchcraft, you acknowledge the witch has not his wonder-working power from God; out then you say, the devil has no such power to give; for if he had, he must be ———. This way of reasoning, as I noted before, is very dangerous, and I think ought not to be used; besides, there is a great fallacy in your dilemma; which, because I perceive you lay the whole weight of the matter upon it, I will evince unto you. The devil, though superlatively arrogant and proud, nevertheless depends on the First Cause for his being, and all his powers, without whose influx he or any other creature cannot subsist a moment, but must either return to their primitive nothing, or be continually preserved by the same power, by the which they were at first produced; therefore the being and powers of all creatures (because they immediately flow from God) are good, and consequently the simple actions, as they proceed from those powers, are in their own nature likewise good, the evil proceeding only from the rebellious will of the creature; wherefore it is no paradox, but a certain truth, that the same action in respect of the first cause is good, but in respect of the second is evil; for instance, the act of copulation is in itself good, instituted by God, and may be explicitly willed and desired by the soul, which sinneth not for exerting the simple act, but for exerting it contrary to the laws prescribed by God: as in wedlock and adultery there is the same special natural action, which, considered simply, as flowing from a power given to man by God, is certainly good; but considered with relation to the rebellious will of the adulterer (who lieth with his neighbour's wife, whom he is forbid to touch) is a very great evil. We may say the same of all human actions; the executioner and the murtherer do the same natural act of striking and killing: the difference consists in the rectitude of the one's, and depravation of the other's, will. These things premised, what more reason have we to conclude that the devil (because he shews signs and wonders to gain belief to lies, which is very contrary to the will of God) must be therefore an independent power, than that the adulterer, the murtherer, or any other sinner (because their actions being evil, of which God cannot be the cause) must be independent beings? The deceit of the last is very palpable, and I doubt not but you will readily acknowledge it; for it is obvious from what has been said, to the meanest capacity, to distinguish between the action itself, which is good, and flows from

God, and the circumstances of the action, the choice whereof proceeds from the iniquity of the will, wherein doth solely consist the sin; the parallel is so exact, that I cannot see the least shadow of reason, why we ought not in like manner to distinguish whatever effect is produced by the devil; to whom (as to man) God, having given powers, and a will to rule those powers, is truly and properly the cause of all the actions (in a natural, but not moral sense) that flow from the powers he has given. Therefore the wonder-working power of the devil, and the effects thereof, considered as acts of one of God's creatures, are not evil but good; the using that power (which proceeds from the rebellion of satan) to bear testimony to a lie, is that one, which constitutes the evil thereof:

And now I have done with your argument, wherein you have indeed shewn great skill and dexterity in turning to your advantage what, being fairly stated, makes against you, as the appearance of angels, &c. observing nicely the rules of art, and particularly that grand one of concealing, nay dissembling, the same art; as when you quote that scripture concerning vain philosophy (of which, though altogether foreign from the matter in hand, yet) you intend to serve yourself with the unthinking, who measure the sense of words by their jingle, not knowing how to weigh the things they signify; and truly herein your end is very artificial: for you intend both to throw dirt at them that differ from you, and at the same time to cover yourself with such a subtle web, through which you may see, and not be seen. What follows is rather a rhetorical lecture, such as the patriots of sects (who commonly explain the holy scriptures according to their own dogmas, and so obtrude human invention for the pure word of God) use with their auditors, to recommend any principle they have a mind to establish, than an impartial and thorough disquisition of a controverted point; wherefore I do not think myself obliged to take any further notice of it: especially seeing truth, which for the most part is little regarded in such florid discourses, and not any prejudice of education, interest or party, did set me about this subject. I have never been used to compliment in points of controversy, therefore I hope you will not be angry because I have given you my thoughts naked and plain. I have not the least motion in my mind of accusing you of any formal design to injure religion; I only observe unto you, that your over eager contention to maintain your principle has hurried you to assert many things of much greater danger, both in themselves and their consequences, than those you would seem to avoid; which do amount to no more than that men, being (in the ordinary course of providence) the depositories of both divine and human laws, may (instead of using them to preserve) pervert them to destroy; which indeed is very lamentable. But it is the inevitable consequence of our depraved nature, and cannot be wholly remedied, till sin, and the grand author of sin, the devil, be entirely conquered, and God be all in all; to whom, with the Son, and Holy Ghost, be glory for ever, Amen.

Sir, your affectionate friend to serve you.

Boston, July 25, 1694.

Boston, August 17, 1694.

Worthy Sir,

Yours of July 25 being in some sort surprising to me, I could do no less than say somewhat, as well to vindicate myself from those many reflections, mistakes and hard censures therein, as also to vindicate what I conceive to be important truth; and to that end find it needful to repeat some part of mine, viz. conclusion

1. That the glorious angels have their mission and commission from the Most High.

2. That without this they cannot appear to mankind.

3. That if the glorious angels have not that power to go till commissioned, or to appear to mortals, then not the fallen angels, who are held in chains of darkness to the judgment of the great day.

4. That when the Almighty Free Agent has a work to bring about for his own glory, or man's good, he can employ not only the blessed angels, but evil ones, in it.

5. That when the Divine Being will employ the agency of evil spirits for any service, it is with him the manner how they shall exhibit themselves, whether to the bodily eye, or intellect only, or whether it shall be more or less formidable.

To deny these three last, were to make the devil an independent power, and consequently a God.

The bare recital of these is sufficient to vindicate me from that reiterated charge, of denying all appearances of angels or devils.

That the good angels cannot appear without mission and commission from the Most High, is, you say, more than follows from the premises; but if you like not such negative deduction. though so natural, it concerns you (if you will assert this power to be in their natures, and their non-appearance only to proceed from the rectitude of their wills, and that without such commission they have a power to appear to mortals, and upon this to build so prodigious a structure, &c.) very clearly to prove it by scripture; for christians have good reason to take the apostle's warning (if some philosophers have taught that man is nothing but matter, and others that 'tis not certain there is any matter at all) to *take heed lest they should be spoiled through vain philosophy*, &c. but that this should be alluded to such as never heard of either notion, or that it was asserted that those real appearances to Joseph, and to the apostle, were through the ministry of the senses, is as vain as such philosophy. As to the dead being raised, had I used art or rhetorick enough to explain my meaning to you, I needed not now to rejoin, that 'tis as good an argument to say, that because holy prophets have raised the dead, therefore wicked men have a power to raise the dead, as 'tis to say, because good angels have appeared, therefore the evil have a power to appear; for who call doubt, but if the Almighty shall commission a wicked man to it, he also shall raise the dead? as is intimated, *Matt.* vii. 22, *And in thy name done many wonderful works.* As to comparisons being odious, particularly that concerning Samson, I think it needful here to add these scriptures further to confirm the fourth conclusion. *2 Sam.* xxiv. 1, compared with *1 Chron.* xxi. 1. In one 'tis *God moved*, &c. and in the other *Satan provoked David to number the people. 2 Chron.* xviii. 21, *And the Lord said, thou shalt entice him, and thou shalt also prevail; go out and do even so;* all which, with many more that might be produced, will shew the truth of the conclusion; so that 'tis no odious comparison to say, that as the Almighty can make use of good, so also of evil spirits, for the accomplishing of his own wise ends, and can empower either without the help of a vehicle: for possessions must be numbered among God's afflictive dispensations, who also orders all the circumstances thereof. But if any object, God is not the author of evil, &c. you have furnished me with a very learned answer, by distinguishing between the act, and the evil of the act, and to which 'tis adapt, but will no wise suit where it is placed, till it be first proved that the devil hath of himself such power not only of appearing at pleasure, but of working miracles, and to the Almighty reserved only the power of restraining; for, till this be proved, the dilemma must remain stable. He that asserts, that because good angels have appeared, therefore the fallen angels have a power of themselves to appear to mortals, and that they cannot be employed by the Almighty, nor that he does not order the manner and circumstances of such appearance, what doth he less than make the devil an independent power, and consequently a God? So he that asserts that the devil hath a power of himself, and independent, to work wonders, and miracles, and to empower witches to do like in order to deceive, &c. what doth he less than own him to be an unconquered enemy, and consequently a sovereign deity? and who is he that is culpable? he that ascribes such attributes to the evil one, or he that asserts that the so doing gives him (or ascribes to him) such power as is the prerogative of him only who is almighty? And here, sir, it highly concerns you to consider your foundations, what proof from scripture is to be found for your assertions, and who it is you are contending for: for hitherto nothing like a proof hath been offered from scripture, ,which abounds so with the contrary, that he that runs may read; as, *Shall there be evil in the city, and the Lord hath not done it? Who is he that saith, and it cometh to pass, when the Lord commandeth not? Who among the gods of the heathen* (of which the devil is one) *can give rain? &c.*

But I shall not be tedious in multiplying proofs, to that which all seem to own. For as to that stale plea of universality, do say that I have read of one, if not several, general councils, that have not only disapproved, but anathematised them that have ascribed such powers to the devils. And several national protestant churches at this day, in their exhortations before the sacrament (among other enormous crimes) admonish all that believe any such power in the witch, &c. to withdraw, as unmeet to partake at the Lord's table.

And I believe christians in general, if they were asked, would own that what powers the devil may at any time have to appear, to afflict, destroy, or cause tempests, &c. must be by power or commission from the Sovereign Being; and that, having such a commission, not only hail, but frogs, lice, or fleas, shall be empowered to plague a great king and kingdom. And if so, this sandy structure of the devil's appearance, and working wonders, at pleasure, and of empowering witches to afflict, &c. (for to this narrow crisis is that whole doctrine reduced) the whole disappears at the first shaking.

Thus, worthy sir, I have given you my sentiments, and the grounds thereof, as plainly and as concise as I was able; though 'tis indeed a subject that calls for the ablest pens to discuss, acknowledging myself to be insufficient for these things. However, I think I have done but my duty, for the glory of God, the sovereign being; and have purposely avoided such a reply as some parts of yours required; and pray that not only you and I, but all mankind, may give to the Almighty the glory due unto his name.

 From, sir, yours to command,   R.C.

   Witchcraft is manifestly a work of the flesh.

PART V.

AN IMPARTIAL ACCOUNT

OF THE MOST MEMORABLE

MATTERS OF FACT,

TOUCHING THE SUPPOSED WITCHCRAFT
IN NEW-ENGLAND.

R. PARRIS had been some years a minister in Salem Village,[9] when this sad calamity, as a deluge, overflowed them, spreading itself far and near. He was a gentleman of liberal education; and, not meeting with any great encouragement, or advantage, in merchandising, to which for some time he applied himself, betook himself to the work of the ministry; this Village being then vacant, he met with so much encouragement, as to settle in that capacity among them.

After he had been there about two years, he obtained a grant from a part of the town, that the house and land be occupied, and which had been allotted by the whole people to the ministry, should be and remain to him, &c. as his own estate in fee simple. This occasioned great divisions both between the inhabitants themselves, and between a considerable part of them and their said minister; which divisions were but as a beginning, or prelude, to what immediately followed.

---

9. Mr. Parris was settled over the Village church Nov. 19th, 1689.

It was the latter end of *February*, 1691, when divers young persons[10] belonging to mr. Parris's family, and one or more of the neighbourhood, began to act after a strange and unusual manner, viz. as by getting into holes, and creeping under chairs and stools, and to use sundry odd postures and antick gestures, uttering foolish, ridiculous speeches, which neither they themselves nor any others could make sense of. The physicians that were called could assign no reason for this; but it seems one of them, having recourse to the old shift, told them, he was afraid they were bewitched. Upon such suggestions, they that were concerned applied themselves to fasting and prayer, which was attended not only in their own private families, but with calling in the help of others. *March the* 11*th*, mr. Parris invited several neighbouring ministers to join with him in keeping a solemn day of prayer at his own house. The time of the exercise, those persons were for the most part silent; but after any one prayer was ended, they would act and speak strangely and ridiculously; yet were such as had been well educated, and of good behaviour; the one, a girl of 11 or 12 years old, would sometimes seem to be in a convulsion fit, her limbs being twisted several ways, and very stiff, but presently her fit would be over. A few days before this solemn day of prayer, mr. Parris's Indian man and woman made a cake of rye meal, with the children's water, and baked it in the ashes, and, as is said, gave it to the dog; this was done as a means to discover witchcraft; soon after which, those ill affected or afflicted persons named several that they said they saw, when in their fits, afflicting them.

The first complained of was the said Indian woman, named Tituba: she confessed that the devil urged her to sign a book, which he presented to her, and also to work mischief to the children, &c. She was afterwards committed to prison, and lay there till sold for her fees. The account she since gives of it is, that her master did beat her, and otherways abuse her, to make her confess and accuse (such as he called) her sister-witches; and that whatsoever she said by way of confessing, or accusing others, was the effect of such usage; her master refused to pay her fees, unless she would stand to what she had said.

---

10. Elizabeth Parris, his daughter, aged nine years, and Abigail Williams, his niece, aged eleven years.

The children complained likewise of two other women, to be the authors of their hurt, viz. Sarah Good, who had long been counted a *melancholy* or *distracted* woman; and one Osborn, an old *bed-ridden* woman; which two were persons so ill thought of, that the accusation was the more readily believed; and, after examination before two Salem magistrates, were committed. *March* 9th, mr. Lowson (who had been formerly a preacher at the said village) came thither, and hath since set forth, in print, an account of what then passed; about which time, as he saith, they complained of goodwife Cory, and goodwife Nurse, members of churches at the Village and at Salem, many others being by that time accused.

March 21. Goodwife Cory was examined before the magistrates of Salem, at the meeting house in the Village, a throng of spectators being present to see the novelty. Mr. Noyes, one of the ministers of Salem, began with prayer; after which the prisoner being called, in order to answer to what should be alledged against her, she desired that she might go to prayer; and was answered by the magistrates, that they did not come to hear her pray, but to examine her.

The number of the afflicted were at that time about ten, viz. mrs. Pope, mrs. Putman, good wife Bibber and good wife Goodall, Mary Wolcott, Mercy Lewes (at Thomas Putman's) and Dr. Grigg's maid, and three girls, viz. Elizabeth Parris, daughter to the minister, Abigail Williams, his niece, and Ann Putman; which last three were not only the beginners, but were also the chief, in these accusations. These ten were most of them present at the examination, and did vehemently accuse her of afflicting them, by biting, pinching, strangling, &c. and they said they did in their fits see her likeness coming to them, and bringing a book for them to sign. Mr. Hathorn, a magistrate of Salem, asked her why she afflicted those children. She said, she did not afflict them. He asked her who did then. She said, I do not know, how should I know? She said, they were poor distracted creatures, and no heed ought to be given to what they said. Mr. Hathorn and Mr. Noyes replied that it was the judgment of all that were there present, that they were bewitched, and only she (the accused) said they were distracted. She was accused by them, that the *black man* whispered to her in her ear now (while she was upon examination) and that she had a yellow bird, that did use to suck between her finders, and that the said bird did suck now in the assembly. Order being given to look in that place to see if there were any sign, the girl that pretended to see It said, that It was too late now, for she had removed a pin, and put it on her head; it was upon search found, that a pin was there sticking upright. When the accused had any motion of their body, hands or mouth, the accusers would cry out; as when she bit a lip, they would cry out of being bitten; if she grasped one hand with the other, they would cry out of being pinched by her, and would produce marks; so of the other motions of her body, as complaining of being prest, when she leaned to the seat next her; if she stirred her feet, they would stamp, and cry out of pain there. After the hearing, the said Cory was committed to Salem prison, and then their crying out of her abated.

March 24, goodwife Nurse[11] was brought before mr. Hathorn and mr. Curwiil (magistrates) in the meeting house. Mr. Hale,[12] minister of Beverly, began with prayer; after which she, being accused of much the same crimes, made the like answers, asserting her own innocence with earnestness. The accusers were mostly the same, Thomas Putman's wife, &c.[13] complaining much. The dreadful shrieking from her and others was very amazing, which was heard at a great distance. She was also committed to prison. A child of Sarah Good's was likewise apprehended, being between 4 and 5 years old. The accusers said this child bit them, and would shew such like marks, as those of a small set of teeth, upon their arms: as many of

---

11. The folly and madness of the witchcraft delusion was strikingly manifested at the examination of goodwife Nurse. Parris, who was taking notes at the time, informs us that the noise of the accusing girls and speakers was so great, that he could not proceed with his minutes. He has, however, given us enough of her examination to show the great distress she was thrown into by her false accusers. Looking around the crowded meeting house, and not discovering one sympathizing countenance, she said, "I have got nobody to look to but God;" and in her agony she lifted her arms and spread out her hands, and exclaimed, "O Lord, help me!" Mr. Hathorn met this appeal to Heaven with this remark,— "It is very awful to see these agonies in an old professor, charged with contracting with the devil."

12. Rev. John Hale, who was more connected with Salem witchcraft than has been generally supposed.

13. Thomas Putman's wife, and her daughter, Ann Junr., as she was called, were most severely afflicted by witches. Thomas was for many years Parish Clerk, and near neighbour to Mr. Parris. Sergt. Thomas Putman, as he was styled, did more to carry forward the witchcraft delusion, than any other person.

the afflicted as the child cast its eye upon, would complain they were in torment: which child they also committed.

Concerning those that had been hitherto examined and committed, it is among other things observed, by Mr. Lawson (in print) that they were by the accusers charged to belong to a company that did muster in arms, and were reported by them to keep days of fast, thanksgiving and sacraments; and that those afflicted (or accusers) did in the assembly cure each other, even with a touch of their hand, when strangled and other ways tortured, and would endeavour to get to the afflicted to relieve them thereby (for hitherto they had not used the experiment of bringing the accused to touch the afflicted, in order to their cure) and could foretel one another's fit to be coming, and would say, look to such a one, she will have a fit presently, and so it happened; and that at the same time when the accused person was present, the afflicted said they saw her spectre or likeness in other places of the meeting-house sucking their familiars.

The said mr. Lawson being to preach at the Village, after the psalm was Sung, Abigail Williams said, *Now stand up and name your text*; after it was read, she said, *it was a long text*. Mrs. Pope in the beginning of sermon said to him, *now there is enough of that*. In sermon, he referring to his doctrine, Abigail Williams said to him, *I know no doctrine you had; if you did name one, I have forgot it*. Ann Putman, an afflicted girl, said, *there was a yellow bird sat on his hat as it hung on the pin in the pulpit.*

March 31, 1692, was set apart as a day of solemn humiliation at Salem, upon the account of this business; on which day Abigail Williams said, *that she saw a great number of persons in the Village at the administration of a mock sacrament, where they had bread as red as raw flesh, and red drink.*

April 1. Mercy Lewis affirmed, *that she saw a man in white, with whom she went into a glorious place,* viz. in her fits, *where was no light of the Sun, much less of candles, yet was full of light and brightness, with a great multitude in white glittering robes, who sang the song in Rev. v. 9. and the* exlix Psalm; *and it was given that she might tarry no longer in this place*. This white man is said to have appeared several times to others of them, and to have given them notice how long it should be before they should have another fit.

April 3. Being sacrament day at the Village, Sarah Cloyce, sister to goodwife Nurse, a member of one of the churches, was (though it seems with difficulty prevailed with to be) present; but being entered the place, and mr. Parris naming his text, *John* vi. 70, *Have not I chosen you twelve? and one of you is a devil*; (for what cause may rest as a doubt, whether upon the account of her sister's being committed, or because of the choice of that text) she rose up and went out; the wind shutting the door forcibly, gave occasion to some to suppose she went out in anger, and might occasion a suspicion of her; however, she was soon after complained of, examined and committed.

April 11. By this time the number of the accused and accusers being much increased, there was a publick examination at Salem, six of the magistrates with several ministers being present. There appeared several who complained against others with hideous clamours and screechings. Goodwife Proctor was brought thither, being accused or cried out against: her husband coming to attend and assist her, as there might be need, the accusers cried out of him also, and that with so much earnestness, that he was committed with his wife. About this time, besides the experiment of the afflicted falling at the sight, &c. they put the accused upon saying the Lord's prayer, which one among them performed, except in that petition, *deliver us from evil*, she exprest it thus, *deliver us from* all *evil*: this was looked upon as if she prayed against what she was now justly under; and being put upon it again, and repeating those words, *hallowed be thy name*, she exprest it, *hollowed be thy name*: this was counted a depraving the words, as signifying to make void, and so a curse rather than a prayer: upon the whole it was concluded that she also could not say it, &c. Proceeding in this work of examination and commitment, many were sent to prison. As an instance, see the following mittimus.

To their Majesties' Gaol-keeper in Salem.

You are in their majesties' names hereby required to take into your care, and safe custody, the bodies of William Hobs and Deborah his wife, Mary Easty, the wife of Isaac Easty, and Sarah Wild, the wife of John Wild, all of Topsfield; and Edward Bishop, of Salem Village, husbandman, and Sarah his wife, and Mary Black, a negro of lieutenant Nathaniel Putman, of Salem Village; also Mary English, the wife of Philip English, merchant, in Salem; who stand charged with high suspicion of sundry acts of witchcraft, done or committed by them lately upon the bodies of Ann Putman, Mary Lewis and Abigail Williams, of Salem Village; whereby great hurt and damage hath been done to the bodies of the said persons, according to the complaint of Thomas Putman and John Buxton, of Salem Village, exhibited; whom you are to secure in order to their further examination.—

Fail not.

John Hathorn, Jona. Curtain, assistants.

Dated Salem, April 22, 1692.

To marshal George Herrick,
 of Salem, Essex.

You are in their majesties' names hereby required to convey the above named to the gaol at Salem.—Fail not.

John Hathorn, Jona. Curtain, assistants.

Dated Salem, April 22, 1692.

The occasion of Bishop's being cried out of, was, he being at an examination in Salem, when at the inn an afflicted Indian was very unruly, whom he undertook, and so managed him, that he was very orderly; after which, in riding home, in company of him and other accusers, the Indian fell into a fit, and clapping hold with his teeth on the back of the man that rode before him, thereby held himself upon the horse; but said Bishop striking him with his stick, the Indian soon recovered, and promised he would do so no more; to which Bishop replied, that he doubted not but he could cure them all, with more to the same effect. Immediately after he was parted from them, he was cried out of, &c.

May 14, 1692. Sir William Phips arrived with commission from their majesties to be governor, pursuant to the new charter, which he now brought with him, the ancient charter having been vacated by king Charles and king James, (by which they had a power not only to make their own laws, but also to choose their own governor and officers) and the country for some years was put under an absolute commission-government, till the Revolution, at which time, though more than two thirds of the people were for reassuming their ancient government, (to which they had encouragement by his then royal highness's proclamation) yet some that might have been better employed (in another station) made it their business (by printing, as well as speaking) to their utmost to divert them from such a settlement; and so far prevailed, that for about seven weeks after the

Revolution, here was not so much as a face of any government; but some few men upon their own nomination would be called a committee of safety; but at length the assembly prevailed with those that had been of the government, to promise that they would reassume; and accordingly a proclamation was drawn, but before publishing it, it was underwritten, that they would not have it understood that they did reassume charter government; so that between government and no government, this country remained till sir William arrived: agents being in this time empowered in England, which no doubt did not all of them act according to the minds or interests of those that empowered them, which is manifest by their not acting jointly in what was done; so that this place is perhaps a single instance (even in the best of reigns) of a charter not restored after so happy a revolution. This settlement by sir William Phips's having come governor put an end to all disputes of these things; and being arrived, and having read his commission, the first thing he exerted his power in, was said to be his giving orders that irons should be put upon those in prison; for though for some time after these were committed, the accusers ceased to cry out of them, yet now the cry against them was renewed, which occasioned such order; and though there was partiality in the executing it (some having them taken off almost as soon as put on) yet the cry of these accusers against such, ceased after this order.

May 24. Mrs. Cary, of Charlestown, was examined and committed. Her husband, mr. Jonathan Cary, has given account thereof, as also of her escape, to this effect:

"I having heard, some days, that my wife was accused of witchcraft, being much disturbed at it, by advice we went to Salem Village, to see if the afflicted knew her; we arrived there 24th May; it happened to be a day appointed for examination; accordingly, soon after our arrival, mr. Hathorn and mr. Curwin, &c. went to the meeting-house, which was the place appointed for that work; the minister began with prayer; and having taken care to get a convenient place, I observed that the afflicted were two girls of about ten years old, and about two or three others, of about eighteen; one of the girls talked most, and could discern more than the rest. The prisoners were called in one by one, and as they came in were cried out of, &c. The prisoners were placed about seven or eight feet from the justices, and the accusers between the justices and them; the prisoners were ordered to stand right before the justices, with an officer appointed to hold each hand, lest they should therewith afflict them; and the prisoners' eyes must be constantly on the justices; for if they looked on the afflicted, they would either fall into their fits, or cry out of being hurt by them. After an examination of the prisoners, who it was afflicted these girls, &c. they were put upon saying the Lord's prayer, as a trial of their guilt. After the afflicted seemed to be out of their fits, they would look steadfastly on some one person, and frequently not speak; and then the justices said they were struck dumb: and after a little time would speak again; then the justices said to the accusers, Which of you will go and touch the prisoner at the bar? Then the most courageous would adventure, but before they had made three steps would ordinarily fall down as in a fit. The justices ordered that they should be taken up and carried to the prisoner, that she might touch them; and as soon as they were touched by the accused, the justices would say, they are well, before I could discern any alteration; by which I observed that the justices understood the manner of it. Thus far I was only as a spectator; my wife also was there part of the time, but no notice taken of her by the afflicted, except once or twice they came to her and asked her name.

"But I having an opportunity to discourse mr. Hale (with whom I had formerly acquaintance) I took his advice what I had best to do, and desired of him that I might have an opportunity to speak with her that accused my wife; which he promised should be, I acquainting him that I reposed my trust in him. Accordingly he came to me after the examination was over, and told me I had now an opportunity to speak with the said accuser, viz. Abigail Williams, a girl of 11 or 12 years old; but that we could not be in private at mr. Parris's house, as he had promised me; we went therefore into the alehouse, where an Indian man attended us, who it seems was one of the afflicted; to him we gave some cider: he shewed several scars, that seemed as if they had been long there, and shewed them as done by witchcraft, and acquainted us that his wife, who also was a slave, was imprisoned for witchcraft. And now, instead of one accuser, they all came in, and began to tumble down like swine; and then three women were called in to attend them. We in the room were all at a stand, to see who they would cry out of; but in a short time they cried out, Cary; and immediately after a warrant was sent from the justices to bring my wife before them, who were sitting in a chamber near by, waiting for this.

"Being brought before the justices, her chief accusers were two girls. My wife declared to the justices, that she never had any knowledge of them before that day. She was forced to stand with her arms stretched out. I requested that I might bold one of her hands, but it was denied me; then she desired me to wipe the tears from her eyes, and the sweat from her face, which I did; then she desired she might lean herself on me, saying she should faint.

"Justice Hathorn replied, she had strength enough to torment those persons, and she should have strength enough to stand. I speaking something against their cruel proceedings, they commanded me to be silent, or else I should be turned out of the room. The Indian before mentioned was also brought in, to be one of her accusers: being come in, he now (when before the justices) fell down and tumbled about like a hog, but said nothing. The justices asked the girls who afflicted the Indian; they answered, she, (meaning my wife) and that she now lay upon him; the justices ordered her to touch him, in order to his cure, but her head must be turned another way, lest, instead of curing, she should make him worse, by her looking on him, her hand being guided to take hold of his; but the Indian took hold of her hand, and pulled her down on the floor, in a barbarous manner; then his hand was taken off; and her hand put on his, and the cure was quickly wrought. I, being extremely troubled at their inhuman dealings, uttered a hasty speech, *That God would take vengeance on them, and desired that God would deliver us out of the hands of unmerciful men.*

Then her mittimus was writ. I did with difficulty and charge obtain the liberty of a room, but no beds in it; if there had been, could have taken but little rest that night. She was committed to Boston prison; but I obtained a habeas corpus to remove her to Cambridge prison, which is in our county of Middlesex. Having been there one night, next morning the jailer put irons on her legs (having received such a command;) the weight of them was about eight pounds: these irons and her other afflictions soon brought her into convulsion fits, so that I thought she would have died that night. I sent to entreat that the irons might be taken off; but all entreaties were in vain, if it would have saved her life, so that in this condition she must continue. The trials at Salem coming on, I went thither, to see how things were managed; and finding that the spectre evidence was there received, together with idle, if not malicious stories, against people's lives, I did easily perceive which way the rest would go; for the same evidence that served for one, would serve for all the rest. I acquainted her with her danger; and that if she were carried to Salem to be tried, I feared she would never return. did my utmost that she might have her trial in our own county, I with several others petitioning the judge for it, and were put in hopes of it; but I soon saw so much, that I understood thereby it was not intended, which put me upon consulting the means of her escape; which through the goodness of God was effected, and she got to Rhode-Island, but soon found herself not safe when there, by reason of the pursuit after her; from thence she went to New-York, along with some others that had escaped their cruel hands; where we found his excellency Benjamin Fletcher, esq. governor, who was very courteous to us. After this, some of my goods were seized in a friend's hands, with whom I had left them, and myself imprisoned by the sheriff; and kept in custody half a day, and then dismissed; but to speak of their usage of the prisoners, and the inhumanity shewn to them at the time of their execution, no sober christian could bear. They had also trials of cruel mockings; which is the more, considering what a people for religion, I mean the profession of it, we have been; those that suffered being many of them church members, and most of them unspotted in their conversation, till their adversary the devil took up this method for accusing them.

"Per JONATHAN CARY."

May 31. Capt. John Aldin was examined in Salem, and committed to Boston prison. The prison-keeper, seeing such a man committed, of whom he had a good esteem, was after this the more compassionate to those that were in prison on the like account; and refrained from such hard things to the prisoners, as before he had used. Mr. Aldin himself has given an account of his examination, in these words:

An account how John Aldin, senior, was dealt with at Salem Village.

John Aldin, senior, of Boston, in the county of Suffolk, mariner, on the 28th day of May, 1692, was sent for by the magistrates of Salem, in the county of Essex, upon the accusation of a company of poor distracted or possessed creatures or witches; and being sent by mr. Stoughton, arrived there the 31st of May, and appeared at Salem Village, before mr. Gidney, mr. Hathorn and mr. Curwin.

Those wenches being present, who played their juggling tricks, falling down, crying out, and staring in people's faces; the magistrates demanded of them several times, who it was of all the people in the room that hurt them: one of these accusers pointed several times at one captain Hill, there present, but spake nothing; the same accuser had a man standing at her back to hold her up; he stooped down to her ear, then she cried out, Aldin, Aldin afflicted her; one of the magistrates asked her if she had ever seen Aldin, she answered no; he asked how she knew it was Aldin; she said the man told her so.

Then all were ordered to go down into the street, where a ring was made; and the same accuser cried out, There stands Aldin, a bold fellow, with his hat on before the judges; he sells powder and shot to the Indians and French, and lies with the Indian squaws, and has Indian papooses. Then was Aldin committed to the marshal's custody, and his sword taken from him; for they said he afflicted them with his sword. After some hours Aldin was sent for to the meeting-house in the Village, before the magistrates; who required Aldin to stand upon a chair, to the open view of all the people.

The accusers cried out that Aldin pinched them, then, when he stood upon the chair, in the sight of all the people, a good way distant from them. One of the magistrates bid the marshal to hold open Aldin's hands, that he might not pinch those creatures. Aldin asked them why they should think that he should come to that Village to afflict those persons that he never knew or saw before. Mr. Gidney bid Aldin confess, and give glory to God. Aldin said, he hoped he should give glory to God, and hoped he should never gratify the devil; but appealed to all that ever knew him, if they ever suspected him to be such a person, and challenged anyone, that could bring in any thing upon their own knowledge, that might give suspicion of his being such an one. Mr. Gidney said he had known Aldin many years, and had been at sea with him, and always looked upon him to be an honest man, but now he saw cause to alter his judgment. Aldin answered, he was sorry for that, but he hoped God would clear up his innocency, that he would, recal that judgment again; and added, that he hoped that he should with Job maintain his integrity till he died. They bid Aldin look upon the accusers, which he did, and then they fell down. Aldin asked mr. Gidney what reason there could be given, why Aldin's looking upon *him* did not strike *him* down as well; but no reason was given that I heard. But the accusers were brought to Aldin to touch them, and this touch they said made them well. Aldin began to speak of the providence of

God, in suffering these creatures to accuse innocent persons. Mr. Noyes asked Aldin why he would offer to speak of the providence of God: God by his providence (said mr. Noyes) governs the world, and keeps it in peace; and so went on with discourse, and stopt Aldin's mouth as to that. Aldin told Mr. Gidney, that he could assure him that there was a lying spirit in them, for I can assure you that there is not a word of truth in all these say of me. But Aldin was again committed to the marshal, and his mittimus written, which was as follows:

To mr. John Arnold, keeper of the prison in Boston, in the county of Suffolk.

Whereas captain John Aldin, of Boston, mariner, and Sarah Rice, wife of Nicholas Rice, of Reading, husbandman, have been this day brought before us, John Hathorn and Jonathan Curwin, esquires; being accused and suspected of perpetrating divers acts of witchcraft, contrary to the form of the statute, in that case made and provided: these are therefore, ill their majesties king William and queen Mary's names, to will and require you to take into your custody the bodies of the said John Aldin and Sarah Rice, and them safely keep, until they shall be delivered by due course of law, as you will answer the contrary at your peril; and this shall be your sufficient warrant. Given under our hands at Salem Village, the 31st of May, in the fourth year of the reign of our sovereign lord and lady, William and Mary, now king and queen over England, &c. Anno Domini 1692.

John Hathorn, Jona. Curwin, assistants.

To Boston, Aldin was carried by a constable; no bail would be taken for him; but was delivered to the prison-keeper, where he remained fifteen weeks; and then, observing the manner of trials, and evidence then taken, was at length prevailed with to make his escape, and being returned, was bound over to answer at the superior court at Boston, the last Tuesday in April, anno 1693; and was there cleared by proclamation, none appearing against him.

Per JOHN ALDIN.

At the examination, and at other times, it was usual for the accusers to tell of the black man, or of a spectre, as being then on the table, &c. The people about would strike with swords, or sticks, at those places. One justice broke his cane at this exercise; and sometimes the accusers would say, they struck the spectre, and it is reported several of the accused were hurt and wounded thereby, though at home at the same time.

The Justices proceeding in these works of examination and commitment to the end of May, there were by that time about a hundred persons imprisoned upon that account.

June 2. A special commission of oyer and terminer having been issued out, to mr. Stoughton, the new lieutenant governor, major Saltonstall, major Richards, major Gidney, mr. Wait Winthrop, captain Sewall, and mr. Sergeant, a quorum of whom sat at Salem this day, where the most that was done this week was the trial of one Bishop[14], alias Oliver, of Salem; who had long undergone the repute of a witch, occasioned by the accusations of one Samuel Gray; he, about twenty years since, having charged her with such crimes; and though upon his deathbed he testified his sorrow and repentance for such accusations, as being wholly groundless, yet the report, taken up by his means, continued, and she being accused by those afflicted, and upon search a teat, as they call it, being found, she was brought in guilty by the jury; she received her sentence of death, and was executed June 10, but made not the least confession of any thing relating to witchcraft.

June 15. Several ministers in and near Boston, having been to that end consulted by his excellency, exprest their minds to this effect, viz.

That they were affected with the deplorable state of the afflicted; that they were thankful for the diligent care of the rulers to detect the abominable witchcrafts which have been committed in the country, praying for a perfect discovery thereof; but advised to a cautious proceeding, lest many evils ensue, &c. and that tenderness be used towards those accused, relating to matters presumptive and convictive, and also to privacy in examinations; and to consult mr. Perkins and mr. Bernard what tests to make use of in the scrutiny: that presumptions and convictions ought to have better grounds than the accusers affirming that they see such persons' spectres

---

14. Bridget Bishop kept a small beer-shop on the old Ipswich road, at Danvers Plains, where Messrs. Perley & Currier's store now stands. Rev. John Hale, of Beverly, in his deposition, given on the 20th of May, 1692, says that he was informed by the wife of John, that Bridget entertained people in her house at night, in drinking and playing shovel-board.

afflicting them; and that the devil may afflict in the shape of good men; and that falling at the sight, and rising at the touch, of the accused, is no infallible proof of guilt; that seeing the devil's strength consists in such accusations, our disbelieving them may be a means to put a period to the dreadful calamities. Nevertheless they humbly recommend to the government, the speedy and vigorous prosecution of such as have rendered themselves obnoxious, according to the direction given in the laws of God, and the wholesome statutes of the English nation, for the detection of witchcraft.

This is briefly the substance of what may be seen more at large in *Cases of Conscience*. (*ult.*) And one of them since taking occasion to repeat some part of this advice, (*Wonders of the Invisible World*, p. 83) declares (notwithstanding the dissatisfaction of others) that if his said book may conduce to promote thankfulness to God for such executions, he shall rejoice, &c.

The 30th of June, the court according to adjournment again sat; five more were tried, viz. Sarah Good and Rebecca Nurse, of Salem Village; Susanna. Martin, of Amsbury; Elizabeth How of Ipswich; and Sarah Wildes of Topsfield: these were all condemned that session, and were all executed on the 19th of July.

At the trial of Sarah Good, one of the afflicted fell in a fit; and after coming out of it she cried out of the prisoner, for stabbing her in the breast with a knife, and that she had broken the knife in stabbing of her; accordingly a piece of the blade of a knife was found about her. Immediately information being given to the court, a young man was called, who produced a haft and part of the blade, which the court having viewed and compared, saw it to be the same; and upon inquiry the young man affirmed, that yesterday he happened to break that knife, and that he cast away the upper part. This afflicted person being then present, the young man was dismissed, and she was bidden by the court not to tell lies; and was improved after (as she had been before) to give evidence against the prisoners.

At the execution, Mr. Noyes urged Sarah Good to confess, and told her she was a witch, and she knew she was a witch; to which she replied, you are a liar; I am no more a witch than you are a wizard; and if you take away my life, God will give you blood to drink.

At the trial of Rebecca Nurse, it was remarkable that the jury brought in their verdict not guilty; immediately all the accusers in the court, and suddenly after all the afflicted out of court, made an hideous outcry, to the amazement not only of the spectators, but the court also seemed strangely surprised: one of the judges exprest himself not satisfied; another of them, as he was going off the bench, said they would have her indicted anew. The chief judge said he would not impose upon the jury; but intimated as if they had not well considered one expression of the prisoner when she was upon trial, viz. that when one Hobbs, who had confessed herself to be a witch, was brought into the court to witness against her, the prisoner, turning her head to her, said, *What, do you bring her? she is one of us*, or to that effect; this, together with the clamours of the accusers, induced the jury to go out again, after their verdict, not guilty. But not agreeing, they came into the court; and she being then at the bar, her words were repeated to her, in order to have her explanation of them; and she making no reply to them, they found the bill, and brought her in guilty; these words being the inducement to it, as the foreman has signified in writing, as follows:

July 4, 1692. I, Thomas Fisk, the subscriber hereof, being one of them that were of the jury last week at Salem court, upon the trial of Rebecca Nurse, &c.[15] being desired by some of the relations to give a reason why the jury brought her in guilty, after her verdict not guilty; I do hereby give my reasons to be as follows, viz.

When the verdict was, not guilty, the honoured court was pleased to object against it, saying to them, that they think they let slip the words which the prisoner at the bar spake against herself, which were spoken in reply to goodwife Hobbs and her daughter, who had been faulty in setting their hands to the devil's book, as they had confessed formerly; the words were, *What do these persons give in evidence against me now? they used to come among us.* After the honoured court had manifested their dissatisfaction of the verdict, several of the jury declared themselves desirous to go out again, and thereupon the court gave leave; but when we came to consider of the case, I could not tell how to take her words as an evidence against her, till she had a further opportunity to put her sense upon them, if she would take it; and then, going into court, I mentioned the words

---

15. A most estimable and intelligent woman, who, with her amiable and excellent sister, Mary Esty, of Topsfield, were executed.—
Their sister, Mary Cloyce, escaped with imprisonment.

aforesaid, which by one of the court were affirmed to have been spoken by her, she being then at the bar, but made no reply, nor interpretation of them; whereupon these words were to me a principal evidence against her.

THOMAS FISK.

When goodwife Nurse was informed what use was made of these words, she put in this following declaration into the court:

These presents do humbly shew to the honoured court and jury, that I being informed that the jury brought me in guilty, upon my saying that goodwife Hobbs and her daughter were of our company; but I intended no otherways, than as they were prisoners with us, and therefore did then, and yet do, judge them not legal evidence against their fellow prisoners. And I being something hard of hearing, and full of grief, none informing me how the court took up my words, and therefore had no opportunity to declare what I intended, when I said they were of our company.

REBECCA NURSE.

After her condemnation she was by one of the ministers of Salem excommunicated; yet the governor saw cause to grant a reprieve; which when known (and some say immediately upon granting) the accusers renewed their dismal outcries against her, insomuch that the governor was by some Salem gentlemen prevailed with to recall the reprieve, and she was executed with the rest.

The testimonials of her christian behaviour, both in the course of her life and at her death, and her extraordinary care in educating her children, and setting them good examples, &c. under the hands of so many, are so numerous, that for brevity they are here omitted.

It was at the trial of these that one of the accusers cried out publicly of Mr. Willard, minister in Boston, as afflicting of her: she was sent out of the court, and it was told about she was mistaken in the person.

August 5, the court again sitting, six more were tried on the same account, viz. mr. George Burroughs, sometime minister of Wells, John Proctor, and Elizabeth Proctor his wife, with John Willard, of Salem Village, George Jacobs senior, of Salem, and Martha Carrier, of Andover; these were all brought in guilty, and condemned; and were all executed, *August* 19, except Proctor's wife, who pleaded pregnancy.

Mr. Burroughs was carried in a cart with the others, through the streets of Salem to execution. When he was upon the ladder, he made a speech for the clearing of his innocency, with such solemn and serious expressions, as were to the admiration of all present: his prayer (which he concluded by repeating the Lord's prayer) was so well worded, and uttered with such composedness, and such (at least seeming) fervency of spirit, as was very affecting, and drew tears from many, so that it seemed to some that the spectators would hinder the execution. The accusers said the black man stood and dictated to him. As soon as he was turned off, mr. Cotton Mather, being mounted upon a horse, addressed himself to the people, partly to declare that he [Burroughs] was no ordained minister, and partly to possess the people of his guilt, saying that the devil has often been transformed into an angel of light; and this somewhat appeased the people, and the executions went on. When he was cut down, he was dragged by the halter to a hole, or grave, between the rocks, about two feet deep, his shirt and breeches being pulled off and an old pair of trowsers of one executed put on his lower parts; he was so put in, together with Willard and Carrier, that one of his hands and his chin, and a foot of one of them, were left uncovered.

John Willard had been employed to fetch in several that were accused; but taking dissatisfaction from his being sent to fetch up some that he had better thoughts of, he declined the service; and presently after he himself was accused of the same crime, and that with such vehemency, that they sent after him to apprehend him. He had made his escape as far as Nashawag, about forty miles from Salem; yet it is said those accusers did then presently tell the exact time, saying, Now Willard is taken.

John Proctor[16] and his wife being in prison, the sheriff came to his house and seized all the goods, provisions and cattle that he could come at, and sold some of the cattle at half price, and killed others, and put them up for the West-Indies; threw out the beer out of a barrel, and carried away the barrel; emptied a pot of broth, and took away the pot, and left nothing in the house for the support of

---

16. John Proctor was a respectable farmer; and great efforts were made by his friends, not only at Salem Village, but also at Ipswich, his native town, to save his life; but they were unsuccessful. A copy of his will, made during his imprisonment and while under sentence of death, is in the Probate-Court Records at Salem.

the children. No part of the said goods are known to be returned. Proctor earnestly requested mr. Noyes to pray with and for him; but it was wholly denied, because he would not own himself to be a witch.

During his imprisonment he sent the following letter, in behalf of himself and others.

Salem Prison, July 23, 1692.

Mr. Mather, Mr. Allen, Mr. Moody, Mr. Willard, and Mr. Baily.

Reverend Gentlemen,

The innocency of our case, with the enmity of our accusers and our judges and jury, whom nothing but our innocent blood will serve, having condemned us already before our trials, being so much incensed and enraged against us by the devil, makes us bold to beg and implore your favourable assistance of this our humble petition to his excellency, that if it be possible our innocent blood may be spared, which undoubtedly otherwise will be shed, if the Lord doth not mercifully step in; the magistrates, ministers, juries, and all the people in general, being so much enraged and incensed against us by the delusion of the devil, which we can term no other, by reason we know in our own consciences we are all innocent persons. Here are five persons who have lately confessed themselves to be witches, and do accuse some of us of being along with them at a sacrament, since we were committed into close prison, which we know to be lies. Two of the five are (Currier's sons) young men, who would not confess any thing till they tied them neck and heels, till the blood was ready to come out of their noses; and it is credibly believed and reported this was the occasion of making them confess what they never did, by reason they said one had been a witch a month, and another five weeks, and that their mother had made them so, who has been confined here this nine weeks. My son William Proctor, when he was examined, because he would not confess that he was guilty, when he was innocent, they tied him neck and heels till the blood gushed out at his nose, and would have kept him so twenty-four hours, if one, more merciful than the rest, had not taken pity on him, and caused him to be unbound. These actions are very like the popish cruelties. They have already undone us in our estates, and that will not serve their turns without our innocent blood. If it cannot be granted that we can have our trials at Boston, we humbly beg that you would endeavour to have these magistrates changed, and others in their rooms; begging also and beseeching you would be pleased to be here, if not all, some of you, at our trials, hoping thereby you may be the means of saving the shedding of our innocent blood. Desiring your prayers to the Lord in our behalf, we rest your poor afflicted servants,

JOHN PROCTOR, &c.

He pleaded very hard at execution for a little respite of time, saying that he was not fit to die; but it was not granted.

Old Jacobs[17] being condemned, the sheriff and officers came and seized all he had; his wife had her wedding ring taken from her, but with great difficulty obtained it again. She was forced to buy provisions of the sheriff, such as he had taken, towards her own support, which not being sufficient, the neighbours in charity relieved her. Margaret Jacobs being one that had confessed her own guilt, and testified against her grandfather Jacobs, mr. Burroughs and John Willard, she the day before execution came to Mr. Burroughs, acknowledging that she had belied them, and begged mr. Burroughs's forgiveness; who not only forgave her, but also prayed with and for her. She wrote the following letter to her father:

From the dungeon in Salem prison, Aug. 20, 1692.

Honoured Father,

After my humble duty remembered to you, hoping in the Lord of your good health, as blessed be God I enjoy, though in abundance of affliction, being close confined here in a loathsome dungeon; the Lord look down in mercy upon me, not knowing how soon I shall be put to death, by means of the afflicted persons; my grandfather having suffered already, and all his estate seized for the king. The reason of my confinement is this: I having, through the magistrates' threatenings, and my own vile and wretched heart, confessed several things contrary to my conscience and knowledge, though to the wounding of my own soul, (the Lord pardon me for it); but oh! the terrors of a wounded conscience who can bear? But blessed be the Lord, he would not let me go on in my sins, but in mercy, I hope, to my soul, would not suffer me to keep it in any longer, but I was forced to confess the truth of all before the magistrates, who would not believe me; but 'tis their pleasure to put me in here, and God

---

17. George Jacobs, Sen., after his execution, was buried on his farm, at Danvers Port, where his grave is to be seen at this day

knows how soon I shall be put to death. Dear father, let me beg your prayers to the Lord on my behalf and send us a joyful and happy meeting in heaven. My mother, poor woman, is very crazy, and remembers her kind love to you, and to uncle, viz. D.A. So leaving you to the protection of the Lord, I rest your dutiful daughter,

MARGARET JACOBS.

At the time appointed for her trial, she had an imposthume in her head, which was her escape.

September 9, six more were tried, and received sentence of death, viz. Martha Cory, of Salem Village; Mary Easty, of Topsfield; Alice Parker and Ann Pudeater, of Salem; Dorcas Hoar, of Beverly, and Mary Bradberry, of Salisbury. Sept. 16, Giles Cory was prest to death.

September 17, nine more received sentence of death, viz. Margaret Scot, of Rowley; goodwife Reed, of Marblehead; Samuel Wardwell and Mary Parker, of Andover; also Abigail Falkner, of Andover, who pleaded pregnancy; Rebecca Eames, of Boxford, Mary Lacy and Ann Foster, of Andover, and Abigail Hobbs, of Topsfield. Of these, eight were executed, Sept. 22, viz. Martha Cory, Mary Easty, Alice Parker, Ann Pudeater, Margaret Scot, William Reed, Samuel Wardwell and Mary Parker.

Giles Cory[18] pleaded not guilty to his indictment, but would not put himself on trial by the jury (they having cleared none upon trial) and knowing there would be the same witnesses against him, rather chose to undergo what death they would put him to. In pressing, his tongue being prest out of his mouth, the sheriff with his cane forced it in again when he was dying. He was the first in New-England that was ever prest to death.

The cart, going to the hill with these eight to execution, was for some time at a set; the afflicted and others said, that the devil hindered it, &c.

---

18. Giles Cory was executed Sept. 19th, 1692, about noon. The day following, Sergt. Thomas Putman, of Salem Village, sent a letter to Judge Sewall, informing him of a revelation from his daughter Ann, wherein a spectre revealed to her the fact that Giles Cory, some seventeen years before, was suspected of causing the death of a man in his employ. The coroner's jury, which sat upon the body, rendered a verdict of murder, by bruising,—he having, as they expressed it, "clodders of blood about the heart." We may suppose that the remembrance of this occurrence may have prejudiced the minds of many against Cory, although there was not a particle of evidence that he caused, or was knowing to, the death of the man in his employ, and living in his house. The courts took no notice of the affair, and it was generally forgotten, until recalled by his prosecution for witchcraft. The story of the murder seems to have been used at the time to palliate the dreadful deed of pressing him to death, by inducing the public to believe that he suffered a just punishment, in consequence of his having, seventeen years before, pressed a man to death with his feet.

It is generally supposed, and we think correctly, that Giles Cory, seeing that no one escaped, and that a trial was but a farce, refused to plead. But Ann Putman informs us, that the ghost of the man, whom it was said Cory murdered, appeared to her the night before his execution, and told her that when goodman Cory made his witch-covenant, the devil stipulated with him, and gave him assurance, that he should never be hanged, let what would come; but was careful not to tell him he should be pressed to death. The ghost in the winding sheet further informed Ann, that Cory's heart was hardened that he should not hearken to the importunity of the court to plead either guilty or not guilty, so that he might at least die a more easy death than by pressing— Because, continued the spectre, it must be done to him as he has done to me, the ghost of the murdered man!

Martha Cory, wife to Giles Cory, protesting her innocency, concluded her life with an eminent prayer upon the ladder.

Wardwell, having formerly confessed himself guilty, and after denied it, was soon brought upon his trial; his former confession and spectre testimony was all that appeared against him. At execution, while he was speaking to the people, protesting his innocency, the executioner being at the same time smoking tobacco, the smoke coming in his face interrupted his discourse; those accusers said that the devil did hinder him with smoke.

Mary Easty, sister also to Rebecca Nurse, when she took her last farewell of her husband, children and friends, was, as is reported by them present, as serious, religious, distinct and affectionate as could well be exprest, drawing tears from the eyes of almost all present. It seems, besides the testimony of the accusers and confessors, another proof, as it was counted, appeared against her: it having been usual to search the accused for teats, upon some parts of her body, not here to be named, was found an excrescence, which they called a teat. Before her death she presented the following petition:

"To the honourable judge and bench now sitting in judicature in Salem, and the reverend ministers, humbly sheweth, That whereas your humble poor petitioner, being condemned to die, doth humbly beg of you to take it into your judicious and pious consideration, that your poor and humble petitioner, knowing my own innocency (blessed be the Lord for it) and seeing plainly the wiles and subtilty of my accusers, by myself, cannot but judge charitably of others, that are going the same way with myself, if the Lord step not mightily in. I was confined a whole month on the same account that I am now condemned, and then cleared by the afflicted persons, as some of your honours know; and in two days time was cried out upon by them again, and have been confined, and now am condemned to die. The Lord above knows my innocence then, and likewise doth now, as at the great day will be known by men and angels. I petition to your honours not for my own life, for I know I must die, and my appointed time is set; but the Lord he knows if it be possible that no more innocent blood be shed, which undoubtedly cannot be avoided in the way and course you go in. I question not but your honours do to the utmost of your powers, in the discovery and detecting of witchcraft and witches, and would not be guilty of innocent blood for the world; but by my own innocency I know you are in the wrong way. The Lord in his infinite mercy direct you in this great work, if it be his blessed will, that innocent blood be not shed. I would humbly beg of you, that your honours would be pleased to examine some of those confessing witches, I being confident there are several of them have belied themselves and others, as will appear, if not in this world, I am sure in the world to come, whither I am going; and I question not but yourselves will see an alteration in these things. They say, myself and others have made a league with the devil; we cannot confess; I know and the Lord knows (as will shortly appear) they belie me, and so I question not but they do others; the Lord alone, who is the searcher of all hearts, knows, as I shall answer it at the tribunal seat, that I know not the least thing of witchcraft, therefore I cannot, I durst not, belie my own soul. I beg your honours not to deny this my humble petition, from a poor dying, innocent person, and I question not but the Lord will give a blessing to your endeavours.

MARY EASTY."

After execution, mr. Noyes, turning him to the bodies, said, What a sad thing it is to see eight firebrands of hell hanging there!

In October, 1692, one of Wenham complained of mrs. Hale, whose husband, the minister of Beverly, had been very forward in these prosecutions; but being fully satisfied of his wife's sincere christianity caused him to alter his judgment; for it was come to a stated controversy, among the New-England divines, whether the devil could afflict in a good man's shape; it seems nothing else could convince him, yet when it came so near to himself he was soon convinced, that the devil might so afflict. Which same reason did afterwards prevail with many others, and much influenced to the succeeding change at trials.

October 7. Edward Bishop and his wife having made their escape out of prison, this day mr. Corwin, the sheriff, came and seized his goods and chattels, and had it not been for his second son (who borrowed ten pound and gave it him) they had been wholly lost. The receipt follows; but it seems they must be content with such a receipt as he would give them:

> Received, this 7th day of October, 1692, of Samuel Bishop, of the town of Salem, of the county of Essex, in New-England, cordwainer, in full satisfaction, a valuable sum of money, for the goods and chattels of Edward Bishop, senior, of the town and county aforesaid, husbandman; which goods and chattels

being seized, for that the said Edward Bishop, and Sarah his wife, having been committed for witchcraft and felony, have made their escape; and their goods and chattels were forfeited unto their majesties, and now being in possession of the said Samuel Bishop; and in behalf of their majesties, I do hereby discharge the said goods and chattels, the day and year above written, as witness my hand,

GEORGE CORWIN, *Sheriff.*

But before this, the said Bishop's eldest son having married into that family of the Putmans, who were chief prosecutors in this business, he holding a cow to be branded lest it should be seized, and having a push or boil upon his thigh, with his straining it broke; this is that that was pretended to be burnt with the said brand, and is one of the bones thrown to the dogmatical to pick, in *Wonders of the Invisible World*, p. 143. The other, of a corner of a sheet, pretended to be taken from a spectre; it is known that it was provided the day before by that afflicted person; and the third bone of a spindle is almost as easily provided, as the piece of the knife; so that Apollo needs not herein be consulted, &c.

Mr. Philip English, and his wife, having made their escape out of prison, mr. Corwin, the sheriff, seized his estate, to the value of about fifteen hundred pound, which was wholly lost to him, except about three hundred pound value (which was afterward restored.)

After goodwife Hoar was condemned, her estate was seized, and was also bought again for eight pound.

George Jacobs, son to old Jacobs, being accused, he fled; then the officers came to his house; his wife was a woman crazy in her senses, and had been so several years. She it seems had been also accused. There were in the house with her only four small children, and one of them sucked her eldest daughter, being in prison: the officer persuaded her out of the house, to go along with him, telling her she should speedily return; the children ran a great way after her, crying.

When she came where the afflicted were, being asked, they said they did not know her; at length one said, Don't you know *Jacobs*, the old witch? and then they cried out of her, and fell down in their fits. She was sent to prison, and lay there ten months; the neighbours of pity took care of the children to preserve them from perishing.

About this time a new scene was begun; one Joseph Balard, of Andover, whose wife was ill (and after died of a fever) sent to Salem for some of those accusers, to tell him who afflicted his wife; others did the like: horse and man, were sent from several places to fetch those accusers who had the spectral sight, that they might thereby tell who afflicted those that were any ways ill.

When these came into any place where such were, usually they fell into a fit: after which, being asked who it was that afflicted the person, they would, for the most part, name one who they said sat on the head, and another that sat on the lower parts, of the afflicted. Soon after Ballard's sending (as above) more than fifty of the people of Andover were complained of; for afflicting their neighbours. Here it was that many accused themselves of riding upon poles through the air; many parents believing their children to be witches, and many husbands their wives, &c. When these accusers came to the house of any upon such account, it was ordinary for other young people to be taken in fits, and to have the same spectral sight.

Mr. Dudley Bradstreet, a justice of peace in Andover, having granted out warrants against, and committed, thirty or forty to prison, for the supposed witchcrafts, at length saw cause to forbear granting out any more warrants. Soon after which, he and his wife were cried out of; himself was (by them) said to have killed nine persons by witchcraft, and he found it his safest course to make his escape.

A dog being afflicted at Salem Village, those that had the spectral sight being sent for, they accused mr. John Bradstreet (brother to the justice) that he afflicted the said dog, and now rid upon him. He made his escape into Piscatuqua government, and the dog was put to death, and was all of the afflicted that suffered death.

At Andover, the afflicted complained of a dog, as afflicting them, and would fall into their fits at the dog's looking upon them; the dog was put to death.

A worthy gentleman of Boston being about this time accused by those at Andover, he sent by some particular friends a writ to arrest those accusers in a thousand pound action for defamation, with instructions to them to inform themselves of the certainty of the proof, in doing which their business was perceived, and from thenceforward the accusations at Andover generally ceased.

In October some of these accusers were sent for to Gloucester, and occasioned four women to be sent to prison; but Salem prison being so full it could receive no more, two were sent to Ipswich prison. In November they were sent for again by lieutenant

Stephens, who was told that a sister of his was bewitched; in their way passing over Ipswich-bridge, they met with an old woman, and instantly fell into their fits. But by this time the validity of such accusations being much questioned, they could not that encouragement they had done elsewhere, and soon withdrew.

These accusers swore that they saw three persons sitting upon lieutenant Stephens's sister till she died; yet bond was accepted for those three.

And now nineteen persons having been hanged, and one prest to death, and eight more condemned, in all twenty-eight, of which above a third part were members of some of the churches in New-England, and more than half of them of a good conversation in general, and not one cleared; about fifty having confest themselves to be witches, of which not one executed; above an hundred and fifty in prison, and above two hundred more accused; the special commission of oyer and terminer comes to a period, which has no other foundation than the governor's commission; and had proceeded in the manlier of swearing witnesses, viz. by holding up the hand, (and by receiving evidences in writing) according to the ancient usage of this country; as also having their indictments in English. In the trials, when any were indicted for afflicting, pining and wasting the bodies of particular persons by witchcraft, it was usual to hear evidence of matter foreign, and of perhaps twenty or thirty years standing, about oversetting carts, the death of cattle, unkindness to relations, or unexpected accidents befalling after some quarrel. Whether this was admitted by the law of England, or by what other law, wants to be determined; the executions seemed mixt, in pressing to death for not pleading, which most agrees with the laws of England; and sentencing women to be hanged for witchcraft, according to the former practice of this country, and not by burning, as is said to have been the law of England. And though the confessing witches were many, yet not one of them that confessed their own guilt, and abode by their confession, was put to death.

Here followeth what account some of those miserable creatures give of their confession under their own hands:

"We, whose names are under written, inhabitants of Andover, when as that horrible and tremendous judgment beginning at Salem Village, in the year 1692, (by some called witchcraft) first breaking forth at mr. Parris's house, several young persons being seemingly afflicted, did accuse several persons for afflicting them, and many there believing it so to be; we being informed that if a person were sick, the afflicted person could tell what or who was the cause of that sickness: Joseph Ballard, of Andover (his wife being sick at the same time) he either from himself, or by the advice of others, fetched two of the persons, called the afflicted persons, from Salem Village to Andover: which was the beginning of that dreadful calamity that befel us in Andover. And the authority in Andover, believing the said accusations to be true, sent for the said persons to come together to the meeting-house in Andover (the afflicted persons being there.) After mr. Barnard had been at prayer, we were blindfolded, and our hands were laid upon the afflicted persons, they being in their fits, and falling into their fits at our corning into their presence (as they said) and some led us and laid our hands upon them, and then they said they were well, and that we were guilty of afflicting of them; whereupon we were all seized as prisoners, by a warrant from a justice of the peace, and forthwith carried to Salem. And by reason of that sudden surprisal, we knowing ourselves altogether innocent of that crime, we were all exceedingly astonished and amazed, and affrighted even out of our reason; and our nearest and dearest relations, seeing us in that dreadful condition, and knowing our great danger, apprehending that there was no other way to save our lives, as the case was then circumstanced, but by our confessing ourselves to be such and such persons, as the afflicted represented us to be, they out of tender love and pity persuaded us to confess what we did confess. And indeed that confession, that it is said we made, was no other than what was suggested to us by some gentlemen; they telling us, that we were witches, and they knew it, and we knew it, and they knew that we knew it, which made us think that it was so; and our understanding, our reason and our faculties almost gone, we were not capable of judging our condition; as also the hard measures they used with us rendered us uncapable of making our defence; but said any thing and every thing which they desired; and most of what we said was but in effect a consenting to what they said. Sometime after, when we were better composed, they telling of us what we had confessed, we did profess that we were innocent, and ignorant of such things. And we hearing that Samuel Wardwell had renounced his confession, and quickly after was condemned and executed, some of us were told that we were going after Wardwell.

Mary Osgood, Abigail Barker, Mary Tiler, Sarah Wilson, Deliv. Dane, Hannah Tiler."

It may here be further added, concerning those that did confess, that besides that powerful argument, of life (and freedom from hardships, not only promised, but also performed to all that owned their guilt) there are numerous instances, too many to be here inserted, of the tedious examinations before private persons, many hours together; they all that time urging them to confess (and taking turns to persuade them) till the accused were wearied out by being forced to stand so long, or for want of sleep, &c. and so brought to give an assent to what they said; they then asking them, were you at such a witch-meeting? or, Have you signed the Devil's book? &c. Upon their replying, Yes, the whole was drawn into form, as their confession.

But that which did mightily further such confessions was, their nearest relations urging them to it. These, seeing no other way of escape for them, thought it the best advice that could be given; hence it was that the husbands of some, by counsel often urging, and utmost earnestness, and children upon their knees intreating, have at length prevailed with them to say they were guilty.

As to the manner of trials, and the evidence taken for convictions at Salem, it is already set forth in print, by the rev. mr. Cotton Mather, in his *Wonders of the Invisible World*, at the command of his excellency sir William Phips; with not only the recommendation, but thanks, of the lieutenant governor; and with the approbation of the rev. mr. I.M. in his postscript to his *Cases of Conscience*; which last book was set forth by the consent of the ministers in and near Boston. Two of the judges have also given their sentiments in these words, p. 147.

> The reverend and worthy author having, at the direction of his excellency the governor, so far obliged the publick, as to the some account of the sufferings brought upon the country by witchcrafts, and of the trials which have passed upon several executed tor the same:
>
> Upon perusal thereof, we find the matters of fact and evidence truly reported, and a prospect given of the methods of conviction, used in the proceedings of the court at Salem.
>
> WILLIAM STOUGHTON, SAMUEL SEWALL.

Boston, Oct. 11, 1692.

And considering that this may fall into the hands of such as never saw those *Wonders*, it may be needful to transcribe the whole account he has given thereof, without any variation (but with one of the indictments annexed to the trial of each) which is thus prefaced, pp. 81, 82, 83.

"But I shall no longer detain my reader from his expected entertainment, in a brief account of the trials which have passed upon some of the malefactors lately executed at Salem for the witchcrafts whereof they stood convicted. For my own part I was not present at any of them; nor ever had I any personal prejudice against the persons thus brought upon the stage; much less, at the surviving relations of those persons, with and for whom I would be as hearty a mourner, as any man living in the world: *The Lord comfort them!* But having received a command so to do, I can do no other than shortly relate the chief matters of fact, which occurred in the trials of some that were executed, in an abridgment collected out of the court-papers, on this occasion put into my hands. You are to take the truth, just as it was; and the truth will hurt no good man. There might have been more of these; and if some other worthy hands did not perhaps intend something further in these collections; for which cause I have only singled out four or five, which may serve to illustrate the way of dealing, wherein witchcrafts use to be concerned: and I report matters, not as an advocate, but as an historian.

" These were some of the gracious words inserted in the advice, which many of the neighbouring ministers did this summer humbly lay before our honourable judges: we cannot but with all thankfulness acknowledge the success, which the merciful God has given unto the sedulous and assiduous endeavours of our honourable rulers, to detect the abominable witchcrafts which have been committed in the country; humbly praying that the discovery of those mysterious and mischievous wickednesses may be perfected. If, in the midst of the many dissatisfactions among us, the publication of these trials may promote such a pious thankfulness unto God, for justice being so far executed among us, I shall rejoice that God is glorified; and pray that no wrong steps of ours may ever sully any of his glorious works."

The Indictment of George Burroughs.

Essex ss.   *Anno Regni Regis & Reginæ: Willielmi & Mariæ, nunc Angliæ, &c. quarto.*———

The jurors for our sovereign lord and lady the king and queen present, that George Burroughs, late of Falmouth, in the province of the Massachusetts Bay, in New England, clerk, the 9th day of May, in the fourth year of the reign of our sovereign lord and lady William and Mary, by the grace of God, of England, Scotland, France and Ireland, king and queen, defenders of the faith, &c. and divers other days and times, as well before as after, certain detestable arts, called witchcrafts and sorceries, wickedly and feloniously hath used, practised and exercised, at and within the township of Salem, in the county of Essex, aforesaid, in, upon and against one Mary Wolcott, of Salem Village, in the county of Essex, single woman; by which said wicked arts the said Mary Wolcott, the 9th day of May, in the fourth year abovesaid, and divers other days and times, as well before as after, was and is tortured, afflicted, pined, consumed, wasted and tormented, against the peace of our sovereign lord and lady, the king and queen, and against the form of the statute in that case made and provided.

Witnesses, *Mary Wolcott, Sarah Vibber, Mercy Lewis, Ann Putman, Eliz. Hubbard.*

Endorsed by the grand jury, *Billa Vera.*

There was also a second indictment, for afflicting Elizabeth Hubbard. The witnesses to the said indictment were *Elizabeth Hubbard, Mary Wolcott* and *Ann Putman.*

The third indictment was for afflicting Mercy Lewis: the witnesses, the said *Mercy Lewis, Mary Wolcott, Elizabeth Hubbard* and *Ann Putman.*

The fourth, for acts of witchcraft on Ann Putman: the witnesses, the said *Ann Putman, Mary Wolcott, Elizabeth Hubbard* and *Mary Warren.*

MATTERS

The Trial of G.B.[19] as printed in Wonders of the Invisible World, from p. 94 to 104.

Glad should I have been, if I had never known the name of this man. or never had this occasion to mention so much as the first letters of his name; but the government requiring some account of his trial to be inserted in this book, it becomes me with all obedience to submit unto the order.

1. This G.B. was indicted for witchcrafts; and, in the prosecution of the charge against him, he was accused by five or six of the bewitched, as the author of their miseries; he was accused by eight of the confessing witches, as being a head actor at some of their hellish rendezvous, and who had the promise of being a king In satan's

---

19. The trial of Rev. George Burroughs appears to have attracted general notice, from the circumstance of his being a former clergy man in Salem village, and supposed to be a leader amongst the witches.— Dr. Cotton Mather says he was not present at any of the trials for witchcraft; how he could keep away from that of Burroughs, we cannot imagine.— His father, Dr. Increase Mather, informs us that he attended this single trial, and says, "had I been one of George Burrough's judges, I could not have acquitted him; for several persons did upon oath testify, that they saw him do such things as no man that had not a devil to be his familiar, could perform." Burroughs was apprehended in Wells, in Maine; so say his children. They also inform us, that he was buried by his friends after the inhuman treatment of his body from the hands of his executioners, at Gallows Hill, in Salem. He is represented as being a small, black haired, dark complexioned man, of quick passions, and possessing great strength. His power of muscle, which discovered itself early when Burroughs was a member of Cambridge College, and which we notice in the flight rebutting evidence offered by his friends at his trial, convinces us that he lifted the gun, and the barrel of molasses by the power of his own well-strung muscles, and not by any help from the devil, as was supposed by the Mathers, both father and son. Alas! that a man's own strong arm should thus prove his ruin. in regard to the reputation of Rev. George Burroughs, Judge Sullivan, in his history of Maine, says:— "He was a man of bad character, and of a cruel disposition."—Our researches lead us to form a very different opinion. And all the weight of character enlisted against him, fails to counteract the favourable impression made by his christian conduit, during his imprisonment, and at the time of his execution. We find Georgius Burroughs in the Harvard catalogue list of graduates for the year 1670.

kingdom, now going to be erected; he was accused by nine persons, for extraordinary lifting, and such feats of strength as could not be done without a diabolical assistance; and for other such things he was accused, until about thirty testimonies were brought in against him; nor were these judged the half of what might have been considered, for his conviction: however, they were enough to fix the character of a witch upon him, according to the rules of reasoning, by the judicious Gallic in that case directed.

2. The court being sensible that the testimonies of the parties bewitched used to have a room among the suspicions, or presumptions, brought in against one. indicted for witchcraft, there were now heard the testimonies of several persons who were most notoriously bewitched, and every day tortured by invisible hands, and these now all charged the spectres of G.B. to have a share in their torments. At the examination of this G.B. the bewitched people were grievously harassed with preternatural mischiefs, which could not possibly be dissembled; and they still ascribed it unto the endeavours of G.B. to kill them. And now, upon his trial, one of the be witched persons testified, that in her agonies a little black-haired man came to her, saying his name was B. and bidding her set her hand unto a book, which he shewed unto her; and bragging that he was a conjurer above the ordinary rank of witches; that be often persecuted her with the offer of that book, saying, she should be well, and need fear nobody, if she would but sign it: but he inflicted cruel pains and hurts upon her, because of her denying so to do. The testimonies of the other sufferers concurred with these; and it was remarkable~ that whereas biting was 'one of the ways which the witches used for the vexing of the sufferers, when they cried out of G.B. biting them, the print of his teeth would be seen on the flesh of the complainers; and just such a set of teeth as G.B's would then appear upon them, which could be distinguished from those of some other men's.

Others of them testified, that in their torments G.B. tempted them to go unto a sacrament, unto which they perceived him with a sound of trumpet summoning other witches; who quickly after the sound would come from all quarters unto the rendezvous. One of them, falling into a kind of a trance, afterwards affirmed, that G. B. had carried her into a very high mountain, where he showed her mighty and glorious kingdoms, and said he would give them all to her, if she would write in his book; but she told him, they were none of his to give, and refused the motion, enduring much misery for that refusal.

It cost the court a wonderful deal of trouble to hear the testimonies of the sufferers; for when they were going to give in their depositions, they would for a long while be taken with fits, that made them uncapable of saying any thing. The chief judge asked the prisoner, who he thought hindered these witnesses from giving their testimonies; and he answered, he supposed it was the devil. That honourable person then replied, How comes the devil so loth to have any testimony borne against you? which cast him into very great confusion.

3. It hath been a frequent thing for the bewitched people to be entertained with apparitions of ghosts of murdered people, at the same time that the spectres of the witches trouble them. These ghosts do always affright the beholders; more than all the other spectral representations; and when they exhibit themselves, they cry out of being murdered by the witchcrafts or other violences of the persons who are then in spectre present. It is further considerable, that once or twice these apparitions have been seen by others, at the very same time they have shown themselves to the bewitched; and seldom have there been these apparitions, but when something unusual and suspected hath attended the death of the party thus appearing. Some, that have been accused by these apparitions, accosting the bewitched people, who had never heard a word of any such persons ever being in the world, have, upon a fair examination, freely and fully confessed the murders of those very persons, although these also did not know how the apparitions had complained of them. Accordingly several of the bewitched had given in their testimony, that they had been troubled with the apparitions of two women, who said they were G.B.'s two wives; and that he had been the death of them; and that the magistrates must be told of it, before whom, if B. upon his trial denied it, they did not know but that they should appear again in the court. Now G.B. had been infamous, for the barbarous usage of his two successive wives, all the country over. Moreover, it was testified, the spectre of G.B. threatening the sufferers, told them he had killed (besides others) mrs. Lawson and her daughter Ann. And it was noted, that these were the virtuous wife and daughter of one, at whom this G.B. might have a prejudice, for being serviceable at Salem Village, from whence himself had in ill terms removed some years before; and that

when they died, which was long since, there were some odd circumstances about them, which made some of the attendants there suspect something of witchcraft, though none imagined from what quarter it should come.

Well, G.B. being now upon his trial, one of the bewitched persons was cast into horror at the ghosts of B's two deceased wives, then appearing before him, and crying for vengeance against him. Hereupon several of the bewitched persons were successively called in, who all, not knowing what the former had seen and said, concurred in their horror of the apparition, which they affirmed that he had before him. But he, though much appalled, utterly denied that he discerned any thing of it, nor was it any part of his conviction.

4. Judicious writers have assigned it a great place in the conviction of witches, when persons are impeached by other notorious witches to be as ill as themselves, especially if the persons have been much noted for neglecting the worship of God. Now, as there might have beea testimonies enough of G.B.'s antipathy to prayer, and the other ordinances of God, though by his profession singularly obliged thereunto; so there now came in against the prisoner, the testimonies of several persons, who confessed their own having been horrible witches, and, ever since their confessions, had been themselves terribly tortured by the devils and other witches, even like the other sufferers, and therein undergone the pains of many deaths for their confessions.

These now testified, that G.B. had been at witch-meetings with them; and that he was the person who had seduced and compelled them into the snares of witchcraft; that he promised them fine clothes for doing it; that he brought poppets to them, and thorns to stick into those poppets, for the afflicting of other people; and that he exhorted them, with the rest of the crew, to bewitch all Salem Village; but be sure to do it gradually, if they would prevail in what they did.

When the Lancashire witches were condemned, I do not remember that there was any considerable further evidence, than that of the bewitched, and than that of some that had confessed. We see so much already against G.B. But this being indeed not enough, there were other things to render what had already been produced credible.

5. A famous divine recites this among the convictions of a witch; the testimony of the party bewitched, whether pining or dying; together with the joint oaths of sufficient persons, that have seen certain prodigious pranks, or feats, wrought by the party accused. Now, God had been pleased so to leave G.B. that he had ensnared himself, by several instances, which he had formerly given, of a preternatural strength; and which were now produced against him. He was a very puny man, yet he had often done things beyond the strength of a giant. A gun of about seven feet barrel, and so heavy that strong men could not steadily hold it out, with both hands; there were several testimonies given in by persons of credit and honour, that he made nothing of taking up such a gun behind the lock with but one hand, and holding it out, like a pistol at arm's end. G.B. in his vindication was so foolish as to say, that an Indian was there, and held it out, at the same time; whereas, none of the spectators ever saw any such Indian; but they supposed the black man (as the witches call the devil, and they generally say he resembles an Indian) might give him that assistance. There was evidence likewise brought in, that he made nothing of taking up whole barrels filled with molasses, or cider, in very disadvantageous postures, and carrying them off, through the most difficult places, out of a canoe to the shore. Yea, there were two testimonies, that G.B. with only putting the fore-finger of bis right band into the muzzle of an heavy gun, a fowling piece of about six or seven feet barrel, lined up the gun, and held it out at arm's end; a gun which the deponents, though strong men, could not with both hands lift up, and hold out at the but-end, as is usual. Indeed one of these witnesses was over-persuaded by some persons to be out of the way upon G.B.'s trial; but he came afterwards, with sorrow for his withdrawing, and gave in his testimony, Nor were either of these witnesses made use of as evidence in the trial.

There came in several testimonies, relating to the domestic affairs of G.B. which had a very hard aspect upon him; and not only proved him a very ill man, but also confirmed the belief of the character which had been already fastened on him. 'Twas testified, that, keeping his two successive wives in a strange kind of slavery, he would, when he came home from abroad, pretend to tell the talk which any had with them: that he has brought them to the point or death, by his harsh dealings with his wives, and then made the people about him to promise that in case death should happen they would say nothing of it: that he used all means to make his wives write, sign, seal and swear a covenant never to reveal any of his secrets: that his wives had privately complained unto the neighbours about frightly apparitions of evil spirits, with which their house was sometimes infested; and that many such things had been whispered among the neighbourhood. There were also some other testimonies, relating to the death of people, whereby the consciences of an impartial jury were convinced that G.B. had bewitched the persons mentioned in the complaints. But I am forced to omit several such passages in this as well as in all the succeeding trials, because the scribes who took notice of them have not supplied me.

7. One Mr. Ruck, brother-in-law to this G.B. testified, that G.B. and he himself, and his sister, who was G.B.'s wife, going out for two or three miles, to gather strawberries, Ruck, with his sister, the wife of G.B. rode home very softly, with G.B. on foot, in their company; G.B. stept aside a little into the bushes, whereupon they halted and hollowed for him: he not answering, they went away homewards, with a quickened pace, without any expectation of seeing him in a considerable while; and yet, when they were got near home, to their astonishment they found him on foot, with them, having a basket of strawberries. G.B. immediately then fell to chiding his wife, on the account of what she had been speaking to her brother of him on the road; which when they wondered at, he said, he. knew their thoughts. Ruck, being startled at that, made some reply, intimating that the devil himself did not know so far; but G.B. answered, my God makes known your thoughts unto me. The prisoner now at the bar had nothing to answer unto what was thus witnessed against him, that was worth considering; only he said, Ruck and his wife left a man with him, when they left him; which Ruck now affirmed to be false; and when the court asked G.B. what the man's name was, his countenance was much altered, nor could he say who it was. But the court began to think that he then stept aside, only that by the assistance of the black man he might put on his invisibility, and in that fascinating mist gratify his own jealous humour to hear what they said of him: which trick of rendering themselves invisible, our witches do in their confessions pretend that they sometimes are masters of; and it is the more credible, because there is demonstration that they often render many other things utterly invisible.

8. Faultering, faulty, unconstant and contrary answers, upon judicial and deliberate examination, are counted some unlucky symptoms of guilt in all crimes, especially in witchcrafts. Now there never was a prisoner more eminent for them than G.B. both at his examination and on his trial. His tergiversations, contradictions and falsehoods were very sensible; he had little to say, but that he had heard some things, that he could not prove, reflecting upon the reputation of some or the witnesses: only he gave in a paper to the jury, wherein, although he had many times before granted, not only that there are witches, but also that the present sufferings of the country are the effects of horrible witchcrafts, yet he now goes to evince it, that there neither are, nor ever were, witches, that, having made a compact with the devil, can send a devil to torment other people at a distance. This paper was transcribed out of Ady; which the court presently knew, as soon as they heard it. But he said, he had taken none of it out of any book; for which his evasion afterwards was, that a gentleman gave him the discourse in a manuscript, from whence he transcribed it.

9. The jury brought him in guilty; but when he came to die, he utterly denied the fact, whereof he had been thus convicted.

The Indictment of Bridget Bishop.

Essex ss.   *Anno Regni Regis & Reginæ: Willielmi & Mariæ, nunc Angliæ, &c. quarto.*————

The jurors for our sovereign lord and lady the king and queen present, that Bridget Bishop, alias Oliver, the wife of Edward Bishop, in Salem, in the county of Essex, sawyer, the nineteenth day of April, in the fourth year of the reign of our sovereign lord and lady William and Mary, by the grace of God, of England, Scotland, France and Ireland, king and queen, defenders of the faith, &c. and divers other days and times, as well before as after, certain detestable arts, called witchcrafts and sorceries, wickedly and feloniously hath used, practised and exercised, at and within the township of Salem, in the county of Essex, aforesaid, in, upon and against one Mercy Lewis, of Salem Village, in the county aforesaid, single woman; by which said wicked arts the said Mercy Lewis, the said 19th day of April, in the fourth year abovesaid, and divers other days and times, as well before as after, was and is hurt, tortured, afflicted, pined, consumed, wasted and tormented, against the peace of our sovereign lord and lady, the king and queen, and against the form of the statute in that case made and provided.

Endorsed, *Billa Vera.*

Witnesses, *Mercy Lewis, Nathaniel Ingersoll, mr. Samuel Parris, Thomas Putman,* junior, *Mary Wolcott,* junior, *Ann Putman,* junior, *Eliz. Hubbard, and Abigail Williams.*

There was also a second indictment, on the said Bishop, for afflicting and practising witchcraft on *Abigail Williams.* Witnesses to the said indictment were, the said Abigail Williams, mr. Parris, Nathaniel Ingersoll, Thomas Putman, Ann Putman, Mary Wolcott, Elizabeth Hubbard.

The third indictment was for afflicting *Mary Wolcott*; witnesses to which said indictment were, Mary Wolcott, Mary Lewis, mr. Samuel Parris, Nathaniel Ingersoll, Thomas Putman, Ann Putman, Elizabeth Hubbard, Abigail Williams.

The fourth indictment was for afflicting *Elizabeth Hubbard*; witnesses to which said indictment were, the said Elizabeth Hubbard, Mercy Lewis, mr. Parris, Nathaniel Ingersoll, Thomas Putman, Ann Putman, Mary Wolcott, Abigail Williams.

The fifth indictment was for afflicting *Ann Putman*; witnesses to which said indictment were the said Ann Putman, mr. Samuel Parris, Nathaniel Ingersoll, Thomas Putman, Mercy Lewis, Mary Wolcott, Abigail Williams, Elizabeth Hubbard.

The Trial of BRIDGET BISHOP, *as printed in Wonders of the Invisible World, June 2, 1692, from p. 104 to p. 114.*

1. She was indicted for bewitching several persons in the neighbourhood. The indictment being drawn up, according to the form in such cases usual, and pleading not guilty, there were brought in several persons, who had long undergone many kinds of miseries, which were preternaturally inflicted, and generally ascribed unto an horrible witchcraft. There was little occasion to prove the witchcraft, it being evident and notorious to all beholders. Now to fix the witchcraft on the prisoner at the bar, the first thing used was the testimony of the bewitched; whereof several testified, that the shape of the prisoner did oftentimes very grievously pinch them, choke them, bite them, and afflict them; urging them to write their names in a book, which the said spectre called *ours*. One of them did further testify, that it was the shape of this prisoner, with another,

which one day took her from her wheel, and, carrying her to the river side, threatened there to drown her, if she did not sign the book mentioned; which yet she refused.. Others of them did also testify, that the said shape did, in her threats, brag to them, that she had been the death of sundry persons, then by her named. Another testified, the apparition of ghosts unto the spectre of Bishop, crying out, *You murdered us*. About the truth whereof, there was in the matter of fact but too much suspicion.

2. It was testified, that at the examination of the prisoner, before the magistrates, the bewitched were extremely tortured. If she did but cast her eyes on them, they were presently struck down; and this in such a manner as there could be no collusion in the business. But upon the touch of her hand upon them, when they lay in their swoons, they would immediately revive; and not upon the touch of anyone's else. Moreover, upon some special actions of her body, as the shaking of her head, or the turning of her eyes, they presently and painfully fell into the like postures. And many of the like accidents now fell out, while she was at the bar; one at the same time testifying, that she said, she could not be troubled to see the afflicted thus tormented.

3. There was testimony likewise brought in, that a man striking once at the place where a bewitched person said the shape of this Bishop stood, the bewitched cried out that he had torn her coat, in the place then particularly specified; and the woman's coat was found to be torn in the very place.

4. One Deliverance Hobbs, who had confessed her being a witch, was now tormented by the spectres for her confession. And she now testified, that this Bishop tempted her to sign the book again, and to deny what she had confessed. She affirmed, that it was the shape of this prisoner which whipped her with iron rods, to compel her thereunto. And she affirmed, that this Bishop was at a general meeting of the witches in a field, at Salem Village, and there partook of a diabolical sacrament, in bread and wine, then administered.

5. To render it further unquestionable, that the prisoner at the bar was the person truly charged in this witchcraft, there were produced many evidences of other witchcrafts, by her perpetrated. For instance, John Cook testified, that about five or six years ago, one morning about sunrise, he was, in his chamber, assaulted by the shape of this prisoner; which looked on him, grinned at him, and very much hurt him with a blow on the side of the head; and that on

the same day, about noon, the same shape walked in the room where he was, and an apple strangely flew out of his hand into the lap of his mother, six or eight feet from him.

6. Samuel Gray testified, that about fourteen years ago, he waked on a night, and saw the room where he lay full of light; and that he then saw plainly a woman between the cradle and the bedside, which looked upon him. He rose, and it vanished, though he found the doors all fast. Looking out at the entry door, he saw the same woman in the same garb again; and said, *In God's name, what do you come for?* He went to bed, and had the same woman again assaulting him. The child in the cradle gave a great screech, and the woman disappeared. It was long before the child could be quieted; and though it were a very likely, thriving child, yet from this time it pined away, and after divers months died in a sad condition. He knew not Bishop, nor her name; but when he saw her after this, he knew by her countenance, and apparel, and all circumstances, that it was the apparition of this Bishop, which had thus troubled him.

7. John Bly and his wife testified, that he bought a sow of Edward Bishop, the husband of the prisoner, and was to pay the price agreed unto another person. This prisoner, being angry that she was thus hindered from fingering the money, quarrelled with Bly; soon after which the sow was taken with strange fits, jumping, leaping, and knocking her head against the fence; she seemed blind and deaf, and would neither eat nor be sucked. Whereupon a neighbour said, she believed the creature was *overlooked*; and sundry other circumstances concurred, which made the deponents believe that Bishop had bewitched it..

8. Richard Coman testified, that eight years ago, as he lay awake in his bed, with a light burning in the room, he was annoyed with the apparition of this Bishop, and of two more that were strangers to him, who came and oppressed him, so that he could neither stir himself, nor wake any one else; and that he was the night after molested again in the like manner, the said Bishop taking him by the throat, and pulling him almost out of the bed. His kinsman offered for this cause to lodge with him; and that night, as they were awake, discoursing together, this Coman was once more visited by the guests which had formerly been so troublesome, his kinsman being at the same time struck speechless, and unable to move hand or foot. He had laid his sword by him; which those unhappy spectres did strive much to wrest from him, but he held too fast for them. He

then grew able to call the people of his house; but although they heard him, yet they had not power to speak or stir, until at last one of the people crying out, What's the matter? the spectres all vanished.

9. Samuel Shattock testified, that in the year 1680, this Bridget Bishop often came to his house upon such frivolous and foolish errands, that they suspected she came indeed with a purpose of mischief; presently whereupon, his eldest child, which was of as promising health and sense as any child of its age, began to droop exceedingly; and the oftener that Bishop came to his house, the worse grew the child. As the child would be standing at the door, he would be thrown and bruised against the stones, by an invisible hand, and in like sort knock his face against the sides of the house, and bruise it after a miserable manner. Afterwards this Bishop would bring him things to dye, whereof he could not imagine any use; and when she paid him a piece of money, the purse and money were unaccountably conveyed out of a locked box, and never seen more. The child was immediately hereupon taken with terrible fits, whereof his friends thought he would have died: indeed he did nothing but cry and sleep, for several months together; and at length his understanding was utterly taken away. Among other symptoms of an enchantment upon him, one was, that there was a board in the garden, whereon he would walk; and all the invitations in the world would never fetch him off. About seventeen or eighteen years after, there came a stranger to Shattock's house, who, seeing the child, said, *This poor child is bewitched; and you have a neighbour living not far off who is a witch.* He added, *Your neighbour has had a falling out with your wife; and she said in her heart, your wife is a proud woman, and she would bring down her pride in this child.* He then remembered that Bishop had parted from his wife in muttering and menacing terms, a little before the child was taken ill. The abovesaid stranger would needs carry the bewitched boy with him to Bishop's house, on pretence of buying a pot of cider. The woman entertained him in a furious manner; and flew also upon the boy, scratching his face till the blood came, and saying, *Thou rogue, what! dost thou bring this fellow here to plague me?* Now it seems the man had said, before he went, that he would fetch blood of her. Ever after the boy was followed by grievous fits, which the doctors themselves generally ascribed unto witchcraft; and wherein he would be thrown still into fire or water, if he were not constantly looked after; and it was verily believed that Bishop was the cause of it.

10. John Louder testified, that upon some little controversy with Bishop about her fowls, going well to bed, he awaked in the night by moonlight, and clearly saw the likeness of this woman grievously oppressing him; in which miserable condition she held him, unable to help himself till near day. He told Bishop of this, but she utterly denied it, and threatened him very much. Quickly after this, being at home on a Lord's day, with the doors shut about him, he saw a black pig approach him; at which he going to kick, it vanished away. Immediately after, sitting down, he saw a black thing jump in at the window, and come and stand before him: the body was like that of a monkey, the feet like a cock's, but the face much like a man's. He being so extremely frighted that he could not speak, this monster spoke to him, and said, *I am a messenger sent unto you, for I understand that you are in some trouble of mind, and if you will be ruled by me, you shall want for nothing in this world.* whereupon he endeavoured to clap his hands upon it; but he could feel no substance, and it jumped out of the window again; but immediately came in by the porch, though the doors were shut, and said, *You had better take my counsel.* He then struck at it with a stick, but struck only the groundsel, and broke the stick. The arm with which he struck was presently disenabled, and it vanished away. He presently went out at the back door, and spied this Bishop, in her orchard, going towards her house; but he had not power to set one foot forward unto her. Whereupon, returning into the house, he was immediately accosted by the monster he had seen before; which goblin was now going to fly at him; whereat he cried out, *The whole armour of God be between me and you!* so it sprang back, and flew over the apple-tree, shaking many apples off the tree in its flying over. At its leap, it flung dirt with its feet against the stomach of the man; whereon he was then struck dumb, and so continued for three days together. Upon the producing of this testimony, Bishop denied that she knew this deponent. Yet their two orchards joined, and they had often had their little quarrels for some years together.

11. William Stacy testified, that receiving money of this Bishop for work done by him, he was gone but about three rods from her, and, looking for his money, found it unaccountably gone from him. Some time after, Bishop asked him whether his father would grind her grist for her. He demanded why. She replied, Because folks count me a witch. He answered, No question but he will grind it for you. Being then gone about six rods from her, with a small load in his

cart, suddenly the off wheel slumpt, and sunk down into an hole, upon plain ground, so that the deponent was forced to get help for the recovering of the wheel. But stepping back to look for the hole which might give him this disaster, there was none at all to be found. Some time after he was awakened in the night; but it seemed as light as day; and he perfectly saw the shape of this Bishop in the room, troubling him; but upon his going out, all was dark again. He charged Bishop afterwards with it, and she denied it not, but was very angry. Quickly after, this deponent having been threatened by Bishop, as he was in a dark night going to the barn, he was very suddenly taken or lifted up from the ground, and thrown against a stone wall; after that he was again hoisted up, and thrown down a bank, at the end of his house. After this, again passing by this Bishop, his horse, with a small load, striving to draw, all his gears flew to pieces, and the cart fell down; and this deponent going then to lift a bag of corn, of about two bushels, could not lift it with all his might.

Many other pranks of this Bishop, this deponent was ready to testify. He also testified, that he verily believed the said Bishop was the instrument of his daughter Priscilla's death; of which suspicion, pregnant reasons were assigned.

12. To crown all, John Bly and William Bly testified, that, being employed by Bridget Bishop to help take down the cellar-wall of the old house, wherein she formerly lived, they did in holes of the said old wall find several poppets made up of rags and hogs' bristles, with headless pins in them, the points being outward: whereof she could now give no account unto the court, that was reasonable or tolerable.

13. One thing that made against the prisoner was, her being evidently convicted of gross lying in the court, several times, while she was making her plea. But besides this, a jury of women found a preternatural teat upon her body; but upon a second search, within three or four hours, there was no such thing to be seen. There was also an account of other people, whom this woman had afflicted; and there might have been, many more, if they had been inquired for; but there was no need of them.

14. There was one very strange thing more, with which the court was newly entertained. As this woman was, under a guard, passing by the great and spacious meeting house of Salem, she gave a look towards the house; and immediately a dæmon, invisibly entering the meeting-house, tore down a part of it; so that though there were no

person to be seen there, yet the people, at the noise running in, found a board, which was strongly fastened with several nails, transported unto another quarter of the house.

The Indictment of Susanna Martin.

Essex ss.   *Anno Regni Regis & Reginæ: Willielmi & Mariæ, nunc Angliæ, &c. quarto.*———

The jurors for our sovereign lord and lady the king and queen present, that Susanna Martin, of Amesbury, in the county of Essex, widow, the second day of May, in the fourth year of the reign of our sovereign lord and lady William and Mary, by the grace of God, of England, Scotland, France and Ireland, king and queen, defenders of the faith, &c. and divers other days and times, as well before as after, certain detestable arts, called witchcrafts and sorceries, wickedly and feloniously hath used, practised and exercised, fit and within the township of Salem, in the county of Essex, aforesaid, in, upon and against one Mary Wolcott, of Salem Village, in the county of Essex, single woman; by which said wicked arts the said Mary Wolcott, the second day of May, in the fourth year aforesaid, and at divers other days and times, as well before as after, was and is tortured, afflicted, pined, consumed, wasted and tormented; as also for sundry other acts of witchcraft by said Susanna Martin committed and done before and since that time, against the peace of our sovereign lord and lady, William and Mary, king and queen of England, their crown and dignity, and against the form of the statute, in that case made and provided.

Returned by the grand jury, *Billa vera.*

Witnesses—*Sarah Vibber, Mary Wolcott, Samuel Parris, Elizabeth Hubbard* and *Mercy Lewis.*

The second indictment was for afflicting *Mercy Lewis.*

Witnesses—Samuel Parris, Ann Putman, Sarah Vibber, Elizabeth Hubbard, Mary Wolcott and Mercy Lewis.

The Trial of SUSANNA MARTIN, *June* 29, 1692; *as is printed in* Wonders of the Invisible World, *from p.* 114 *to p.* 116.

1. Susanna Martin pleading not guilty to the indictment of witchcraft brought in against her, there were produced the evidences of many persons very sensibly and grievously bewitched, who all complained of the prisoner at the bar, as the person whom they

believed the cause of their miseries. And now, as well as in the other trials, there was an extraordinary endeavour by witchcrafts, with cruel and frequent fits, to hinder the poor sufferers from giving in their complaints; which the court was forced with much patience to obtain, by much waiting and watching for it.

There was now also an account given of what had passed at her first examination before the magistrates; the cast of her eye then striking the afflicted people to the ground, whether they saw that cast or no. There were these among other passages between the magistrates and the examinant:

Magistrate. Pray, what ails these people?

Martin. I don't know.

Mag. But, what do you think ails them?

Martin. I do not desire to spend my judgment upon it.

Mag. Don't you think they are bewitched?

Martin. No, I do not think they are.

Mag. Tell us your thoughts about them, then.

Martin. No, my thoughts are my own when they are in, but when they are out they are another's. Their master——

Mag. Their master! Who do you think is their master?

Martin. If they be dealing in the black art, you may know as well as I.

Mag. Well, what have you done towards this?

Martin. Nothing at all.

Mag. Why, 'tis you or your appearance.

Martin. I can't help it.

Mag. Is it not your master? How comes your appearance to hurt these?

Martin. How do I know? He that appeared in the shape of Samuel, a glorified saint, may appear in anyone's shape.

It was then also noted in her, as in others like her, that if the afflicted went to approach her, they were flung down to the ground; and when she was asked the reason of it, she said, I cannot tell; it may be the devil bears me more malice than another.

The court accounted themselves alarmed by these things to inquire further into the conversation of the prisoner, and see what there might occur to render these accusations further credible. Whereupon John Allen, of Salisbury, testified, that he refusing, because of the weakness of his oxen, to cart some staves at the request of this Martin, she was displeased at it, and said, it had been as good that he had, for his oxen should never do him much more service. Whereupon this deponent said, Dost thou threaten me, thou old witch? I'll throw thee into the brook; which to avoid, she flew over the bridge, and escaped. But as he was going home, one of his oxen tired, so that he was forced to unyoke him that he might get him home. He then put his oxen, with many more, upon Salisbury-beach, where cattle used to get flesh. In a few days, all the oxen upon the beach were found by their tracks to have run unto the mouth of Merrimack-river, and not returned; but the next day they were found come ashore upon Plum-island. They that sought them used all imaginable gentleness; but they would still run away with a violence that seemed wholly diabolical, till they came near the mouth of Merrimack river, when they ran right into the sea, swimming as far as they could be seen. One of them then swam back again, with a swiftness amazing to the beholders, who stood ready to receive him, and help up his tired carcass; but the beast ran furiously up into the island, and from thence through the marshes, up into Newbury-town, and so up into the woods; and after a while was found near Amesbury. So that, of fourteen good oxen, there was only this saved: the rest were all cast up, some in one place, and some in another, drowned.

4. John Atkinson testified, that he exchanged a cow with a son of Susanna Martin, whereat she muttered, and was unwilling he should have it. Going to receive this cow, though he hamstringed her, and haltered her, she of a tame creature grew so mad, that they could scarce get her along. She broke all the ropes that were fastened unto her; and though she was tied fast unto a tree, yet she made her escape, and gave them such further trouble, as they could ascribe to no cause but witchcraft.

5. Bernard Peache testified, that, being in bed, on a Lord's-day night, he heard a scrabbling at the window, whereat he then saw Susanna Martin come in, and jump down upon the floor. She took hold of this deponent's feet, and, drawing his body up into an heap, she lay upon him near two hours; in all which time he could neither speak nor stir. At length, when he could begin to move, he laid hold on her hand, and pulling it up to his mouth, he bit three of her

fingers, as he judged, to the bone; whereupon she went from the chamber down the stairs, out at the door. This deponent thereupon called unto the people of the house to advise them of what passed; and he himself followed her. The people saw her not; but there being a bucket at the left hand of the door, there was a drop of blood on it, and several more drops of blood upon the snow, newly fallen abroad. There was likewise the print of her two feet, just without the threshold; but no more sign of any footing further off.

At another time this deponent was desired by the prisoner to come to husking of corn, at her house; and she said, *If he did not come, it were better that he did.* He went not; but the night following, Susanna Martin, as he judged, and another, came towards him. One of them said, *Here he is;* but he, having a quarterstaff, made a blow at them: the roof of the barn broke his blow; but, following them to the window, he made another blow at them, and struck them down; yet they got up, and got out, and he saw no more of them.

About this time, there was a rumour about the town, that Martin had a broken head; but the deponent could say nothing to that.

The said Peache also testified, the bewitching of cattle to death, upon Martin's discontents.

6. Robert Downer testified, that this prisoner being some years ago prosecuted at court for a witch, he then said unto her, *he believed she was a witch.* Whereat she being dissatisfied, said, *that some she-devil would shortly fetch him away;* which words were heard by others, as well as himself. The night following, as he lay in his bed, there came in at the window, the likeness of a cat, which flew upon him, and took fast hold of his throat, lay on him a considerable while, and almost killed him; at length he remembered what Susanna Martin had threatened the day before, and with much striving he cried out, *Avoid, thou she-devil; in the name of God the Father, the Son, and the Holy Ghost, avoid:* whereupon it left him, leaped on the floor, and flew out at the window.

And there also came in several testimonies, that, before ever Downer spoke a word of this accident, Susanna Martin and her family had related how this Downer had been handled.

7. John Kembal testified, that Susanna Martin, upon a causeless disgust, had threatened him about a certain cow of his, that she should never do him any more good, and it came to pass accordingly; for soon after the cow was found stark dead on the dry

ground, without any distemper to be discerned upon her; upon which he was followed. with a strange death upon more of his cattle; whereof he lost, in one spring, to the value of 30 *l*. But the said John Kembal had a further testimony to give in against the prisoner, which was truly admirable. Being desirous to furnish himself with a dog, he applied himself to buy one of this Martin, who had a bitch with whelps in her house; but she not letting him have his choice, he said he would supply himself then at one Blezdel's. Having marked a puppy which he liked at Blezdel's, he met George Martin, the husband of the prisoner, going by, who asked whether he would not have one of his wife's puppies; and he answered, no. The same day one Edmund Eliot, being at Martin's house, heard George Martin relate where this Kembal had been, and what he had said; whereupon Susanna Martin replied, *If I live I'll give him puppies enough*. Within a few days after this, Kembal coming out of the woods, there arose a little black cloud in the N. W. and Kembal immediately felt a force upon him, which made him not able to avoid running upon the stumps of trees that were before him, although he had a broad, plain cart-way before him; but though he had his axe on his shoulder to endanger him in his falls, he could not forbear going out of his way to tumble over them. When he came below the meeting-house, there appeared to him a little thing like a puppy, of a darkish colour, and it shot backwards and forwards between his legs. He had the courage to use all possible endeavours to cut it with his axe, but he could not hit it; the puppy gave a jump from him, and went, as to him it seemed, into the ground. Going a little further, there appeared unto him a black puppy, somewhat bigger than the first, but as black as a coal. Its motions were quicker than those of his axe. It flew at his belly, and at his throat, so over his shoulders one way, and then over his shoulders another way. His heart now began to fail him, and he thought the dog would have tore his throat out; but he recovered himself and called upon God in his distress, and naming the name of Jesus Christ, it vanished away at once. The deponent spoke not one word of these accidents, for fear of affrighting his wife. But the next morning, Edmund Eliot going into Martin's house, this woman asked him where Kembal was.

He replied, At home, a-bed, for ought he knew. She returned, They say he was frighted last night. Eliot asked, With what? She answered, With puppies. Eliot asked where she heard of it; for he had heard nothing of it. She rejoined, About the town; although Kembal had mentioned the matter to no creature living.

3. William Brown testified, that Heaven having blessed him with a most pious and prudent wife, this wife of his one day met with Susanna Martin; but when she approached just unto her, Martin vanished out of sight, and left her extremely affrighted. After which time the said Martin often appeared unto her, giving her no little trouble; and when she did come, she was visited with birds, that sorely pecked and pricked her; and sometimes a bunch like a pullet's egg would rise on her throat, ready to choke her, till she cried out, *Witch, you shan't choke me!* While this good woman was in this extremity, the church appointed a day of prayer on her behalf; whereupon the trouble ceased; she saw not Martin as formerly; and the church, instead of their fast, gave thanks for her deliverance. But a considerable while after, she being summoned to give in some evidence at the court against this Martin, quickly this Martin came behind her, while she was milking her cow, and said unto her, *For thy defaming me at court, I'll make thee the miserablest creature in the world.* Soon after which, she fell into a strange kind of distemper, and became horribly frantic, and uncapable of any reasonable action; the physicians declaring that her distemper was preternatural, and that some devil had certainly bewitched her; and in that condition she now remained.

9. Sarah Atkinson testified, that Susanna Martin came from Amesbury, to their house at Newbury, in an extraordinary season, when it was not fit for anyone to travel. She came (as she said to Atkinson) all that long way on foot. She bragged and showed how dry she was; nor could it be perceived that so much as the soles of her shoes were wet. Atkinson was amazed at it, and professed that she should herself have been wet up to the knees, if she had then come so far; but Martin replied, *she scorned to be drabbled.* It was noted that this testimony, upon her trial, cast her into a very singular confusion.

10. John Pressy testified, that being one evening very unaccountably bewildered near a field of Martin, and several times as one under an enchantment, returning to the place he had left, at length he saw a marvellous light, about the bigness of an half bushel, near two rods out of the way. He went and struck at it with a stick, and laid it on with all his might. He gave it near forty blows, and felt it a palpable substance. But, going from it, his heels were struck up,

and he was laid with his back on the ground; sliding, as he thought, into a pit; from whence he recovered, by taking hold on a bush; although afterwards no could find no such pit in the place. Having after his recovery gone five or six rods, he saw Susanna Martin standing on his left hand, as the light had done before; but they changed no words with one another. He could scarce find his house in his return; but at length he got home, extremely affrighted. The next day it was upon inquiry understood, that Martin was in a miserable condition, by pains and hurts that were upon her.

It was further testified by this deponent, that after he had given in some evidence against Susanna Martin many years ago, she gave him foul words about it, and said, *he should never prosper; more particularly, that he should never have more than two cows: that though he were ever so likely to have more, yet he should never have them;* and, that, from that very day to this, namely for twenty years together, he could never exceed that number, but some strange thing or other still prevented his having any more.

11. Jarvis Ring testified, that about seven years ago he was oftentimes grievously oppressed in the night, but saw not who troubled him, until at length he, lying perfectly awake, plainly saw Susanna Martin approach him: she came to him, and forcibly bit him by the finger; so that the print of the bite is now, so long after, to be seen upon him.

12. But, besides all these evidences, there was a most wonderful account of one Joseph Ring produced on this occasion. This man has been strangely carried-about by dæmons, from one witch-meeting to another, for near two years together; and for one quarter of this time they made him and kept him dumb, though he is now again able to speak. There was one T. H. who, having, as 'tis judged, a design of engaging this Joseph Ring in a snare of devilism, contrived a wile to bring this Ring two shillings in debt unto him. Afterwards this poor man would be visited with unknown shapes, and this T.H. sometimes among them: which would force him away with them, unto unknown places, where he saw meetings, feasting, dancings; and after his return, wherein they hurried him along through the air, he gave demonstrations to the neighbours, that he had been so transported. When he was brought unto these hellish meetings, one of the first things they still did unto him was, to give him a knock on the back, whereupon he was ever, as if bound with chains, uncapable of stirring out of the place, till they should release him. He related,

that there often came to him a man, who presented him a book, whereto he would have him set his hand; promising him that he should then have even what he would; and presenting him with all the delectable things, persons and places that he could imagine; but he refusing to subscribe, the business would end with dreadful shapes, noises and screeches, which almost scared him out of his wits. Once, with a book, there was a pen offered him, and an inkhorn, with liquor in it, that seemed like blood; but he never touched it.

This man did now affirm, that he saw the prisoner at several of these hellish rendezvous.

Note. This woman was one of the most impudent, scurrilous, wicked creatures, in the world: and she now, throughout her whole trial, discovered herself to be such an one. Yet when she was asked what she had to say for herself, her chief plea was, that she had led a most virtuous and holy life.

The Indictment of Elizabeth How.

Essex ss. *Anno Regni Regis & Reginæ: Willielmi & Mariæ, nunc Angliæ, &c. quarto.*———

The jurors for our sovereign lord and lady the king and queen present, that Elizabeth How, wife of James How, of Ipswich, in the county of Essex, the thirty-first day of May, in the fourth year of the reign of our sovereign lord and lady William and Mary, by the grace of God, of England, Scotland, France and Ireland, king and queen, defenders of the faith, &c. and divers other days and times, as well before as after, certain detestable arts, called witchcrafts and sorceries, wickedly and feloniously hath used, practised and exercised, at and within the township of Salem, in the county of Essex, aforesaid, in, upon and against one Mary Wolcott, of Salem Village, in the county aforesaid, single woman; by which said wicked arts the said Mary Wolcott, the said thirty-first day of May, in the fourth year abovesaid, and divers other days and times, as well before as after, was and is tortured, afflicted, pined, consumed, wasted and tormented; and also for sundry other acts of witchcrafts, by said Elizabeth How committed and done before and since that time, against the peace of our sovereign lord and lady, the king and queen, and against the form of the statute in that case made and provided.

Witnesses—*Mary Wolcott, Ann Putman, Abigail Williams, Samuel Pearly, and his wife Ruth, Joseph Andrews, and wife Sarah, John Sherrin, Joseph Safford, Francis Lane, Lydia Foster, Isaac Cummins,* junior.

There was also a second indictment for afflicting *Mercy Lewis*. Witnesses——Mercy Lewis, Mary Wolcott, Ann Putman, Samuel Pearly and wife, Joseph Andrews and wife, John Sherrin, Joseph Safford, Francis Lane, Lydia Foster.

The Trial of ELIZABETH HOW, *June* 30, 1692; *as is printed in Wonders of the Invisible World, from p.* 126 *to p.* 132, *inclusively.*

1. Elizabeth How, pleading not guilty to the indictment of witchcrafts then charged upon her, the court, according to the usual proceeding of the courts in England in such cases, began with hearing the deposition of several afflicted people, who were grievously tormented by sensible and evident witchcrafts, and all complained of the prisoner as the cause of their trouble. It was also found that the sufferers were not able to bear her look; as likewise that in their greatest swoons they distinguished her touch from other people's, being thereby raised out of them. And there was other testimony of people, to whom the shape of this How gave trouble nine or ten years ago.

2. It has been a most usual thing for the bewitched persons, at the same time that the spectres representing the witches troubled them, to be visited with apparitions of ghosts, pretending to have been murdered by the witches then represented, and sometimes the confessions of the witches afterwards acknowledged those very murders, which these apparitions charged upon them, although they had never heard what information had, been given by the sufferers. There were such apparitions of ghosts testified by some of the present sufferers, and the ghosts affirmed that this How had murdered them: which things were feared, but not proved.

3. This How had made some attempts of joining to the church at Ipswich, several years ago; but she was denied an admission into that holy society, partly through a suspicion of witchcraft, then urged against her. And there now came in testimony of preternatural mischiefs presently befalling some that had been instrumental to debar her from the communion whereupon she was intruding.

4. There was a particular deposition' of Joseph Safford, that his wife had conceived an extreme aversion to this How, on the reports

of her witchcrafts; but How one day taking her by the hand, and saying, *I believe you are not ignorant of the great scandal that I lie under by an evil report raised upon me,* she immediately, unreasonably, and unpersuadably, even like one enchanted, began to take this woman's part., How being soon after propounded, as desiring an admission to the table of the Lord, some of the pious brethren were unsatisfied about her. The elders appointed a meeting, to hear matters objected against her; and no arguments in the world could hinder this goodwife Safford from going to the lecture. She did indeed promise, with much ado, that she would not go to the church-meeting; yet she could not refrain going thither also. How's affairs were so canvassed, that she came off rather guilty, than cleared; nevertheless goodwife Safford could not forbear taking her by the hand, and saying, *Though you are condemned before men, you are justified before God.* She was quickly taken in a very strange manner; frantic, raving, raging, and crying out, *Goody How must come into the church; she is a precious saint; and though she be condemned before men, she is justified before God.* So she continued for the space of two or three hours, and then fell into a trance. But, coming to herself, she cried out, *Ha! I was mistaken!* afterwards again repeated, *Ha! I was mistaken!* Being asked by a stander-by wherein, she replied, *I thought goody How had been a precious saint of God, but now I see she is a witch: she has bewitched me and my child, and we shall never be well till there be testimony for her, that she may be taken into the church.*

And How said, afterwards, *That she was very sorry to see Safford at the church-meeting mentioned.* Safford, after this, *declared herself to be afflicted by the shape of How, and that front that shape she endured many miseries.*

5. John How, brother to the husband of the prisoner, testified, that he refusing to accompany the prisoner unto her examination as was by her desired, immediately some of his cattle were bewitched to death, leaping three or four feet high, turning about, squeaking, falling and dying at once; and going to cut off an ear, for an use that might as well perhaps have been omitted, the hand wherein he held his knife was taken very numb; and so it remained, and full of pain, for several days, being not well at this very time. And he suspected this prisoner for the author of it.

6. Nehemiah Abbot testified, that unusual and mischievous accidents would befall his cattle, whenever he had any difference with this prisoner. Once particularly she wished his ox choked; and

within a little while, that ox was choked with a turnip in his throat. At another time, refusing to lend his horse at the request of her daughter, the horse was in a preternatural manner abused. And several other odd things of that kind were testified.

7. There came in testimony, that one goodwife Sherwin, upon some difference with How, was bewitched, and that she died charging this How of having an hand in her death; and that other people had their barrels of drink unaccountably mischiefed, spoiled, and spilt, upon their displeasing her.

The things in themselves were trivial; but there being such a course of them, it made them the more to be considered. Among others, Martha Wood gave her testimony, that a little after her father had been employed in gathering an account of this How's conversation, they once and again lost great quantities of drink out of their vessels, in such a manner as they could ascribe to nothing but witchcraft; as also that How giving her some apples, when she had eaten of them she was taken with a very strange kind of a maze, insomuch that she knew not what she said or did.

8. There was likewise a cluster of depositions, that one Isaac Cummins refusing to lend his mare to the husband of this How, the mare was within a day or two taken in a strange condition. The beast seemed much abused, being bruised, as if she had been running over the rocks, and marked where the bridle went, as if burnt with a red hot bridle. Moreover, one using a pipe of tobacco for the cure of the beast, a blue flame issued out of her, took hold of her hair, and not only spread and burnt on her, but it also flew upwards towards the roof of the barn, and had like to have set the barn on fire. And the mare died very suddenly.

9. Timothy Pearly and his wife testified, not only that unaccountable mischiefs befel their cattle upon their having differences with this prisoner, but also that they had a daughter destroyed by witchcrafts; which daughter still charged How as the cause of her affliction; and it was noted that she would be struck down whenever How was spoken of. She was often endeavoured to be thrown into the fire, and into the water, in her strange fits; though her father had corrected her for charging How with bewitching her, yet (as was testified by others also) she said she was sure of it, and must die standing to it. Accordingly she charged How to the very death; and said, *Though How could afflict and torment her body, yet she*

could not hurt her soul, and that the truth of this matter would appear when she should be dead and gone.

10. Francis Lane testified, that being hired by the husband of this How to get him a parcel of posts and rails, this Lane hired John Pearly to assist him. This prisoner then told Lane, that she believed the posts and rails would not do, because John Pearly helped him; but that if he had gotten them alone without John Pearly's help, they might have done well enough. When James Hew came to receive his posts and rails of Lane, How taking them up by the ends, they, though good and sound, yet unaccountably broke off, so that Lane was forced to get thirty or forty more. And this prisoner being informed of it, she said, she told him so before, because Pearly helped about them.

11. Afterwards there came in the confessions of several other (penitent) witches, which affirmed this How to be one of those who with them had been baptized by the devil in the river, at Newbury-falls; before which, he made them there kneel down by the brink of the river, and worship him.

The Indictment of Martha Carrier.

Essex ss.   *Anno Regni Regis & Reginæ: Willielmi & Mariæ, nunc Angliæ, &c. quarto.*————

The jurors for our sovereign lord and lady the king and queen present, that Martha Carrier, wife of Thomas Carrier, of Andover, in the county of Essex, husbandman, the thirty-first day of May, in the fourth year of the reign of our sovereign lord and lady William and Mary, by the grace of God, of England, Scotland, France and Ireland, king and queen, defenders of the faith, &c, and divers other days and times, as well before as after, certain detestable arts, called witchcrafts and sorceries, wickedly and feloniously hath used, practised and exercised, at and within the township of Salem, in the county of Essex, aforesaid, in, upon and against one Mary Wolcott, of Salem Village, in the county of Essex, single woman; by which said wicked arts the said Mary Wolcott, the thirty-first day of May, in the fourth year aforesaid, and at divers other days and times, as well before as after, was and is tortured, afflicted, pined, consumed, wasted and tormented; against the peace of our sovereign lord and lady, William and Mary, king and queen of England, their crown and dignity, and against the form of the statute, in that case made and provided.

Witnesses—*Mary Wolcott, Elizabeth Hubbard, Ann Putman.*

There was also a second indictment for afflicting *Elizabeth Hubbard*, by witchcraft. Witnesses—Elizabeth Hubbard, Mary Wolcott, Ann Putman, Mary Warren.

The Trial of MARTHA CARRIER, *August* 2, 1692; *as may be seen in Wonders of the Invisible World, from p.* 132, *to p.* 138.

1. Martha Carrier was indicted for the bewitching of certain persons, according to the form usual in such cases. pleading not guilty to her indictment, there were first brought in a considerable number of the bewitched persons; who not only made the court sensible of an horrid witchcraft committed upon them, but also deposed, that it was Martha Carrier, or her shape, that grievously tormented them, by biting, pricking, pinching and choking them. It was further deposed, that while this Carrier was on her examination before the magistrates, the poor people were so tortured, that every one expected their death upon the very spot; but that upon the binding of Carrier they were eased. Moreover the looks of Carrier then laid the afflicted people for dead; and her touch, if her eyes at the same time were off them, raised them again, which things were also now seen upon her trial. And it was testified that upon the mention of some having their necks twisted almost round by the shape of this Carrier, she replied, *Its no matter, though their necks had been twisted quite off.*

2. Before the trial of this prisoner, several of her own children had frankly and fully confessed, not only that they were witches themselves, but that their mother had made them so. This confession they made with great shows of repentance, and with much demonstration of truth. They related place, time and occasion; they gave an account of journeys, meetings and mischiefs by them performed, and were very credible in what they said. Nevertheless, this evidence was not produced against the prisoner at the bar, in as much as there was other evidence enough to proceed upon.

3. Benjamin Abbot gave in his testimony, that, last March was a twelve-month, this Carrier was very angry with him, upon laying out some land near her husband's. Her expressions in this anger were, that she would stick as close to Abbot as the bark stuck to the tree;

and that he should repent of it before seven years came to an end, so as doctor Prescot should never cure him. These words were heard by others besides Abbot himself, who also heard her say, she would hold his nose as close to the grindstone as ever it was held since his name was Abbot. Presently after this he was taken with a swelling in his foot, and then with a pain in his side, and exceedingly tormented. It bred a sore, which was lanced by Dr. Prescot, and several gallons of corruption ran out of it. For six weeks it continued very bad; and then another sore bred in his groin, which was also lanced by Dr. Prescot. Another sore bred in his groin, which was likewise cut, and put him to very great misery. He was brought to death's door, and so remained until Carrier was taken and carried away by the constable; from which every day he began to mend, and so grew better every day, and is well ever since.

Sarah Abbot also, his wife, testified, that her husband was not only all this while afflicted in his body, but also that strange, extraordinary and unaccountable calamities befel his cattle; their death being such as they could guess no natural reason for.

4. Allin Toothaker testified, that Richard, the son of Martha Carrier, having some difference with him, pulled him down by the hair of the head; when he rose again, he was going to strike at Richard Carrier, but fell down flat on his back to the ground, and had not power to stir hand or foot, until he told Carrier he yielded; and then he saw the shape of Martha Carrier go off his breast.

This Toothaker had received a wound in the wars; and he now testified, that Martha Carrier told him, he should never be cured. Just before the apprehending of Carrier, he could thrust a knitting-needle into his wound four inches deep; but presently after her being seized, he was thoroughly healed.

He further testified, that when Carrier and he sometimes were at variance, she would clap her hands at him, and say, he should get nothing by it. Whereupon he several times lost his cattle by strange deaths, whereof no natural causes could be given.

5. John Roger also testified, that, upon the threatening words of this malicious Carrier, his cattle would be strangely bewitched; as was more particularly then described.

6, Samuel Preston testified, that about two years ago, having some difference with Martha Carrier, he lost a cow in a strange, preternatural, unusual manner; and about a month after this, the said

Carrier having again some difference with him, she told him he had lately lost a cow, and it should not be long before he lost another; which accordingly came to pass; for he had a thriving and well-kept cow, which without any known cause quickly fell down and died.

7. Phebe Chandler testified, that about a fortnight before the apprehension of Martha Carrier, on a Lord's-day, while the psalm was singing in the church, this Carrier then took her by the shoulder, and shaking her, asked her where she lived: she made her no answer, although, as Carrier lived next door to her father's house, she could not in reason but know who she was. Quickly after this, as she was at several times crossing the fields, she heard a voice that she took to be Martha Carrier's, and it seemed as if it were over her head. The voice told her, *she should within two or three days be poisoned:* accordingly, within such a little time, one half of her right hand became greatly swollen and very painful, as also part of her face; whereof she can give no account how it came. It continued very bad for some days; and several times since she has had a great pain in her breast; and been so seized on her legs, that she has hardly been able to go. She added, that lately going well to the house of God, Richard, the son of Martha Carrier, looked very earnestly upon her, and immediately her hand, which has formerly been poisoned, as is abovesaid, began to pain her greatly, and she had a strange burning at her stomach; but was then struck deaf, so that she could not hear any of the prayer, or singing, till the two or three last words of the psalm.

8, One Foster, who confessed her own share in the witchcraft, for which the prisoner stood indicted, affirmed, that she had seen the prisoner at some of their witch-meetings, and that it was this Currier who persuaded her to be a witch. She confessed that the devil carried them on a pole to a witch-meeting; but the pole broke, and she hanging about Carrier's neck, they both fell down, and she then received an hurt by the fall, whereof she was not at this very time recovered.

9. One Lacy, who likewise confessed her share in this witchcraft, now testified; that she and the prisoner were once bodily present at a witch-meeting in Salem Village, and that she knew the prisoner to be a witch, and to have been at a diabolical sacrament, and that the prisoner was the undoing of her and her children, by enticing them into the snare of the devil.

10, Another Lacy, who also confessed her share in this witchcraft, now testified, that the prisoner was at the witch-meeting in Salem Village, where they had bread and wine administered to them.

11. In the time of this prisoner's trial, one Susanna Shelden, in open court, had her hands unaccountably tied together with a wheel-band so fast that without cutting it could not be loosened. It was done by a spectre; and the sufferer affirmed it was the prisoner's.

Memorandum. This *rampant hag*, Martha Carrier, was the person of whom the confessions of the witches, and of her own children among the rest, agreed that the devil had promised her she should be queen of hell.

Thus far the account given in *Wonders of the Invisible World*; in which (setting aside such words as these, in the trial of G.B. viz. "They, i.e. the witnesses, were enough to fix the character of a witch upon him"—in the trial of Bishop, these words, "But there was no need of them," i.e. of further testimony—in the trial of How, where it is said, "And there came in testimony of preternatural mischiefs presently befalling some that had been instrumental to debar her from the communion, whereupon she was intruding,") Martin is called one of the most impudent, scurrilous, wicked creatures in the world; in his account of Martha Carrier, he is pleased to call her a *rampant hag*, &c.

These expressions, as they manifest that he wrote more like an advocate than an historian, so also that those that were his employers were not mistaken in their choice of him for that work, however he may have missed it in other things: as, in his owning (in the trial of G.B.) that the testimony of the bewitched, and confessors, was not enough against the accused; for it is known that not only in New-England such evidence has been taken for sufficient, but also in England, as himself there owns, and , will also hold true of Scotland, &c. they having proceeded upon such evidence, to the taking away of the lives of many. To assert that this is not enough, is to tell the world that such executions were but so many bloody murders; which surely was not his intent to say.

His telling that the court began to think that Burroughs stept aside to put on invisibility, is a rendering them so mean philosophers, and such weak christians, as to be fit to be imposed upon by any silly pretender.

His calling the evidence against How trivial, and others against Burroughs he accounts no part of his conviction, and that of lifting a gun with one finger, its being not made use of as evidence, renders the whole but the more perplext. (Not to mention the many mistakes therein contained.)

Yet all this (and more that might have been hinted at) does not hinder, but that his account of the manner of trials of those for witchcraft is as faithfully related as any trials of that kind, that were ever yet made public; and it may also be reasonably thought that there was as careful a scrutiny, and as unquestioned evidences improved, as had been formerly used in the trials of others, for such crimes, in other places. Though indeed a second part might be very useful, to set forth which was the evidence convictive in these trials; for it is not supposed that romantic or ridiculous stories should have any influence; such as biting a spectre's finger so that the blood flowed out; or such as Shattock's story of twelve years standing, which yet was presently eighteen years or more, and yet a man of so excellent memory as to be able to recall a small difference his wife had with another woman when eighteen years were past.

As it is not to be supposed that such as these could influence any judge or jury, so not unkindness to relations, or God's having given to one man more strength than to some others; the oversetting of carts, or the death of cattle; nor yet excrescences (called teats) nor little bits of rags tied together (called poppets;) much less any person's illness, or having their clothes rent, when a spectre has been well hanged; much less the burning the mare's fart, mentioned in the trial of How.

None of these being in the least capable of proving the indictment, the supposed criminals were indicted for afflicting, &c. such and such particular persons by witchcraft, to which none of these evidences have one word to say; and the afflicted and confessors being declared not enough, the matter needs yet further explaining.

But to proceed. The general court having set and enacted laws, particularly one against witchcraft, assigning the penalty of death to any that shall feed, reward or employ, &c. evil spirits, though it has not yet been explained what is intended thereby, or what it is to feed, reward or employ devils, &c. yet some of the legislators have given this, instead of an explanation, that they had therein but copied the law of another country.

January 3. By virtue of an act of the general court, the first superior court was held at Salem, for the country of Essex; the judges appointed were mr. William Stoughton (the lieutenant governor) Thomas Danforth, John Richards, Wait Winthrop, and Samuel Sewall, esquires; where ignoramus was found upon the several bills of indictment against thirty, and *billa vera* against twenty-six more; of all these, three only were found guilty by the jury upon trial, two of which were (as appears by their behaviour) the most senseless and ignorant creatures that could be found; besides which, it does not appear what came in against those more than against the rest that were acquitted.

The third was the wife of Wardwell, who was one of the twenty executed, and it seems they had both confessed themselves guilty; but he, retracting his said confession, was tried and executed. It is supposed that this woman, fearing her husband's fate, was not so stiff in her denials of her former confession, such as it was. These three received sentence of death.

At these trials some of the jury made inquiry of the court, what account they ought to make of the spectre evidence; and received for answer, *As much as of chips in wort.*

January 31, 1692–3. The superior court began at Charlestown, for the county of Middlesex, mr. Stoughton, mr. Danforth, mr. Winthrop and mr. Sewall, judges; where several had *ignoramus* returned upon their bills of indictment, and *billa vera* upon others.

In the time the court sat, word was brought in, that a reprieve was sent to Salem, and had prevented the execution of seven of those that were there condemned; which so moved the chief judge, that he said to this effect, *We were in a way to have cleared the land of these, &c. Who it is obstructs the course of justice, I know not; the Lord be merciful to the country;* and so went off the bench, and came no more that court.

The most remarkable of the trials, was of Sarah Daston. She was a woman of about seventy or eighty years of age. To usher her in to her trial, a report went before, that if there were a witch in the world she was one, as having been so accounted of for twenty or thirty years; which drew many people from Boston, &c. to hear her trial. There were a multitude of witnesses produced against her; but what testimony they gave in seemed wholly foreign, as of accidents, illness, &c. befalling them, or theirs, after some quarrel; what these testified was much of it of actions said to be done twenty years before that time. The spectre evidence was not made use of in these trials, so that the jury soon brought her in not guilty. Her daughter and granddaughter, and the rest that were then tried, were also acquitted. After she was cleared, judge Danforth admonished her in these words, *Woman, woman, repent; there are shrewd things come in against you.* She was remanded to prison for her fees, and there in a short time expired. One of Boston, that had been at the trial of Daston, being the same evening in company with one of the judges in a public place, acquainted him that some, that had been both at the trials at Salem and at this at Charlestown,. had asserted, *That there was more evidence against the said Daston than against any at Salem;* to which the said judge conceded, saying, *that it was so.* It was replied by that person, *That he dare give it under his hand, that there was not enough come in against her to bear a just reproof.*

April 25, 1693. The first superior court was held at Boston, for the county of Suffolk; the judges were the lieutenant Governor, mr. Danforth, mr. Richards, and mr. Sewall, esquires; where (besides the acquitting mr. John Aldin by proclamation) the most remarkable was, what related to Mary Watkins, who had been a servant, and lived about seven miles from Boston, having formerly accused her mistress of witchcraft, and was supposed to be distracted; she was threatened, if she persisted in such accusations, to be punished. This, with the necessary care to recover her health, had that good effect, that she not only had her health restored, but also wholly acquitted her mistress of any such crimes, and continued in health till the return of the year, and then again falling into melancholy humours, she was found strangling herself; her life being hereby prolonged, she immediately accused herself of being a witch; was carried before a magistrate, and committed. At this court a bill of indictment was brought to the grand jury against her, and her confession upon her examination given in as evidence; but these, not wholly satisfied herewith, sent for her, who gave such account of herself, that they (after they had returned into the court to ask some questions) twelve of them agreed to find *ignoramus*, but the court was pleased to send them out again, who again at coming in returned it as before. She was continued for some time in prison, &c. and at length was sold to Virginia. About this time the prisoners in all the prisons were released.

To omit here the mentioning of several wenches in Boston, &c. who pretended to be afflicted, and accused several, the ministers often visiting them, and praying with them, concerning whose affliction narratives are in being, in manuscript; not only these, but the generality of those accusers, may have since convinced the ministers, by their vicious courses, that they might err in extending too much charity to them.

The conclusion of the whole in the Massachusetts colony was, sir William Phips, governor, being called home, before he went he pardoned such as had been condemned, for which they gave about thirty shillings each to the king's attorney.

In August, 1697, the superior court sat at Hartford, in the colony of Connecticut, where one mistress Benom was tried for witchcraft. She had been accused by some children that pretended to the spectral sight; they searched her several times for teats; they tried the experiment of casting her into the water, and after this she was excommunicated by the minister of Wallinsford. Upon her trial nothing material appeared against her, save spectre evidence. She was acquitted, as also her daughter, a girl of twelve or thirteen years old, who had been likewise accused; but upon renewed complaints against them, they both flew into New-York government. Before this, the government issued forth the following proclamation:

By the honourable the lieutenant governor, council and assembly of his majesty's province of the Massachusetts-bay, in general court assembled.

Whereas the anger of God is not yet turned away, but his hand is still stretched out against his people in manifold judgments, particularly in drawing out to such a length the troubles of Europe, by a perplexing war; and more especially respecting ourselves in this province, in that God is pleased still to go on in diminishing our substance, cutting short our harvest, blasting our most promising undertakings more ways than one, unsettling us, and by his more immediate hand snatching away many out of our embraces by sudden and violent deaths, even at this time when the sword is devouring so many both at home and abroad, and that after many days of public and solemn addressing him: and although, considering the many sins prevailing in the midst of us, we cannot but wonder at the patience and mercy moderating these rebukes, yet we cannot but also fear that there is something still wanting to accompany our supplications; and doubtless there are some particular sins, which

God is angry with our Israel for, that have not been duly seen and resented by us, about which God expects to be sought, if ever he turn again our captivity:

Wherefore it is commanded and appointed, that Thursday, the fourteenth of January next, be observed as a day of prayer, with fasting, throughout this province; strictly forbidding all servile labour thereon; that so all God's people may offer up fervent supplications unto him, for the preservation and prosperity of his majesty's royal person and government, and success to attend his affairs both at home and abroad; that all iniquity may be put away, which hath stirred God's holy jealousy against this land; that he would shew us what we know not, and help us wherein we have done amiss to do so no more; and especially that whatever mistakes on either hand have been fallen into, either by the body of this people, or any orders of men, referring to the late tragedy, raised among us by satan and his instruments, through the awful judgment of God, he would humble us therefor, and pardon all the errors of his servants and people, that desire to love his name; that he would remove the rod of the wicked from off the lot of the righteous; that he would bring in the American heathen, and cause them to hear and obey his voice.

Given at Boston, December 17, 1696, in the eighth year his Majesty's reign.
ISAAC ADDINGTON, *Secretary.*

Upon the day of the fast, in the full assembly at the south meeting-house in Boston, one of the honourable judges, who had sat in judicature in Salem, delivered in a paper, and while it was in reading stood up; but the copy being not to be obtained at present, it can only be reported by memory to this effect, viz. It was to desire the prayers of God's people for him and his; and that God having visited his family, &c. he was apprehensive that he might have fallen into some errors in the matters at Salem, and pray that the guilt of such miscarriages may not be imputed either to the country in general, or to him or his family in particular.

Some, that had been of several juries, have given forth a paper, signed with their own hands, in these words:

"We, whose names are under written, being in the year 1692 called to serve as jurors in court at Salem on trial of many, who were by Some suspected guilty of doing acts of witchcraft upon the bodies of sundry persons:

"We confess that we ourselves were not capable to understand, nor able to withstand, the mysterious delusions of the powers of darkness, and prince of the air; but were, for want of knowledge in ourselves, and better information from others, prevailed with to take up with such evidence against the accused, as, on further consideration and better information, we justly fear was insufficient for the touching the lives, of any, (*Deut.* xvii. 6) whereby we fear we have been instrumental, with others, though ignorantly and unwittingly, to bring upon ourselves and this people of the Lord the guilt of innocent blood; which sin the Lord saith, in scripture, he would not pardon, (*2 Kings*, xxiv. 4) that is, we suppose, in regard of his temporal judgments. We do therefore hereby signify to all in general (and to the surviving sufferers in special) our deep sense of, and sorrow for, our errors, in acting on such evidence to the condemning of any person; and do hereby declare, that we justly fear that we were sadly deluded and mistaken; for which we are much disquieted and distressed in our minds; and do therefore humbly beg forgiveness, first of God for Christ's sake, for this our error; and pray that God would not impute the guilt of it to ourselves, nor others; and we also pray that we may be considered candidly, and aright, by the living sufferers, as being then under the power of a strong and general delusion, utterly unacquainted with, and not experienced in, matters of that nature.

"We do heartily ask forgiveness of you all, whom we have justly offended; and do declare, according to our present minds, we would none of us do such things again on such grounds for the whole world; praying you to accept of this in way of satisfaction for our offence, and that you would bless the inheritance of the Lord, that he may be entreated for the land.

Foreman,	*Thomas Fisk*,	*Th. Pearly*, sen.
	William Fisk,	*John Peabody*,
	John Bacheler,	*Thomas Perkins*,
	Thomas Fisk, jun.	*Samuel Sayer*,
	John Dane,	*Andrew Eliot*.
	Joseph Evelith,	*A. Herrick*, sen."

POSTSCRIPT.

SINCE making the foregoing collections of letters, to the rev. mr. Cotton Mather, and others, &c. (which as yet remain unanswered) a book is come to hand intitled, "THE LIFE OF SIR WILLIAM PHIPS," printed in London, 1697: which book, though it bears not the author's name, yet the style, manner and matter are such, that, were there no other demonstration or token to know him by, it were no witchcraft to determine that the said mr. Cotton Mather is the author of it. But that he, who has *encountered enchantments*, and gone through the *Wonders of the Invisible World*, and *discovered the devil*—that he should step aside into a remote country to put on invisibility, though the reason of this be not so manifest, yet it may be thought to be to gratify some peculiar fancies. And why may not this be one, that he might with the better grace extol the actions of Mr. Increase Mather, as agent in England, or as president of Harvard college, not forgetting his own? As to sir William, it will be generally acknowledged, that notwithstanding the meanness of his parentage and education, he attained to be master of a ship, and that he had the good hap to find a Spanish wreck, not only sufficient to repair his fortunes, but, to raise him to a considerable figure; which king James so far assisted, as to make him a knight; and that after this, in the reign of his present majesty, he took up with those of the agents, that were for accepting the new charter, whereby himself became governor.

It is not doubted, but that he aimed at the good of the people; and great pity it is that his government was so sullied (for want of better information and advice from those whose duty it was to have given it) by that hobgoblin monster, witchcraft, whereby this country was nightmared, and harassed, at such a rate as is not easily imagined.

POSTSCRIPT.

After which, some complaints going to England about mal-administration, in the least matters comparatively, yet were such, that he was called home to give account thereof, where he soon after expired, so finishing his life and government together. Death having thus drawn the curtain, forbidding any further scene, it might have been prudent to let his dust remain without disturbance. But the said book endeavouring to raise a statue to him, i.e. to ascribe to him such achievements as either were never performed by him, or else unduly aggravated, this has opened the mouth, both of friends and enemies, to recount the mistakes in the said book; as also those miscarriages wherewith sir William was chargeable; such as, had it not been for this book would have been buried with him.

In page 3, search is made over the world, to whom to compare him in his advancement; and most unhappily Pizarro is pitched upon, as a match for him; who was a bastard, dropt in a church-porch, put to suck a sow, and, being grown, ran away, and shipt himself for America; there so prospered, as to command an army; and therewith did mighty things, particularly took Atabalipa, one of the kings of Peru, prisoner; and, having received for his ransom, in gold and silver, to the value of ten millions, perfidiously put him to death; and was the death of no man knows how many thousands of innocents, and is certainly one of the worst that could have been pitched upon for such comparison. Though this, together with the rhetorical flourishes and affected strains therein, are instances of the author's variety of learning; for which he is recommended by these three venerable persons in the entrance to the said book; yet the integrity, prudence and veracity thereof are not so manifestly to be seen. Passing over a multitude of misrepresentations that are therein, relating to the acts of sir William, as not designing to rake in the grave of the dead, who is it can see the veracity of those words? p. 40. "He lay within pistol-shot of the enemy's cannon, and beat them from thence, and much battered the town, having his ship shot through in an hundred places, with four and twenty pounders;" when, in the judgment of those present, they were not nearer to the enemy than about half or three quarters of a mile; that there might be in all about seven shot that struck the hull of the vessel, none of them known to be bigger than 18 pounders, the enemy having but one gun that would carry an 18 pound ball.

It were a folly, after such assertions, to take any notice of this bedecked statue, when there was so much the less need of erecting

POSTSCRIPT.

one (as is asserted p. 108) having already been done so well, that even this author himself despairs of doing it better; and that by a man of such diffused and embalmed a reputation, as that his commendations are asserted to be enough to immortalize the reputation of sir William, or whomsoever else he should please to bestow them upon, viz. that reverend person who was the president of the only university then in the English America, p. 109. Which by the way is a much fairer statue, in honour of the president of the university, than that erected for sir William.

For, notwithstanding all this noise, of erecting statues, and the great danger in plucking them down, &c. yet, in p. 89, it is said that even sir William shewed choler enough, leaving it open for others thereby to understand that he was wholly given over to passion and choler. And, in p. 92, it is said he did not affect any mighty shew of devotion. These expressions, with others, may prevail with the unbiassed reader to think that these builders of statues had some further design in it, than to blazon the achievements of sir William Phips, viz. to set forth mr. I. Mather's negotiation in England, his procuring the new charter and sir William to be governor, and himself established president of the college, are the things principally driven at in the book.

Another principal thing is, to set forth the supposed witchcrafts in New-England, and how well Mr. Mather the younger therein acquitted himself.

As to the new charter, for the right understanding that affair, it will be needful to say, that the people that afterwards settled in NewEngland, being about to leave their native soil, God to seek (as the providence of God should direct them) a settlement in remote regions, wherein they might best secure their civil and religious interests, before they entered upon this, (considering it might be needful on many accounts for their future well-being, they obtained a charter to be in the nature of a prime agreement, setting forth the sovereign's prerogative, and the people's privileges; in the enjoyment whereof they long continued, after having purchased the title to their lands of the natives of their country, and settled themselves therein, without any charge to the crown.

That clause in their charter for this country, viz. "Provided that no other christian prince be prepossessed of it," being a tacit acknowledgment, that before settlement, no one christian prince had any right thereto more than another. During this time of New

POSTSCRIPT.

England's prosperity, the government here were very sparing of granting freedoms, except to such as were so and so qualified: whereby the number of non freemen being much increased, they were very uneasy, by their being shut out from any share in the government, or having any votes for their representatives, &c. It rendered many of them ready to join with such as were undermining the government; not duly considering that it had been far more safe to have endeavoured to prevail with the legislators for an enlargement.

So that it will not be wondered at, that in the latter end of the reign of King Charles Il, and of king James, (when most of the charters in England were vacated) this was *quo warranto'd*, and finally judgment entered up against it, and the country was put into such a form of government as was most agreeable to those times, viz. a legislative power was lodged in the governor (or president) and some few appointed to be of his council, without any regard therein either to the laws of England, or those formerly of this colony: thus rendering the circumstances of this country beyond comparison worse than those of any corporation in England; the people of those corporations being acknowledged still to have a right to *magna charta*, when their particular charters were made void; but here, when *magna charta* has been pleaded, the people have been answered, that they must not expect that *magna charta* would follow them to the end of the world; not only their estates, but their lives, being thereby rendered wholly precarious. And Judge Palmer has set forth in print, that the king has power to grant such a commission over his people.

It is not hard to imagine, that under such a commission, not only the people were liable to be oppressed by taxes, but also by confiscations, and seizing of lands, unless patents were purchased at excessive prices) with many other exorbitant innovations.

The first that accepted this commission was mr. Dudley, a gentleman born in this country, who did but prepare the way for sir Edmond Andros; in whose time things bad grown to such extremities, not only here, but in England, as rendered the succeeding revolution absolutely necessary; the revolution here being no other than an acting according to the precedent given by England.

During the time of sir Edmond's government, mr. Increase Mather, teacher of the north church in Boston, having undergone some trouble by fobb-actions laid upon him, &c. (though with some

POSTSCRIPT.

difficulty) he made his escape, and got passage for England, being therein assisted by some particular friends; where being arrived, he applied himself to king James for redress of those evils the country then groaned under; and meeting with a seeming kind reception, and some promises, it was as much as might at that time be reasonably expected.

Upon the day of the revolution here, though the greatest part of the people were for reassuming their ancient government, pursuant to his royal highness's proclamation, yet matters were so clogged, that the people were dismissed without it, who did not in the least mistrust but that those, who were put out of the government by mr. Dudley, would reassume; mr. Bradstreet, who had been then governor, being heard to say that evening, when returned home, that had not he thought they would have reassumed, he would not have stirred out of his house that day. But after this, some that were driving at other matters, had opportunities by threats and other ways not only to prevail with that good old gentleman, but with the rest of the government, wholly to decline it; which some few observing, they took the opportunity to call themselves a committee of safety, and so undertook to govern such as would be governed by them.

It has been an observation of long continuance, that matters of state seldom prosper, when managed by the clergy. Among the opposers of the reassuming, few were so strenuous as some of the ministers; and among the ministers, none more vehement than mr. Cotton Mather, pastor of the north church in Boston, who has charged them, as they would answer it another day, not to reassume. Among his arguments against it, one was, that it would be to put a slight upon his father, who, he said, was in England, labouring for a complete restoration of charter privileges, not doubting but they would be speedily obtained. Any man that knows New-England cannot but be sensible, that such discourses, from such men, have always been very prevalent. And hence it was, that even those that would think themselves wronged, if they were not numbered among the best friends to New-England, and to its charter, would not so much as stoop to take it up, when there was really nothing to hinder them from the enjoyment thereof.

After the committee of safety had continued about seven weeks, or rather after anarchy had been so long triumphant, an assembly having been called came to this resolution, and laid it before those gentlemen that had been of the government,—that if they would not

POSTSCRIPT.

act upon the foundation of the charter, that, pursuant to it, the assembly would appoint some others in that station. The answer to which was, that they would accept, &c. And when a declaration, signifying such a reassuming, was prepared, with the good liking of the deputies, in order to be published, some, that were opposers, so terrified those gentlemen, that, before publishing, it was underwritten that they would not have it understood that they did reassume charter government, to the no small amazement of the people, and disappointment of the deputies, who, if these had not promised so to act, had taken other care, and put in those that would.

The next principal thing done was, they chose two of their members, viz. one of the upper house, the other of the lower, both of them gentlemen of known integrity as well as ability, to go to England, in order to obtain their resettlement; and in regard mr. I. Mather was already there, they joined him, as also a certain gentleman in London, with these other two. Those from hence being arrived in London, they all united for the common interest of the country, though without the desired effect. They were in doubt whether it were best to improve their utmost for a reversal of the judgment in a course of law, or to obtain it in a parliamentary way, or to petition his majesty for a new grant of former privileges; and, considering that the two first might prove dilatory and expensive, as well as for other reasons, they resolved upon the latter, and petitioned his majesty for the country's resettlement, with former privileges, and what further additions his majesty in his princely wisdom should think fit. Accordingly it pleased his majesty to declare in council his determination, viz. That there should be a charter granted to New-England. But the minutes then taken thereof, and a draught of the new charter, being seen, it was the opinion of the two gentlemen sent from hence, that it were best to tarry his majesty's return from Flanders, in hopes then to obtain ease in such things as might be any ways deemed grievous. And this was the result of the advice of such as were best able to give it, that they could meet with; and accordingly they wholly desisted taking it out of the offices.

But mr. Mather and that other gentleman had, as it is said, other advice given them, which they strenuously pursued; and his majesty having left it (as is asserted in the life of sir William, p. 57) to them to nominate a governor, they pitched upon sir William Phips, who was then in England, as the most likely and able to serve the king's interests among the people there, under the changes, in some things unacceptable, now brought upon them, p. 62; and, without tarrying for the concurrence of those other agents, the charter was taken out, &c.

But mr. Mather, perhaps fearing he should have but small thanks here for his having so far an hand in bringing upon them those unacceptable changes, wrote, and caused to be printed, an account of his negotiation; but, surely by some error in the conception, it proved only an embryo, and was stilled as soon as born. One indeed, designed to be as it were a posthumous, was left with mr. Bailey, formerly of Boston, and a member of the north church, with a charge not to suffer it to be seen till he were gone to New-England; yet it seems some other person got a sight of it, which was the occasion of mr. Mather's sending him that minatory epistle, by some called a bull. But besides this, for fear of the worst, mr. Mather got several non-con. ministers to give him a testimonial, or letters of commendation, for his great service herein.

In the mean time, mr. Cotton Mather, being in some doubt of the same thing, handed about a paper of fables; wherein his rather, under the name of Mercurius, and himself under the name of Orpheus, are extolled, and the great actions of Mercurius magnified; the present charter exalted, by trampling all the former, as being very defective, and all those called unreasonable that did not readily agree with the new one. And indeed the whole country are compared to no better than beasts, except Mercurius and Orpheus; the governor himself must not escape being termed an elephant, though as good as he was great; and the inferiors told by Orpheus, that for the quiet enjoyment of their land, &c. they were beholding to Mercurius. Though this paper was judged not convenient to be printed, yet some copies were taken, the author having shewn variety of heathen learning in it.

This is in short that eminent service for which the said mr. I.M. is in the present book so highly extolled, in so many pages, that to repeat them, were to transcribe a considerable part of the said book.

And no doubt he deserves as much thanks as dr. Sharp did, when he was sent by the presbytery of Scotland to procure the settlement of their kirk by king Charles II at his restoration.

POSTSCRIPT.

Not but that the present charter of New-England is indeed truly valuable, as containing in it peculiar privileges, which abundantly engages this people to pay the tribute of thankfulness to his majesty, and all due subjection to whom it shall please him to substitute as governor over us; and to pray that the King of kings would pour out his richest blessings upon him, giving him a long and prosperous reign over the nations, under the benign influences whereof oppression and tyranny may flee away.

And if his majesty hath put this people into the present form of government, that they might be in the better condition of defence in a time of war, or that they might better understand the privilege of choosing their own governor by the want of it, and should be graciously pleased (the war being over) to restore to these, as has been already granted to the rest of his majesty's subjects, the full enjoyment of their ancient privileges, it would be such an obligation upon them to thankfulness and duty, as could never be forgotten, nor sufficiently exprest, and would rather abate than increase charge to the crown.

As to the supposed witchcrafts in New-England, having already said so much thereof, there is the less remains to be added.

In the rimes of sir Edmond Andros's government, goody Glover, a despised, crazy, ill-conditioned old woman, an Irish Roman Catholic, was tried for afflicting Goodwin's children; by the account of which trial, taken ill short hand for the use of the jury, it may appear that the generality of her answers were nonsense, and her behaviour like that of one distracted. Yet the doctors, finding her as she had been for many years, brought her in *compos mentis*; and setting aside her crazy answers to some ensnaring questions, the proof against her was wholly deficient. The jury brought her in guilty.

Mr. Cotton Mather was the most active and forward of any Minister in the country in those matters, taking home one of the children, and managing such intrigues with that child, and printing such an account of the whole in his *Memorable Providences*, as conduced much to the kindling of those flames, that in sir William's time threatened the destruction of this country.

King Saul in destroying the witches out of Israel is thought by many to have exceeded, and in his zeal to have slain the Gibeonites wrongfully under that notion; yet went after this to a witch to know his fortune. For his wrongfully destroying the Gibeonites (besides

POSTSCRIPT.

the judgments of God upon the land) his sons were hanged; and for his going to the witch, himself was cut off. Our sir William Phips did not do this; but, as appears by this book, had first his fortune told him, (by such as the author counts no better) and though be put it off (to his pastor, who he knew approved not thereof) as if it were brought to him in writing, without his seeking, &c. yet by his bringing it so far, and safe keeping it so many years, it appears he made some account of it; for which he gave the writer, after he had found the wreck, as a reward, more than two hundred pounds. His telling his wife, (p. 6) that he should be a commander, should have a brick house in Greenlane, &c. might be in confidence of some such prediction; and that he could foretel to him (p. 90) that he should be governor of New-England, was probably such an one, the scriptures not having revealed it. Such predictions would have been counted, at Salem, pregnant proofs of witchcraft, and much better than what were against several that suffered there. But sir William, when the witchcrafts at Salem began (in his esteem) to look formidable, that he might act safely in this affair, asked the advice of the ministers in and near Boston. The whole of their advice and answer is printed in *Cases of Conscience,* the last pages. But lest the world should be ignorant who it was that drew the said advice, In this book of the life of sir William Phips, p. 77, are these words, *The ministers made to his excellency and the council a return, drawn up at their desire, by mr. Mather the younger, as I have been informed.* Mr. C.M. therein intending to beguile the world, and make them think that another, and not himself, had taken that notice of his (supposed) good service done therein, which otherwise would have been ascribed to those ministers in general; though indeed the advice then given looks most like a thing of his composing, as carrying both fire to increase, and water to quench, the conflagration; particularly after the devil's testimony, by the supposed afflicted, had so prevailed, as to take away the life of one, and the liberty of an hundred, and the whole country set into a most dreadful consternation, then this advice is given, ushered in with thanks for what was already done, and in conclusion putting the government upon a speedy and vigorous prosecution, according to the laws of God, and the wholesome statutes of the English nation; so adding oil, rather than water, to the flame: for who so little acquainted with the proceedings of England, as not to know that they have taken some methods, with those here used, to discover who were witches? The rest of the advice, consisting of cautions and directions, is inserted in this book of the life of sir

POSTSCRIPT.

William: so that if sir William, looking upon the thanks for what was past, and exhortation to proceed, went on to take away the lives of nineteen more, this is according to the advice said to be given him by the ministers; and if the devil, after those executions, be affronted, by disbelieving his testimony, and by clearing and pardoning all the rest of the accused, yet this also is, according to that advice, but to cast the scale. The same that drew this advice saith, in *Wonders of the Invisible World, Enchantments Encountered*, that to have a hand in any thing that may stifle or obstruct a regular detection of that witchcraft, is what we may well with a holy fear avoid: their majesties' good subjects must not every day be torn to pieces by horrid witchcraft, and those bloody felons be wholly left unprosecuted; the witchcraft is a business that will not be shammed. The pastor of that church, of which sir William was a member, being of this principle, and thus declaring it, after the former advice, no wonder though it cast the scale against those cautions. It is rather a wonder that no more blood was shed; for if that advice of his pastor could still have prevailed with the governor, witchcraft had not been so shammed off as it was. Yet now, in this book of the life of sir William, the pardoning the prisoners when condemned, and clearing the gaols, is called (p. 82) a vanquishing the devil; adding this conquest to the host of the noble achievements of sir William, though performed not only without, but directly against, his pastor's advice. But this is not all; though this book pretends to raise a statue in honour of sir William, yet it appears it was the least part of the design of the author to honour him, but it was rather to honour himself, and the ministers; it being so unjust to sir William, as to give a full account of the cautions given him, but designedly hiding from the reader the encouragements and exhortations to proceed, that were laid before him, (under the name of the ministers' advice;) in effect telling the world that those executions at Salem were without and against the advice of the ministers, exprest in those cautions, purposely hiding their giving thanks for what was already done, and exhorting to proceed; thereby rendering sir William of so sanguinary a complexion, that the ministers had such cause to fear his going on with the tragedy, though against their advice, that they desired the president to write his *Cases of Conscience*, &c, to plead misinformation will not salve here, however it may seem to palliate other things, but is a manifest, designed travesty, or misrepresentation, of the minister's advice to sir William, a hiding the truth, and a wronging the dead, whom the author so much pretends to honour; for which the acknowledgments ought to be as universal as the offence. But though the ministers' advice, or rather mr. Cotton Mather's, was perfectly ambidexter, giving as great or greater encouragement to proceed in those dark methods, than cautions against them; yet many eminent persons being accused, there was a necessity of a stop to be put to it. If it be true, what was said at the council-board in answer to the commendations of sir William for his stopping the proceedings about witchcraft, viz. that it was high time for him to stop it, his own lady being accused; if that assertion were a truth, then New-England may seem to be more beholden to the accusers for accusing her, and thereby necessitating a stop, than to sir William, or to the advice that was given him by his pastor, mr. Cotton Mather, having been very forward to write books of witchcraft, has not been so forward either to explain or to defend the doctrinal part thereof; and his belief (which he had a year's time to compose) he durst not venture, so as to be copied. Yet in this book of the life of sir William he sufficiently testifies his retaining that heterodox belief, seeking by frightful stories of the sufferings of some, and the refined sight of others, &c. (p. 69) to obtrude upon the world, and confirm it in such a belief as hitherto he either cannot or will not defend, as if the blood already shed thereby were not sufficient.

Mr. I. Mather, in his *Cases of Conscience*, p. 25, tells of a bewitched eye, and that such can see more than others. They were certainly bewitched eyes, that could see as well shut as open, and that could see what never was; that could see the prisoners upon the afflicted, harming them, when those whose eyes were not bewitched could have sworn that they did not stir from the bar. The accusers are said to have suffered much by biting, (p. 73) and the prints of just such a set of teeth, as those they accused had, would be seen on their flesh; but such as had not such bewitched eyes have seen the accusers bite themselves, and then complain of the accused. It has also been seen, when the accused, instead of having just such a set of teeth, has not had one in his head. They were such bewitched eyes, that could see the poisonous powder (brought by spectres, p. 70) and that could see in the ashes the print of the brand, there invisibly heating to torment the pretended sufferers wIth, &c.

These, with the rest of such legends, have this direct tendency, viz. to tell the world that the devil is more ready to serve his votaries, by his doing for them things above or against the course of nature, shewing himself to them and making explicit contracts with them, &c. than the Divine Being is to his faithful servants; and that as he is willing, so also able, to perform their desires. The way whereby these people are believed to arrive at a power to afflict their neighbours, is by a compact with the devil, and that they have a power to commission him to those evils, p. 72. However irrational, or unscriptural, such assertions are, yet they seem a necessary part of the faith of such as maintain the belief of such a sort of witches.

As the scriptures know nothing of a covenanting or commissioning witch, so reason cannot conceive how mortals should by their wickedness arrive at a power to commission angels, fallen angels, against their innocent neighbours. But the scriptures are full in it, and the instances numerous, that the Almighty Divine Being has this prerogative, to make use of what instruments he pleaseth, in afflicting any, and consequently to commission devils: and though this word, *commissioning*, in the author's former books, might be thought to be by inadvertency, yet now, after he hath been cautioned of it, still to persist in it seems highly criminal; and therefore, in the name of God, I here charge such belief as guilty of sacrilege in the highest nature, and so much worse than stealing church plate, &c. as it is a higher offence to steal any of the glorious attributes of the Almighty, to bestow them upon mortals, than it is to steal the utensils appropriated to his service. And whether to ascribe such power of commissioning devils to the worst of men, be not direct blasphemy, I leave to others better able to determine. When the Pharisees were so wicked as to ascribe to Beelzebub the mighty works of Christ (whereby he did manifestly shew forth his power and godhead) then it was that our Saviour declared the sin against the Holy Ghost to be unpardonable.

When the righteous God is contending with apostate sinners for their departures from him, by his judgments: as plagues, earthquakes, storms and tempests, sicknesses and diseases, wars, loss of cattle, &c. then not only to ascribe this to the devil, but to charge one another with sending or commissioning those devils to do these things, is so abominable and so wicked, that it requires a better judgment than mine to give it its just denomination.

But that christians, so called, should not only charge their fellow christians therewith; but proceed to trials and executions; crediting that enemy to all goodness, and accuser of the brethren, rather than believe their neighbours in their own defence; this is so diabolical a

POSTSCRIPT.

wickedness, as cannot proceed but from a doctrine of devils; how far damnable it is, let others discuss. Though such things were acting in this country in sir William's time, yet (p. 65) there is a discourse of a guardian angel, as then over-seeing it: which notion, however it may suit the faith of Ethnicks, or the fancies of Trithemius, it is certain that the Omnipresent Being stands not in need, as earthly potentates do, of governing the world by vicegerents. And if sir William had such an invisible pattern to imitate, no wonder though some of his actions were unaccountable: especially those relating to witchcraft: for if there was in those actions an angel superintending, there is little reason to think it was Gabriel, or the spirit of Mercury.; nor Hanael, the angel or spirit of Venus; nor yet Samuel, the angel or spirit of Mars; names feigned by the said Trithemius, &c. It may rather be thought to be Apollyon, or Abaddon.

Objection. But here it will be said, What, are there no witches? Does not the law of God command that they should be extirpated? Is the command vain and unintelligible?

Sol. For any to say that a witch is one that makes a compact with, and commissions devils, &c. is indeed to render the law of God vain and unintelligible, as having provided no way whereby they might be detected, and proved to be such; and how the Jews waded through this difficulty for so many ages, without the supplement of mr. Perkins and Bernard thereto, would be very mysterious. But to him that can read the scriptures without prejudice from education, &c. it will manifestly appear that the scripture is full and intelligible, both as to the crime, and means to detect the culpable. He that shall hereafter see any person, who, to confirm people in a false belief about the power of witches and devils, pretending to a sign to confirm it; such as knocking off of invisible chains with the hand, driving away devils by brushing, striking with a sword or stick, to wound a person at a great distance, &c. may (according to that head of mr. Gaule's, quoted by mr. C.M. and so often herein before recited, and so well proved by scripture) conclude that he has *seen witchcraft performed.*

If Balaam became a sorcerer by sacrificing and praying to the true God against his visible people, then he that shall pray that the afflicted (by their *spectral* sight) may accuse some other persons (whereby their reputations and lives may be endangered) such will justly deserve the name of a *sorcerer*. If any person pretends to know more than can be known by human means, and professeth at the

POSTSCRIPT.

same time that they have it from the *black man, i.e. the devil*, and shall from hence give testimony against the lives of others, they are manifestly such as have a familiar spirit; and if any, knowing them to have their information from the *black man*, shall be inquisitive of them for their testimony against others, they therein are dealing with such as have a *familiar spirit*.

And if these shall pretend to *see the dead* by their *spectral sight*, and others shall be inquisitive of them, and receive their answers what it is the *dead say*, and who it is they accuse, both the one and the other are by scripture *guilty of necromancy*.

These are all of them crimes as easily proved as any whatsoever, and that by such proof as the law of God requires, so that it is *no unintelligible law*.

But if the iniquity of the times be such that these criminals not only escape, being indemnified, but are encouraged in their wickedness, and made use of to take away the lives of others, this is worse than a making the law of God *vain*, it being a rendering of it *dangerous*, against the lives of innocents, and without all hopes of better, so long as these bloody principles remain.

As long as christians do esteem the law of *God to be imperfect*, as not describing that crime that it requires to be punished by death: As long as men suffer themselves to be poisoned in their education, and be grounded in a *false belief by the books of the heathen*:

As long as the devil shall be believed to have *a natural power to act above and against the course of nature:*

As long as the *witches* shall be believed to have a power to *commission him:*

As long as the *devil's testimony*, by the pretended afflicted, shall be received as *more valid to condemn*, than their plea of *not guilty* to acquit:

As long as the accused shall have their *lives and liberties* confirmed and restored to them *upon their confessing themselves guilty:*

As long as the *accused* shall be forced to *undergo hardships and torments* for their not confessing:

As long as *teats* for the *devil to suck* are searched for upon the bodies of the accused, as a token of guilt:

As long as the *Lord's prayer* shall be profaned, by being made a test, who are culpable:

POSTSCRIPT.

As long as *witchcraft, sorcery, familiar spirits, and necromancy,* shall be improved to discover who are witches, &c.

So long it may be expected that innocents will suffer as witches:

So long God will be daily dishonoured, and so long his judgments must be expected to be continued.

F I N I S.

More books in the Supernatural History Series

*The Wonders of the Invisible World,
Being an Account of the Tryals of Several Witches
Lately Executed in New-England*
Cotton Mather

*A Report of the Mysterious Noises Heard in the House
of Mr. John D. Fox in Hydesville, Arcadia, Wayne County*
E.E. Lewis

Hydesville: The Story of the Rochester Knockings
Thomas Olman Todd

Spiritualism: The Open Door to the Unseen Universe
James Robertson

Hydesville: The Story of the Rochester Knockings
Thomas Olman Todd

The Vampire; A Tale
John Polidori

The Were-Wolf
Clemence Housman

Found at foxediting.com/books/ and at online and specialty bookstores.

www.ingramcontent.com/pod-product-compliance
Lightning Source LLC
Chambersburg PA
CBHW030240170426
43202CB00007B/68